Intermediate **Student's Book**

New Headway
English Course

Liz & John Soars

Oxford University Press

Contents LANGUAGE INPUT

SKILLS DEVELOPMENT

LANGUAGE INPUT

SKILLS DEVELOPMENT

1

What a wonderful world!

Auxiliary verbs
Social expressions

Test your grammar

1 Make questions with *you* from the sentences.

Example
I come from Australia. (*Where?*)

Where do you come from?

a I live in a flat near the centre of town. (*Where?*)
b I speak three languages. (*How many?*)
c I'm learning English because I need it for my job. (*Why?*)
d I've been to France, Germany, Sweden, and the United States. (*Which countries?*)
e I was born in Dublin in 1961. (*Where? When?*)
f I've been learning English for three years. (*How long?*)
g I have two brothers and a sister. (*How many?*)
h I've got £10 in my pocket. (*How much?*)
i I went to the cinema last night. (*Where?*)
j I'm wearing jeans and a jumper. (*What?*)

In pairs, ask and answer the questions about *you*. Tell the class about your partner.

2 Make the statements negative.

Example
I smoke.

I don't smoke.

a My mother works in a bank.
b It's raining.
c I went out last night.
d I'm learning Russian.
e We've got a dog.
f I had a shower this morning.
g English is spoken in every country in the world.

PRESENTATION

Auxiliary verbs

1 Answer the questions in the quiz.

General knowledge

QUIZ

1 When did the modern Olympic Games start?
a 1876   b 1888   c 1896

2 How long does it take for the sun's rays to reach Earth?
a 8 minutes   b 8 hours   c 8 days

3 What was Neil Armstrong doing when he said, 'That's one small step for a man, one giant leap for mankind'?

4 What doesn't a vegan eat?

5 If you are buying things with rupees, which country are you in?

6 Where were the first books printed?
a Germany
b Egypt
c China

2 **T.1** Listen and check your answers.

3 Find an example of the following tenses in the quiz.

Present Simple	Past Simple
Present Continuous	Past Continuous
Present Simple passive	Past Simple passive
Present Perfect Simple	

● **Grammar question**

– When do we use the auxiliary verbs *do*, *be*, and *have*?
Think of tenses, negatives and questions.

4 Write some general knowledge questions. Ask the class.

7 In which religion are the gods Brahma, Vishnu and Siva worshipped?

8 Which record album has sold more than any other?

9 What does VIP stand for?

10 Why didn't Ben Johnson get the gold medal for the 100 metres at the Seoul Olympics?

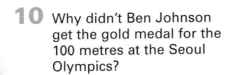

11 What was Abraham Lincoln doing when he was assassinated?

12 How many times has Brazil won the World Cup?

13 How many wings does a butterfly have?

14 If you are eating *sushi*, what exactly are you eating?

PRACTICE

1 Grammar and pronunciation

1 Correct the factual mistakes in sentences a–k and give the right information.

T.2a First listen to the sentence stress in the example.

Example
The sun rises in the west.

> It doesn't rise in the west!
> It rises in the east!

a The Pope comes from Australia.
b The teacher's wearing a swimming costume.
c People drive on the right in Britain.
d My mother has got ten sisters and brothers.
e We went to Iceland on holiday last summer.
f I had a huge breakfast.
g It'll snow tomorrow.
h We're learning Chinese.
i I live in a palace.
j Champagne is made in Scotland.
k Cats and dogs can swim.

T.2b Listen and check your answers.

2 Write questions for the answers.

Example
How many books *did you read* on holiday?
Four.

a What _____ last night?
I stayed in and watched television.

b What sort of books _____ reading?
I like horror stories and science fiction.

c _____ been to America?
Yes, I have. I went there last year. I really enjoyed it.

d What _____ the teacher _____?
She's helping Maria with this exercise.

e _____ your father do?
He works in a bank.

f Why _____ your homework last night?
Because I didn't feel well.

g How long _____ it take you to come to school?
It takes me about twenty minutes. I come by bus.

h What _____ doing next weekend?
I don't know. I haven't got any plans yet.

i _____ you _____ a CD player at home?
No, I haven't. Just a tape recorder.

In pairs, ask and answer the questions about *you*.

2 *is* or *has*?

T.3 Listen to the sentences. They all contain *'s*.
Say if *'s = is* or *'s = has*.

Example
She's got a BMW.   *has*
Peter's waiting near the door.   *is*

3 Short answers

1 **T.4a** Read and listen to the breakfast conversation.

Dad   Morning! Did you sleep well?
Emma   Yes.
Dad   Do you want any breakfast?
Emma   No. I'm not hungry.
Dad   Oh. Have you fed the cat?
Emma   Yes.
Dad   Has the post come?
Emma   No.
Dad   OK. Are you going to be late tonight?
Emma   No. I'll be back at the usual time.

2 **T.4b** Listen to a similar dialogue. What's the difference?

We use short answers in spoken English because *yes* or *no* on its own can sound impolite.
Practise the dialogue using short answers.

3 **T.5** Answer the questions you hear with a short answer.

4 Stand up! Ask three students the following *yes/no* questions. Add one or two questions of your own. Put a tick (✓) or a cross (✗) in the columns. Give short answers in your reply.

	S1	S2	S3
Do you play a musical instrument?			
Does anyone in your family smoke?			
Have you got any pets?			
Can you cook?			
Are you going out tonight?			
Did you watch TV last night?			
Have you been to the cinema recently?			
. . .			
. . .			

4 Reading and tenses

Read the text about *The Times* newspaper. Put the verbs in brackets into the correct tense. There are examples of active and passive sentences.

Example
The Times is printed (print) six days a week, from Monday to Saturday.

The Times, symbol of tradition and establishment

THE TIMES is one of Britain's oldest and most influential newspapers. It (a) _____ (begin) its life in 1785. It (b) _____ (start) by John Walter. In those days it (c) _____ (cost) two and a half old pennies.

In the nineteenth century, The Times (d) _____ (develop) a reputation for accurate reporting and independent editorial views. Now it (e) _____ (sell) over 650,000 copies a day. It (f) _____ (publish)

in London, along with its sister newspaper, The Sunday Times, which (g) _____ (have) at least ten sections and takes all week to read!

'The Times (h) _____ (have) an excellent reputation for over 200 years,' said its editor, who (i) _____ (work) for the paper since 1980, 'and now we (j) _____ (try) our best to continue that tradition in order to produce a newspaper for the twenty-first century.'

5 Speaking

Work in pairs. Your teacher will give you some information about a journalist called Charles Hendrickson, who has worked for The Times and other newspapers. You will not have the same information as your partner.

Ask and answer questions to complete the information.

Example

Student A
Charles Hendrickson was born in … (When?).
He went to school in Paris and Geneva.

Student B
Charles Hendrickson was born in 1940. He went to school in … (Where?).

LANGUAGE REVIEW

Auxiliary verbs

The auxiliary verbs do, be and have are used to express various grammatical functions, for example to form questions and negatives, and to form tenses.

do
Do, does and did are used to form the question and negative in the Present Simple and the Past Simple.

Where **do** you work?
What **does** she do?
Why **did** you go to Paris?

I **don't** like the rain.
He **doesn't** want to go home.
We **didn't** buy anything.

be
Be is used with -ing forms and past participle forms to make continuous and passive verb forms.

She's wearing new shoes.
What **were** you doing this morning?
I've **been** learning English for three years.

The Times **is** published in London.
I **was** born in India.
My money's **been** stolen.

have
Have is used to make perfect verb forms.

Have you ever seen a ghost?
She's **been** waiting for two hours.

📖 **Grammar Reference: page 142.**

● READING AND LISTENING

Pre-reading task

1 In the 2nd century BC a list was made of the most impressive and beautiful man-made objects in the world. These were called **The Seven Wonders of the World**.

Match each picture in the box with its name. How many can we still see today?

The Pharos, lighthouse of Alexandria
The Hanging Gardens of Babylon
The Statue of Zeus at Olympia
The Colossus of Rhodes
The Pyramids of Egypt
The Tomb of Mausolus
The Temple of Diana

2 What do you think are some of the greatest wonders of the twentieth century? Don't just think of buildings!

Reading

1 In the text, the journalist, Ann Halliday, describes what are for her the seven wonders of the modern world. Read about them.

2 In what way does she say modern wonders are different from ancient wonders?

Put them in order, 1 – 7, according to which *you* think is the most important (1 = the most important, 7 = the least important).

☐ computers   ☐ space travel
☐ medical science   ☐ holidays
☐ the Olympic Games   ☐ agriculture
☐ we are still here

Discuss your decisions as a class.

Wonders of the modern world

by Ann Halliday

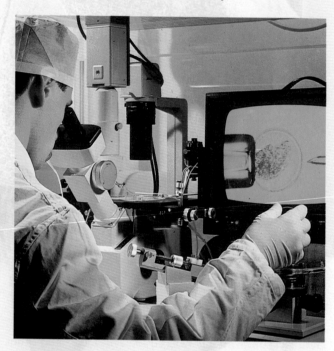

I DON'T believe that today's wonders are similar in kind to the wonders of the Ancient World. They were all buildings and statues. In the last two centuries we have seen unprecedented technical and scientific achievements. These are surely our modern wonders.   5
Here is my list.

1 Computers
They have already revolutionized the way we live and work. But it is early days for computers. We don't know how much they are still changing the world.   10
More computer wonders are yet to come.

2 Space Travel
Only a few years before men were walking on the moon, reputable scientists declared that it was impossible. But in 1969 Neil Armstrong stepped out of his space capsule   15
and made his famous statement: 'That's one small step for a man, one giant leap for mankind'.

3 Medical Science
Surely nothing has done more for the comfort and happiness of mankind than the advance of medical   20
knowledge! How many millions of people have benefited from the humble aspirin? How many lives has penicillin saved? Average life expectancy in Europe has risen dramatically over the last hundred years, from about 50 years in 1906 to about 75 years today.   25

Majorca

4 Holidays

Yes — holidays! In fact there have always been holidays — in ancient Rome there were more than 150 a year — but a holiday used to mean simply a day when you didn't work. Now holidaymakers travel to all parts of the world. Perhaps you don't like so many tourists in your country, but you must agree that a phenomenon which sees the population of Greece treble in summer, and which sends office workers and shop assistants to Spain, Turkey, or the Caribbean is a wonder of the world.

5 The Olympic Games

It is true that the Olympic Games are now commercialized and there is greed and drug abuse. However, it is a competition in which every country in the world takes part. Every four years, for a brief moment, we see these countries come together in peace and friendship. We feel hope again for the future of mankind.

6 Agriculture

In 1724, Jonathan Swift wrote, 'Whoever makes two blades of grass or two ears of corn grow where only one grew before serves mankind better than the whole race of politicians'. In Europe our farmers have done this. In 1709, whole villages in France died of hunger. Now, in Europe we can't eat all the food we produce. If only the politicians could find a way to share it with those parts of the world where there is still famine.

40

45

50

55

7 We are still here

The last wonder of the modern world is simply that we are still here. We have bombs that could destroy the world but we have not used them. This is surely the greatest wonder of all!

60

Comprehension check

Here are seven more statements made by Ann about her choice of wonders. Which statement goes with which wonder? Discuss your answers with a partner.

a Surgeons can perform the most amazing operations.
b We see people from warring countries shake hands.
c Small children can program them, sometimes more easily than adults!
d No government dares to use such weapons.
e Maybe visiting one country a day is not your idea of the best way to see the world!
f We produce enough to feed the world.
g Progress in this area is slower now. Not as much money goes into research as in the 1960s.

Language work

Complete the following with the correct auxiliary verb in the positive or negative form. Check your answers with the text.

1 Computers _____ already revolutionized the way we live and work.

2 We _____ know how much they _____ still changing the world.

3 Only a few years before men _____ walking on the moon, scientists said that it was impossible.

4 How many lives _____ penicillin saved?

5 A holiday used to mean a day when you _____ work.

6 The Olympic Games _____ now commercialized.

Listening

T.6 You will hear three people giving their ideas of the wonders of the modern world.

– Make a list of the wonders they mention.
– What is good about each wonder?
– Are there any problems with it?

● SPEAKING

Discussion

1 What machines are important in your life? In pairs, put the inventions in order. Which do you think is the most important? Which has changed the world the most? Mark them **1** for the most important down to **10** for the least important.

- [ ] the telephone
- [ ] the car
- [ ] the television
- [ ] the plane
- [ ] the space satellite
- [ ] the atom bomb
- [ ] the space rocket
- [ ] the computer
- [ ] the fax machine
- [ ] the washing machine

2 Work in groups of four. Try to persuade the others that your order is the right one!

3 Talk together as a class. What other machines would you add to the list?

● VOCABULARY AND PRONUNCIATION

Sounds and spelling

1 English spelling, as you probably know, is not logical! Words which *look* as though they are pronounced the same *aren't* pronounced the same.

meat /miːt/ and *great* /greɪt/
home /həʊm/ and *some* /sʌm/
know /nəʊ/ and *now* /naʊ/

2 In the following lists of words, three words rhyme, but one is different. <u>Underline</u> the one that's different. The two vowel sounds are given to help you. There is a list of phonetic symbols on the inside back cover of this book.

Example
/uː/ or /ʊ/?
boot   *foot*   shoot   suit

a /iː/ or /e/?
bread   head   read (past)   read (present)

b /ɜː/ or /ɔː/?
work   fork   talk   walk

c /ʌ/ or /əʊ/?
done   phone   son   won

d /e/ or /eɪ/?
paid   made   played   said

e /uː/ or /ʊ/?
good   food   wood   stood

f /eɪ/ or /iː/?
ache   break   take   weak

g /ɪə/ or /eə/?
dear   hear   pear   near

h /əʊ/ or /aʊ/?
cows   knows   owes   rose

T.7   Listen and check your answers.

Silent letters

1 There are many silent letters in English words.
lis~~t~~en   ta~~l~~k   ~~w~~rite   ~~k~~nife

Cross out the silent letters in the following words.

a sign
b honest
c half
d comb

e receipt
f knee
g iron
h lamb

i salmon
j cupboard
k whistle
l answer

2 Here are some words in phonetics. Write the words. Careful! They all have silent letters.

Example /klaɪmd/ = *climbed*

a /ˈkɑːsl/ _____
b /bɒm/ _____
c /ˈsænwɪdʒ/ _____
d /ˈaɪlənd/ _____
e /nɒk/ _____

f /ˈfɒrən/ _____
g /hɑːt/ _____
h /ˈnɒlɪdʒ/ _____
i /saɪˈkɒlədʒɪ/ _____
j /ˈgrænmɑː/ _____

T.8   Listen and check your answers.

A love poem!
Can you read the poem?

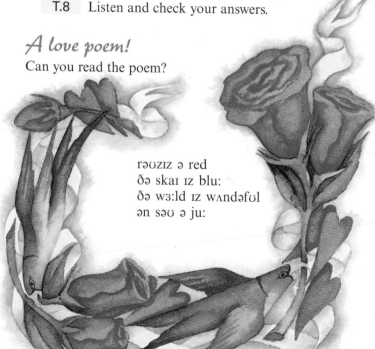

rəʊziz ə red
ðə skaɪ ɪz bluː
ðə wɜːld ɪz wʌndəfʊl
ən səʊ ə juː

● WRITING

Correcting mistakes

1 It is important to try to correct your own mistakes when you write. Look at the letter that a student has written to her friend. Her teacher has used symbols to show her the kind of mistakes she has made.

T	Tense	WW	Wrong word
P	Punctuation	Gr	Grammar
WO	Word order	⋏	Word missing
Prep	Preposition	Sp	Spelling

Read the letter and correct the mistakes.

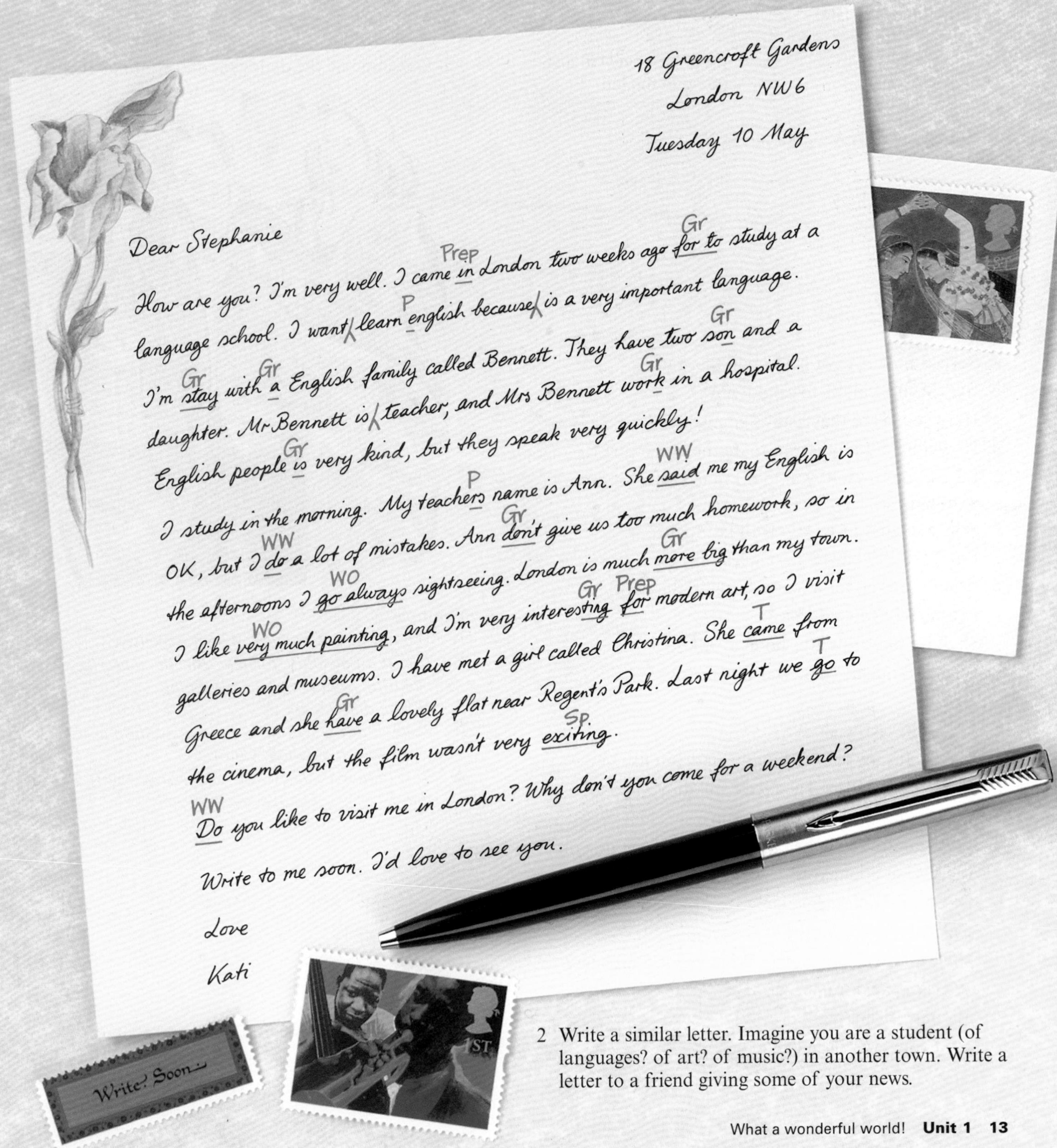

18 Greencroft Gardens
London NW6
Tuesday 10 May

Dear Stephanie

How are you? I'm very well. I came _in_ [Prep] London two weeks ago _for_ [Gr] to study at a language school. I want ⋏ learn _english_ [P] because ⋏ is a very important language. I'm _stay_ [Gr] with _a_ [Gr] English family called Bennett. They have two _son_ [Gr] and a daughter. Mr Bennett is ⋏ teacher, and Mrs Bennett _work_ [Gr] in a hospital. English people _is_ [Gr] very kind, but they speak very quickly!

I study in the morning. My _teachers_ [P] name is Ann. She _said_ [WW] me my English is OK, but I _do_ [WW] a lot of mistakes. Ann _don't_ [Gr] give us too much homework, so in the afternoons I _go always_ [WO] sightseeing. London is much _more big_ [Gr] than my town. I like _very much painting_ [WO], and I'm very _interesting_ [Gr] _for_ [Prep] modern art, so I visit galleries and museums. I have met a girl called Christina. She _came_ [T] from Greece and she _have_ [Gr] a lovely flat near Regent's Park. Last night we _go_ [T] to the cinema, but the film wasn't very _exiting_ [Sp].

_Do_ [WW] you like to visit me in London? Why don't you come for a weekend?

Write to me soon. I'd love to see you.

Love

Kati

Write soon.

2 Write a similar letter. Imagine you are a student (of languages? of art? of music?) in another town. Write a letter to a friend giving some of your news.

Social expressions

1 When we're talking and chatting, we use a lot of idiomatic expressions!

Example

> Hurry up, we're late!

> Hang on a sec. I'm just going to the loo.

Match a line in **A** with a line in **B**.

a _____   e _____   i _____
b _____   f _____   j _____
c _____   g _____   k _____
d _____   h _____

A

a Sorry I'm late. I got held up in the traffic.

b Bye, Mum! I'm off to school now.

c Have you heard that Jenny's going out with Pete Boyd?

d How long did it take you to do the homework?

e I don't know about you, but I'm fed up with this weather.

f Who was that I saw you with last night?

g I'm tired. I'm having next week off.

h Right! Let's go for a ten-mile jog in the park!

i Let me buy you a drink.

j Shall we meet this afternoon at 3.00?

k What a fantastic coat! Was it expensive?

B

1 No, no. It's my round. What would you like?

2 That's a good idea. The break will do you good.

3 Me, too. I'm just longing for some sunshine.

4 Never mind. You're here now. Come and sit down.

5 Ages. What about you?

6 It cost an absolute fortune!

7 Really? I don't know what she sees in him.

8 Sorry. I can't make it then. What about a bit later?

9 Take care, my love. Have a nice day!

10 You must be joking!

11 Mind your own business!

2 **T.9a** Listen and check your answers. Memorize some of the dialogues. Close your books and practise them in pairs.

3 **T.9b** Listen to the sentences. Reply, using one of the lines in column **B**. You will have to change some of them a little.

4 Choose some of the dialogues and continue them.

Example

A *What a fantastic coat! Was it expensive?*

B *It cost an absolute fortune. But the material's beautiful, and it's got a silk lining.*

A *Where did you get it?*

B *I saw it in the window of that new shop in town; you know, it's called 'Chic'.*

A *Yes, I know it. They have some lovely stuff, don't they?*

2 Happiness!

Present states and actions
Active and passive
Numbers

Test your grammar

Look at the pairs of sentences.
Which one is correct? Why?

1 She speaks five languages.
   She's speaking five languages.

2 Look at that man! He wears such
   a funny hat.
   Look at that man! He's wearing
   such a funny hat.

3 Don't take that book back to the
   library. I'm reading it.
   Don't take that book back to the
   library. I read it.

4 They have two daughters and
   two sons.
   They're having two daughters
   and two sons.

5 Do you understand Spanish?
   Are you understanding Spanish?

6 We're thinking opera is boring.
   We think opera is boring.

7 English speaks all over the world.
   English is spoken all over the
   world.

PRESENTATION (1)

Present Simple

1 What do you think is the happiest time of a
   person's life: when you are a child or an adult?

2 A market research organization did a survey to find out who are the
   happiest people in Britain! They interviewed over 5,000 people.

   Here are the results of the survey. At what time in their lives are British
   people happiest? When are they least happy? Why do you think this is?

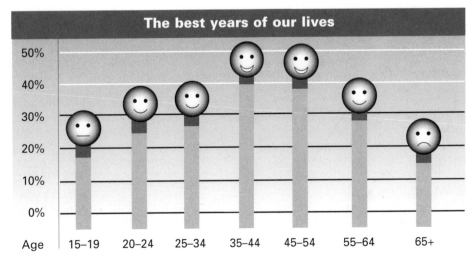

The best years of our lives

Age	15–19	20–24	25–34	35–44	45–54	55–64	65+

The happiest person in Britain

The happiest person in Britain today is a professional married man between the ages of 35 and 54. He *lives* in the south of England but not in London. He *owns* a comfortable, detached house and *has* two children.

What does he do?
He *has* a steady job in an office in London. After a hard day at work, he *relaxes* in front of the television or *watches* a video. He *doesn't go out* every evening, but two evenings a week he *meets* friends for a drink in the local pub. He *owns* a pet, usually a dog, and *takes* it for a walk every day after work. He *spends* on average £120 per week.

Where does he go?
At the weekend, he regularly *eats* in restaurants, *goes* to see shows, and *plays* a sport (usually golf). Most weekends he *puts* on a pair of old blue jeans, and *potters* in the garden. He usually *goes* on holiday abroad more than once a year.

What does his wife do?
His wife is happy, too, but not quite as happy. She *runs* the home and *has* a job, but she *doesn't earn* as much as her husband.

Mr Happy!
John Smith aged 45, an accountant from Surrey

● Grammar questions

– What tense are all the verbs in *italics*? Why?
– Why do the verbs in the text end in *-s*?
– Which auxiliary verb is used to form questions and negatives in the Present Simple?

PRACTICE

Speaking

1 Ask and answer questions about John Smith.

Example
... married?

> Is he married?

> Yes, he is.

a Where ... live?
b What ... do?
c How many children ...?
d How ... relax after work?
e How much ... per week?
f What ... do at the weekend?
g How often ... holiday abroad?

T.11   Listen and check your answers.

2 Ask and answer the same questions with a partner.

> Are you married?

> No, I'm not.

3 John Smith's lifestyle doesn't seem very exciting.

– Why do you think he is so happy?
– Why is his wife less happy?
– Do you think men are generally happier than women in your country?

PRESENTATION (2)

Present Simple and Present Continuous
Active and passive

1 **T.12** Look at the photograph of Roger Dromard, also aged 45, and listen to him talking about himself. Answer the questions.

– What's the best thing that ever happened to him?
– What was his job before? What does he do now?
– Where does he live?
– Is he married?
– What does Fiona do? Does Roger earn more than Fiona?
– What is Roger's hobby? What is Fiona's hobby?
– Does Roger play any sports?
– Are there any problems with his job?
– Does he often eat out in restaurants?
– Is Roger's life like John Smith's? Is he happy?

2 Listen again. Complete the sentences with the exact words Roger uses.

a In summer I *usually* _____ home at about 5.30 in the morning.

b I _____ a small van, and I _____ all my tools and equipment in that.

c It's autumn now so I _____ the gardens and _____ leaves.

d I _____ lots of daffodils and tulips.

e After work I *always* _____ home and _____ in a hot bath.

f I *usually* _____ our evening meal because she (Fiona) _____ home from work after me.

g At weekends we *often* _____ into the country and _____ to antique shops and antique sales.

h We _____ a television! Everybody _____ one these days but we _____ .

i I _____ old radios and Fiona _____ old cookery books.

j I've just bought two 1930s radios and I _____ them and _____ them.

k I *never* _____ any sports.

l I _____ much in autumn and winter so I _____ much at the moment.

Grammar questions

– What tense are the verbs in sentences a and b? Why? Find some more examples of this tense.
– What tense are the verbs which complete sentence c? Why? Find some more examples.
– What part of speech are the words in *italics*? Which tense do they (nearly always) go with?

3 Look at the pictures. Describe what's happening.

Example
Roger's cutting the grass. He's wearing shorts.

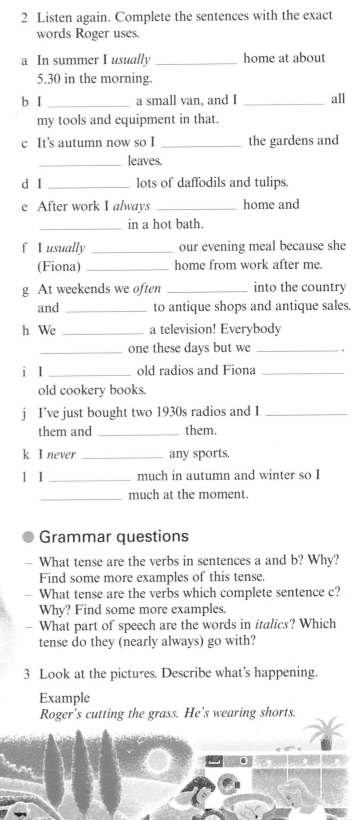

PRACTICE

1 Note-taking and speaking

Write notes about John Smith and Roger Dromard under the headings.

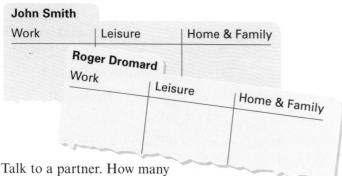

John Smith

Work	Leisure	Home & Family

Roger Dromard

Work	Leisure	Home & Family

Talk to a partner. How many similarities and differences can you find?

2 Dialogues

1 **T.13** Read and listen to the dialogue. Then work in pairs, and read and memorize it.

A What do you do?

B I'm an interior designer. I decorate people's houses, and give them ideas for furniture and lighting.

A And what are you doing at the moment?

B Well, I'm not working on a house. I'm working on a hotel. I'm designing a new dining-room for the Hilton.

2 Work in pairs. Make up similar dialogues with some of the jobs below.

3 Ask each other about your own jobs or studies.

a film director   a mechanic   a football manager   an artist

an architect   a ski instructor   a journalist a traffic warden a travel agent an actor   a plumber   a farmer

3 Discussing grammar

Action and state verbs

1 Some verbs are used in both simple and continuous tenses.

> She usually **drives** to work but today she **isn't driving**, she**'s walking**.

These are called *action* verbs.

2 Some verbs are not usually used in the continuous tenses. These are called *state* verbs.

> I **like** black coffee.
> (NOT *~~I'm liking~~ black coffee.)
>
> Do you **know** the answer?
> (NOT * ~~Are you knowing~~ the answer?)

Work in pairs and discuss your answers.

1 Ten of the verbs in the box are *not* usually used in the Present Continuous.

Underline them.

> go   understand   believe   <u>like</u>   agree   enjoy
> cost   want   listen to   think (= opinion)
> mean   know   play   love   tell

2 Put a tick (✓) if the sentence is right and a cross (✗) if it is wrong. Correct the mistakes.

Example
I don't understand English newspapers. ✓
What are you wanting to drink? ✗
What do you want to drink?

a Jim isn't wanting an ice-cream. He doesn't like it.
b We're enjoying the course very much. We're learning a lot.
c I'm understanding you but I'm not agreeing with you.
d Do you think that Vanessa plays golf well?
e I'm sorry. I'm not knowing the answer.
f I'm not believing you. You're telling lies.
g They know the car costs a lot of money but they want to buy it.
h She listens to a French song but she doesn't understand what it is meaning.

3 Complete the following pairs of sentences using the verb in *italics*. Use the Present Simple for one and the Present Continuous for the other.

a *come*

Alec and Mary are Scottish. They _____ from Glasgow.

They'll be here very soon. They _____ by car.

b *have*

Lisa can't answer the phone. She _____ a bath.

She _____ two new pairs of jeans.

c *think*

I _____ that all politicians tell lies.

I _____ about my girlfriend. She's in New York at the moment.

d *not enjoy*

We _____ this party at all. The music is too loud.

We _____ going to big parties.

e *watch*

Be quiet! I _____ my favourite programme.

I always _____ it on Thursday evenings.

f *see*

John's not at home. He _____ the doctor about his sore throat.

I _____ the problem but I can't help you. Sorry.

g *smell*

Mmmmm! Dinner _____ good. What is it?

Why _____ you _____ those roses? They're plastic!

h *use* (Careful!)

This room _____ usually _____ for big meetings. But today it _____ for a party.

4 Present Simple active or passive?

1 Which of the sentences are active and which are passive?

a I use this room as a study.
b This room is used for meetings.
c We feed our cats twice a day.
d But the dogs are fed just once a day.

2 **One hour is 60 minutes, which is 3,600 seconds. A lot can happen in that time!**

Read about some of the things that happen all over the world. Put the verb in brackets into either Present Simple or Present Simple passive.

Example
Every hour the planet Earth ___*travels*___ (travel) 66,620 miles around the sun.
Eleven earthquakes ___*are felt*___ (feel) somewhere in the world.

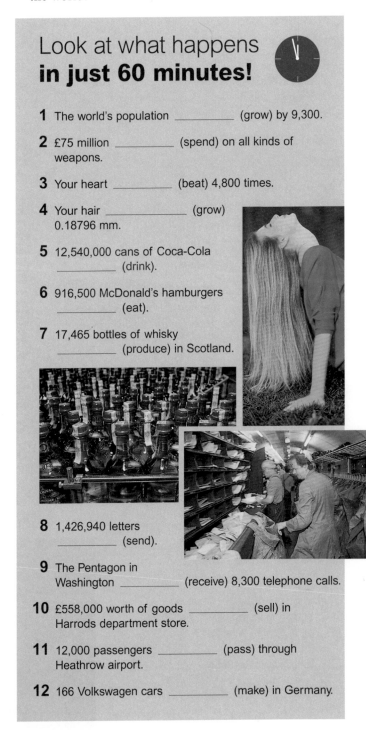

Look at what happens **in just 60 minutes!**

1 The world's population _____ (grow) by 9,300.

2 £75 million _____ (spend) on all kinds of weapons.

3 Your heart _____ (beat) 4,800 times.

4 Your hair _____ (grow) 0.18796 mm.

5 12,540,000 cans of Coca-Cola _____ (drink).

6 916,500 McDonald's hamburgers _____ (eat).

7 17,465 bottles of whisky _____ (produce) in Scotland.

8 1,426,940 letters _____ (send).

9 The Pentagon in Washington _____ (receive) 8,300 telephone calls.

10 £558,000 worth of goods _____ (sell) in Harrods department store.

11 12,000 passengers _____ (pass) through Heathrow airport.

12 166 Volkswagen cars _____ (make) in Germany.

LANGUAGE REVIEW

Present Simple

The Present Simple is used:

1 to express an action which happens again and again, that is, a *habit*. It is often found with these time expressions:

always every day usually
sometimes never

*I **sometimes walk** to work.*
*He **usually wears** a suit.*

2 to express a fact which is always true, or true for a long time.

*I **come** from Argentina.*
*He **works** in a bank.*

Present Continuous

The Present Continuous is used:

1 to express an activity that is in progress now.

*I**'m writing** a postcard to my friend.*
*Thomas **is listening** to the teacher.*

2 to express an activity around now but not necessarily happening at this moment.

*I**'m reading** a good book at the moment.*
*He**'s studying** to be an accountant.*

State Verbs

State verbs are not usually used in the Present Continuous. Here are some state verbs:

like	want	understand
believe	remember	hope
know	need	own
think (opinion)	have (possession)	

Passive

The uses of the Present Simple and the Present Continuous are the same in the passive.

*Champagne **is made** in France.*
*My car **is serviced** every six months.*
*My car **is being serviced** today.*

📖 **Grammar Reference: page 143.**

● READING AND SPEAKING

Pre-reading task

1 What do you think the life of a nun is like? What do they *always* do, *sometimes* do, and *never* do?

2 Which of the following do you think are important to nuns?

sport clothes prayer food and drink children
solitude hotels travel gardening reading
television singing money

Reading

1 Look at the pictures of Sister Wendy.
– What does she look like?
– What is she doing in the pictures?

2 Now read the text. Which of the things in the box above does she mention?

Sister Wendy, TV Star!

Sister Wendy Beckett has been a nun for nearly 50 years, since she was 16. Most of the time she lives in solitary confinement in a caravan in the grounds of a Carmelite monastery in Norfolk, often not speaking to anyone 5 for 22 hours a day. But every few months she leaves her caravan and travels round Europe, staying in international hotels and eating in famous restaurants. Why is she leading this double life? How does a nun who has devoted her life to solitude and prayer become a visitor to the Ritz? 10

Sister Wendy has a remarkable other life. She writes and presents an arts programme for BBC television called 'Sister Wendy's Grand Tour'. In it, she visits European art capitals and gives her personal opinions on 15 some of the world's most famous works of art. She begins each programme with these words: 'For over 20 years I lived in solitude. Now I'm 20 seeing Europe for the first time. I'm visiting the world's most famous art treasures.'

'I think God has been very good to me.'

She speaks clearly and plainly, with none of the
25 academic verbosity of art historians. TV viewers
love her common-sense wisdom, and are
fascinated to watch a kind, elderly, bespectacled,
nun who is so obviously delighted by all she sees.
They are infected by her enthusiasm. Sister
30 Wendy believes that although God wants her to
have a life of prayer and solitary contemplation,
He has also given her a mission to explain art in
a simple manner to ordinary people. She says:

'I think God has been very good to me. Really
35 I am a disaster as a person. Solitude is right for
me because I'm not good at being with other
people. But of course I enjoy going on tour. I
have a comfortable bed, a luxurious bath and
good meals, but the joy is mild compared with
40 the joy of solitude and silent prayer. I always
rush back to my caravan. People find this hard to
understand. I have never wanted anything else; I
am a blissfully happy woman.'

Sister Wendy's love of God and art is matched
45 only by her love of good food and wine. She
takes delight in poring over menus, choosing a
good wine and wondering whether the steak is
tender enough for her to eat because she has no
back teeth. However, she is not delighted by her
50 performance on television.

'I can't bear to watch myself on television. I
feel that I look so silly — a ridiculous black-
clothed figure. Thank God we don't have a
television at the monastery. I suppose I am
55 famous in a way, but as 95% of my time is spent
alone in my caravan, it really doesn't affect me.
I'm unimportant.'

Sister Wendy earned £1,200 for the first series.
The success of this resulted in an increase for the
60 second series. The money is being used to
provide new shower rooms for the Carmelite
monastery. ■

Comprehension check

1 What do these numbers in the text refer to?

16   22   20   95%   50   1,200

2 Are the following statements true (✓) or false (✗)?
Correct the false ones.

a Sister Wendy spends a lot of time alone.
b She travels to art capitals all over the world.
c Her television programmes are popular because she
meets famous art historians and interviews them.
d She believes that God wants her to lead this double life.
e She doesn't enjoy being alone in her caravan any more.
f She only eats plain food and she doesn't drink alcohol.
g Some of her teeth are missing.
h She loves watching herself on television.
i The other nuns at the monastery always watch her
programmes on television.
j Sister Wendy is using the money she has earned to
improve the monastery.

Language work

1 Complete the interview with Sister Wendy.

I   (a) _____ ?

SW   When I was sixteen. Goodness, that's nearly
fifty years ago!

I   (b) _____ ?

SW   In Norfolk. In a Carmelite monastery. Well,
not actually in the monastery but in the
grounds. I have a caravan.

I   (c) _____ ?

SW   No, I don't. Just in Europe—that's far enough!

I   (d) _____ ?

SW   I don't really know. I'm not sure why they're
popular. I feel that I look so silly, but perhaps
people find it funny to watch a silly old nun!

I   (e) _____ ?

SW   Yes, I do. Of course I do. The tours are really
interesting and everybody enjoys a life of
luxury now and then. I love good food and
drink, but you know, I'm happiest on my own
in my caravan.

I   (f) _____ ?

SW   No, I don't! I look ridiculous. I never watch if I
can help it!

I   (g) _____ ?

SW   I'm using it to help the monastery. Some new
shower rooms are being built. That's good, isn't it?

2   T.14   Listen and check your answers.

Discussion

Work in groups. Look at the list in Exercise 2 of the Pre-
reading task. Which of them are important to *you*? Why?

● VOCABULARY AND LISTENING

Sport

1 Make a list of as many sports and leisure activities as you can think of. Use the pictures to help you.

2 Write in *play*, *go*, or *do*. There are three of each.

_____ tennis	_____ athletics	_____ football
_____ exercises	_____ volleyball	_____ fishing
_____ jogging	_____ aerobics	_____ skiing

Can you work out the rules?

3 Choose some of the sports or activities from your list and fill in the columns below. Use your dictionary to look up any new words that you need.

sport/activity	play, go, or do?	people	place	equipment needed
football	play	goalkeeper footballer referee	stadium football pitch	ball boots

4 **T.15** Listen to three people talking about their favourite sport or leisure activity and make notes under the following headings.

- Which sport or activity are they talking about?
- How often do they do it?
- Where do they do it?
- What equipment do they need?

a   b   c

- Which picture goes with which sport?
- Why do they like it?
- Are they good at it?

5 Work in pairs. Ask and answer questions.

What sports do you do? Where? How often ...? Are you good at ...?

● WRITING

Describing a person

1 Think of someone in your family. Write three sentences about them. Read your sentences aloud to the rest of the class.

2 Which relative did you choose? Why did you choose that person? Did you write about their character, appearance, or both?

3 Look at the photograph and read the description of Aunt Emily.

4 Go through the text again and underline like this:

_____ the parts which describe her physical appearance

_ _ _ _ _ _ _ the parts which describe her character

. . . . the parts which describe her habits

5 Find the following words (l. = line):

quite (l. 3) a little (l. 7) rather (l. 7) very (l. 10) extremely (l. 13)

How do they change the meaning of the adjectives which follow them?

My aunt Emily

Of all my relatives, I like my Aunt Emily the best. She's my mother's youngest sister. She has never married, and she lives alone in a small village near Bath. She's in her late fifties, but she's still quite young in spirit. She has a fair complexion, thick brown hair which she
5 wears in a bun, and dark brown eyes. She has a kind face, and when you meet her, the first thing you notice is her lovely, warm smile. Her face is a little wrinkled now, but I think she is still rather attractive. She is the sort of person you can always go to if you have a problem.

She likes reading and gardening, and she goes for long walks over
10 the hills with her dog, Buster. She's a very active person. Either she's making something, or mending something, or doing something to help others. She does the shopping for some of the old people in the village. She's extremely generous, but not very tolerant with people who don't agree with her. I hope that I am as happy and contented as she is when
15 I'm her age.

6 She's 'not very tolerant' (l. 13). This is a nice way of saying she is 'intolerant'. Sometimes we try to be polite by not using a negative adjective. We can say **not very** + the opposite adjective.

Use a tactful way to describe someone who is:

a rude   c mean   e cruel
b boring   d ugly   f stupid

7 Who is 'you' in lines 6 (×2) and 8 in the text?

8 Write a similar description of a member of your family in about 200 words. Include the following:

– your opinion of the person
– physical description
– their character, habits, likes and dislikes.

PostScript

Numbers

1 Read aloud the following numbers.

15   50   406   72   128
90   19   850
1,520   36   247   5,000
100,000   2,000,000

When do we say *and*?

2 Practise the numbers.

Money
£100   50p   £9.40   £47.99
$400   5,000 FF   1,000 DM

Fractions
¼   ¾   ⅔   12½

Decimals and percentages
6.2   17.25   50%
75.7%   100%

Dates
1995   1939   1789
15/7/94   30/10/67

Phone numbers
01865 87676   0171 586 4431
00 44 925 270992

3 T.16a Read the numbers in Exercise 2 aloud. Listen and check your answers after each line.

4 T.16b Work in pairs. You will hear five short conversations. In each one there are some numbers. Write down the numbers you hear. Discuss what each number refers to with your partner.

Telling tales

Past tenses
Active and passive
Giving opinions

Test your grammar

1 Look at the three sentences. What is the difference in meaning?

a When Sylvia arrived home at eight o'clock, Tim cooked the dinner.

b When Sylvia arrived home at eight o'clock, Tim was cooking the dinner.

c When Sylvia arrived home at eight o'clock, Tim had cooked the dinner.

2 Match a picture with a sentence in exercise 1.

PRESENTATION (1)

Past Simple and Past Continuous

1 Look at the pictures. They tell the story of one of Aesop's fables. What can you see? What can you guess about the story?

2 Read the story. Put the verb in brackets into the Past Simple. They are all irregular. Complete the moral of 'The Bald Knight' at the end.

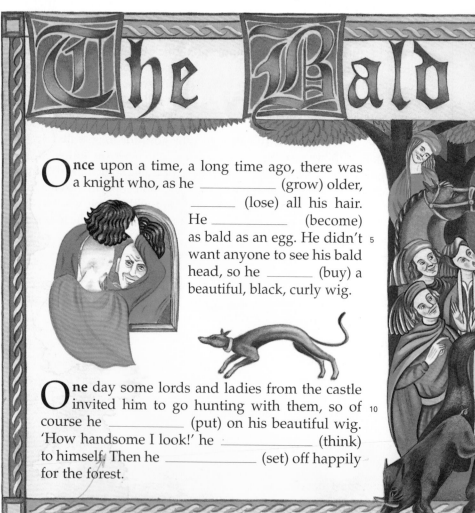

The Bald

Once upon a time, a long time ago, there was a knight who, as he _____ (grow) older, _____ (lose) all his hair. He _____ (become) as bald as an egg. He didn't 5 want anyone to see his bald head, so he _____ (buy) a beautiful, black, curly wig.

One day some lords and ladies from the castle invited him to go hunting with them, so of 10 course he _____ (put) on his beautiful wig. 'How handsome I look!' he _____ (think) to himself. Then he _____ (set) off happily for the forest.

3 The following sentences have been taken from the story. Read it again and decide where they fit.

> a … as he <u>was dressing</u> in front of his mirror.
>
> b He <u>was riding</u> along, singing merrily to himself, when he <u>passed</u> under an oak tree and …
>
> c They <u>were</u> all still <u>laughing</u> when they <u>arrived</u> back at the castle.

4 **T.17** Listen and check your answers.

● **Grammar questions**

– What tense are all the underlined verb forms in Exercise 3?

– What is the difference in meaning between the following two sentences?

  He laughed when he fell off his horse.
  He was laughing when he fell off his horse.

PRACTICE

1 Grammar

<u>Underline</u> the correct verb form in the following sentences.

a While he *rode/was riding* in the forest he *lost/was losing* his wig.

b When I *arrived/was arriving* the party was in full swing. Paul *danced/was dancing* with Mary, and Pat and Peter *drank/were drinking* champagne.

c When I *finished/was finishing* the ironing, I *cooked/was cooking* dinner.

d How fast *did they travel/were they travelling* when their car *had/was having* a puncture?

e A police car *passed/was passing* us on the motorway when we *did/were doing* 80 miles per hour.

f I *took/was taking* a photograph of him while he *ate/was eating* an ice-cream.

g He *didn't like/wasn't liking* the photo when he *saw/was seeing* it.

h I'm sorry I *woke/was waking* you. What *were you dreaming/did you dream* about?

2 Pronunciation

T.18 You will hear twelve regular verbs in the Past Simple. Put them in the right column, according to the pronunciation of *-ed*.

/t/	/d/	/ɪd/

---

15 **H**owever, a terrible thing happened. His wig _____ (catch) on a branch and _____ (fall) off in full view of everyone. How they all laughed at him! At first the poor knight _____ (feel) very foolish but then he _____ (see) the funny side 20 of the situation, and he started laughing, too.

The knight never _____ (wear) his wig again.

THE MORAL OF THIS STORY IS: WHEN PEOPLE LAUGH AT US, IT IS BEST TO …

3 Speaking

1 Read what Sylvia did yesterday.

6.30	woke up
6.45 – 7.15	packed her suitcase
7.30 – 8.30	drove to the airport
9.20 – 10.15	flew to Edinburgh
11.00 – 12.45	had a meeting
1.00 – 2.15	had lunch
2.30 – 4.45	visited a school
6.05 – 6.45	wrote a report on the plane
8.30 – 9.00	cooked a meal
9.30 – 11.00	listened to music

2 Work with a partner. Ask and answer questions about what Sylvia *was doing* at the times below.

Example

> What was she doing at 6 o'clock in the morning?

> > She was sleeping.

7.00 am	11.30 am	6.30 pm
8.00 am	1.30 pm	8.45 pm
9.45 am	3.00 pm	10.00 pm

3 Write a similar list about what you did yesterday. Ask and answer questions with your partner about different times of the day.

Example

> What were you doing at 7 o'clock in the evening?

> > I was having dinner.

4 Life stories

Work in pairs. Join a line in **A** with a word in **B** and a line in **C** to make your own story about the lives of a grandmother and grandfather. Read your story to others in the class.

A	B	C
They met and fell in love		they returned to Britain.
They got married		they were living in Hong Kong.
They had their first son		the Second World War.
They lived in Hong Kong	**when**	they were working abroad.
They had five more sons	**while**	the summer of 1991.
They sent their sons to boarding school	**during**	five years.
They lived in six different countries	**for**	their marriage.
They were happily married		over forty-five years.
My grandfather died		they were working together in Malaysia.

T.19 Listen and check the true story of their lives. How different is your version?

PRESENTATION (2)

Past Simple and Past Perfect

1 Look at the pictures. They tell the story of another of Aesop's fables. What can you see? What do you think the story is about?

2 **T.20** Close your books and listen to the story. Is it the same as yours?

3 Read the story and complete the moral at the end.

The Farmer
and his Sons

There was once an old, dying farmer (1). Before he died he wanted to teach his three sons how to be good farmers. So he called them to him and said, 'My boys, 5 before I die I want you to know that there is a great treasure buried in the vineyard. Promise me that you will look for it when I am dead.'

The sons promised and (2) they began looking for the treasure. They worked very hard in the hot sun (3). In their minds they 10 pictured boxes of gold coins, diamond necklaces and other such things.

4 Where do the following sentences fit in the story?
   Put a number 1–6 in the boxes.

a as soon as their father had died, ☐
b who had worked hard in his vineyard all his life ☐
c what their father had meant by the great treasure, ☐
d and all the time as they were working they
   wondered what their father had left for them ☐
e They felt that all their hard work had been for
   nothing. ☐
f Soon they had dug up every inch of the vineyard. ☐

5 Listen again and check your answers.

(4) But they found not a single penny. They were very
upset. (5) But then the grapes started to appear on the
vines and their grapes were the biggest and best in the
neighbourhood, and they sold them for a lot of money. 15

Now they understood (6) and they lived happily and
wealthily ever after.

THE MORAL OF THIS STORY IS:
HARD WORK BRINGS …

● Grammar questions

– What tense are all the underlined verb forms in
  Exercise 4?

– Which sentence is true?

a *The sons looked for the treasure when their father
   was dying.*
b *The sons looked for the treasure when their father
   had died.*

– What is the difference in meaning between a and b?

PRACTICE

1 Discussing grammar

Work in pairs and discuss your answers.

1 Discuss the difference in meaning between the
   following pairs of sentences.

a When I arrived at the party, they *were drinking*
   champagne.
   When I arrived at the party, they*'d drunk* the
   champagne.

b When I got home, the children *went* to bed.
   When I got home, the children *had gone* to bed.

c They thanked their teacher for everything she *was
   doing* to help them pass the exam.
   They thanked their teacher for everything she*'d
   done* to help them pass the exam.

d He told me that they *were staying* at the Ritz Hotel.
   He told me that they *had stayed* at the Ritz Hotel.

2 Join the sentences using the conjunction in brackets.
   Change one verb into the Past Perfect.

   Example
   The children went to bed. We watched television.
   (After)
   *After the children had gone to bed, we watched
   television.*

a I took an aspirin. My headache disappeared. (when)
b He drove 200 miles. He stopped for a break. (after)
c I couldn't pay for my ticket. A thief stole my wallet.
   (because)
d She passed her driving test. She bought a car.
   (as soon as)
e I didn't go to Italy. I learnt Italian. (until)
f He didn't tell the policeman. He took the money.
   (that)
g We didn't tell Anna. George rang. (that)

2 Dictation and questions

Ask your teacher questions about the gaps in the following text. Write in the replies the teacher gives you to complete the story.

Example
Last summer Wanda and Roy went on holiday to _____ (*Where?*).

> Where did they go?

Last summer Wanda and Roy went on holiday to
(1) _____ (*Where?*). Every day they
(2) _____ and _____ (*What?*). One
morning they were swimming (3) _____ (*Where?*)
when a huge wave (4) _____ (*What/do?*). Wanda
was very upset because (5) _____ (*Why?*).
The next day they were sunbathing (6) _____
(*Where?*) and Wanda was wearing (7) _____
(*What?*) when suddenly there was another huge wave, which
(8) _____ (*What/do?*). She was furious, but then
she looked down and to her amazement she saw
(9) _____ (*What?*).

3 Stress and intonation

1 **Student A** Read out a statement from your list.
  Student B Answer Student A with the correct response from your list.

Student A

I went to the airport but I couldn't catch the plane.
I was homesick while I was living in New York.
I met my boyfriend's/girlfriend's parents last Sunday.
My grandfather had two sons from his first marriage.
I told everyone the good news.
As soon as I saw him I knew something was wrong.

Student B

Hadn't they heard it already?
Oh dear! Had you forgotten your passport?
Really? I didn't know he'd been married before.
Oh! Hadn't you met them before?
Oh dear! What had happened?
Poor you! Had you never lived abroad before?

---

2 **T.21** Listen and check your answers. Pay particular attention to the stress and intonation.

3 Change roles and practise the conversations again. Choose one or two and make them into longer conversations.

LANGUAGE REVIEW

Narrative tenses

The Past Simple

1 The Past Simple is used to express a finished action in the past.

 *We **played** tennis yesterday.*
 *She **saw** Peter last Sunday and they **went** for a walk.*
 *They **met** in 1980 but they **didn't marry** until 1993.*

2 It is also used to express a past habit.

 *When I was a child we **went** to Spain every summer.*
 *I **wore** a uniform at school.*

The Past Continuous

The Past Continuous is used to express an activity in progress in the past.
The events of a story are in the Past Simple, but descriptions and interrupted activities are in the Past Continuous.

*When we arrived, he **was making** some coffee.*
*When we arrived he **made** some coffee.*

*It **was raining** and she **was feeling** miserable when suddenly she **saw** Peter and she **smiled** again.*

The Past Perfect

The Past Perfect is used to make clear that one action in the past happened before another action in the past.

*When we arrived home Anna **had gone** to bed.*
*When we arrived home Anna **went** to bed.*

📖 **Grammar Reference: page 145.**

● VOCABULARY

Art, music and literature

Use your dictionary to look up any new words.

1 Look at the nouns below and write them in the correct column.

composer	poem	author	painter
oil painting	instrument	band	palette	sketch
tune	chapter	orchestra	bugle	biography
brush	detective story	banjo	portrait	fiction
play	drawing	novel	pianist	pop group

ART	MUSIC	LITERATURE

2 Which of the following verbs can go with the nouns in Exercise 1?

read	write	compose	play	play in	draw
paint	conduct	hum	tune		

3 Complete each of the following sentences with a verb in the right tense and a noun.

a Agatha Christie _____ many famous _____ .

b I couldn't put the book down until I _____ the last _____ .

c I don't know the words of the song but I can _____ the _____ .

d The only _____ I can _____ is the piano.

e Picasso often _____ unusual _____ of his girlfriends.

f The _____ of Princess Diana _____ by the journalist, Andrew Morton.

g Listen! The show is starting. Can you hear the _____ ? They _____ their instruments.

h My brother is a soldier. He _____ the bugle in the army _____ .

i Before I painted the picture I _____ a quick _____ in pencil.

4 Work in groups. Do you have a favourite book or poem, piece of music, or painting? Why do you like it? Think about it for a few minutes then compare your favourites with the rest of the class.

● READING AND SPEAKING

The writer, the painter and the musician

Pre-reading task

1 ▢ T.22 You are going to read about the lives of three famous people, Agatha Christie, Pablo Picasso, and Scott Joplin.

– Why were they famous?
– Look at and/or listen to their most popular works. Do you know any more?

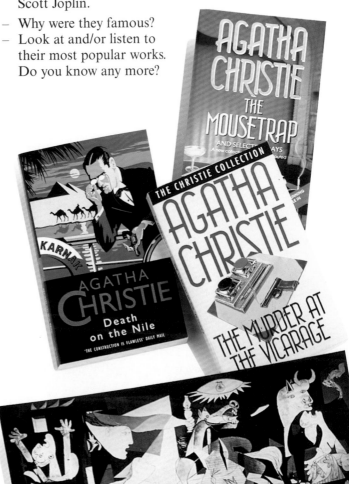

▲ *Guernica 1937* by
Pablo Picasso
© Succession Picasso/DACS 1996.

The Entertainer ▶
by Scott Joplin

2 Discuss the following questions about the people.

– What nationality were they?
– Which century were they born in?
– Which one do you know most/least about?

Reading

Work in three groups.

Group A Read about the writer.
Group B Read about the painter.
Group C Read about the musician.

Read your extract and answer the questions about your person. Try to *guess* the words underlined from the context. Then use your dictionary to check the words.

1 Where was she/he born?
2 When was she/he born?
3 What do you learn about her/his childhood?
4 Which people played a part in her/his career?

5 What do you think were the most important events in her/his life?
6 What do you learn of her/his works?
7 When did she/he die?
8 Which of the following numbers or dates relate to your person? What do they refer to?

50	79	6,000	11	13	14	4,680,000
1882	1920	1926	1937	1952		

When you have finished, find a partner from each of the other groups and go through the questions together, comparing information.

The Writer

Agatha Mary Clarissa Christie is possibly the world's most famous detective story writer. She wrote 79 novels and several plays. Her sales
5 *outnumber those of William Shakespeare. However, behind her 4,680,000 words was a painfully shy woman whose life was often lonely and unhappy.*

10 She was born in 1890 in Devon, the third child of Clarissa and Frederick Miller, and grew into a beautiful and sensitive girl with waist-length golden hair. She didn't
15 go to school but was educated at home by her mother. Her father died when she was 11 and both she and her mother were grief-stricken.

▲ A scene from *The Mousetrap*, which opened in London on 25 November 1952 and is still running today.

During World War I, while she
20 was working in a hospital dispensary, she learned about chemicals and poisons, which proved very useful to her in her later career. She wrote her first detective
25 novel, *The Mysterious Affair at Styles*, in 1920. In it she introduced Hercule Poirot, the Belgian detective who appeared in many subsequent novels. Her other main detective
30 was an elderly spinster called Miss Marple.

In 1914, at the beginning of the war, she had married Archibald Christie but the marriage was
35 unhappy. It didn't last and they divorced in 1926. That year there was a double tragedy in her life because her much-loved mother died. Agatha suffered a nervous breakdown,
40 and one night she abandoned her car and mysteriously disappeared. She went missing for 11 days and was eventually found in a hotel in Harrogate, in the North of England.
45 It is interesting to note that it was while she was suffering so much that she wrote one of her masterpieces, *The Murder of Roger Ackroyd*.

Agatha desperately wanted solitude
50 and developed very bitter feelings towards the media because the newspapers had given her a hard time over her breakdown and disappearance. She was determined
55 never to let them enter her private life again and she buried herself in her work. On 25 November 1952 her play *The Mousetrap* opened in London. Today, over 40 years later, it
60 is still running. It is the longest running show in the whole world.

She enjoyed a very happy second marriage to Max Mallowan, an archaeologist. Her detective skills
65 were a help to him in his excavations in Syria and Iraq. By successfully staying out of the limelight she ultimately found happiness with her beloved husband. She died peacefully
70 in 1976.

The Painter

On 25 October 1881 a little boy was born in Malaga, Spain. It was a difficult birth and to help him breathe, cigar smoke was blown into his nose! But despite
5 being the youngest ever smoker, this baby grew up to be one of the 20th century's greatest painters—**Pablo Picasso**.

Picasso showed his truly exceptional
10 talent from a very young age. His first word was *lápiz* (Spanish for pencil) and he learned to draw before he could talk. He was the only son in the family and very good-looking, so he was thoroughly
15 spoilt. He hated school and often refused to go unless his doting parents allowed him to take one of his father's pet pigeons with him!

Apart from pigeons, his great love was
20 art, and when in 1891 his father, who was an amateur artist, got a job as a drawing teacher at a college, Pablo went with him to the college. He often watched his father paint and sometimes was allowed
25 to help. One evening his father was painting a picture of their pigeons when he had to leave the room. He returned to

find that Pablo had completed the picture, and it was so amazingly beautiful and
30 lifelike that he gave his son his own palette and brushes and never painted again. Pablo was just 13.

From then onwards there was no stopping him. Many people realized that
35 he was a genius but he disappointed those who wanted him to become a traditional painter. He was always breaking the rules of artistic tradition and shocked the public with his strange and
40 powerful pictures. He is probably best known for his 'Cubist' pictures, which used only simple geometric shapes. His paintings of people were often made up of triangles and squares with their
45 features in the wrong place. His work changed our ideas about art, and to millions of people modern art means the work of Picasso. *Guernica*, which he painted in 1937, records the bombing of
50 that little Basque town during the Spanish Civil War, and is undisputedly one of the masterpieces of modern painting.

Picasso created over 6,000 paintings,
55 drawings and sculptures. Today a 'Picasso' costs several million pounds. Once, when the French Minister of Culture was visiting Picasso, the artist accidentally spilt some paint on the
60 Minister's trousers. Picasso apologized and wanted to pay for them to be cleaned, but the Minister said, 'Non! Please, Monsieur Picasso, just sign my trousers!'

65 Picasso died of heart failure during an attack of influenza in 1973.

The Musician

Ever since it was the musical theme in the film 'The Sting', there are few people who have not tapped their feet to the hit piano tune, 'The Entertainer'—the most famous composition of the American musician, Scott Joplin.

5 Scott was born in Texas in 1868, into a poor but musical black family. His father, who was a freed slave, played the violin, and his mother played the banjo and sang. Scott played the violin and bugle but his favourite instrument was his neighbour's piano. His father worked extra
10 hours to buy him a battered old grand piano, and soon Scott was playing by ear negro tunes, blues, and spirituals. Music flowed naturally from his fingers, and he quickly became the talk of the town.

15 Scott didn't learn to read music until he was 11, when an old German music teacher spotted his talent and gave him free, formal piano lessons. He learned to play the works of such composers as Bach, Beethoven, and Mozart as well as his
20 improvised music. Thus when he started to write music, his tunes were a wonderful mixture of classical European and African beat. This unique style was known as Ragtime, and was played everywhere in the USA in the early 1900s by
25 both black and white musicians.

In 1882, when Scott was 14, his mother died and he left home to seek his fortune in St. Louis. In the 1880s, St. Louis was noisy and bustling with life. The waterfront of the Mississippi River was full of gangsters, gamblers, and
30 sailors. The sound of music was everywhere—black, white and mixed. The hot steamy nights were filled with blues, working songs, banjos, and honky tonk pianos. Scott was soon playing Ragtime piano in cheap bars on the waterfront.
35 This was a rough, tough area of the city where arguments over girls, whisky, and money were settled with fists and guns. Scott grew up very fast and his musical talent continued to develop. All in all he wrote about 50 piano rags.

40 Scott Joplin died in 1917. Today he is the undisputed King of Ragtime, thanks to his natural ability, his unusual musical education, and the popularity of the film, *The Sting*.

Comprehension check

1 Read the other two extracts quickly. Help each other with any new words, particularly those words which are <u>underlined</u> in your text.

2 Here are some answers about all three people. Write in the questions.

a What _____ ?
She was beautiful and shy, with long, golden hair.

b Why _____ ?
To help him breathe, after a difficult birth.

c How _____ ?
By working extra hours.

d Why _____ ?
Because they gave her a hard time over her breakdown and disappearance.

e When _____ ?
In 1937.

f Where _____ ?
To St. Louis.

Language work

1 *'The Mousetrap'* **was written** *by Agatha Christie.*

In the sentence above, *was written* is an example of the Past Simple passive.
Find some more examples of this in the texts on pages 30 and 31, and put a box ☐ around them.

📖 Grammar Reference: page 144.

2 Put the auxiliaries *was*, *had*, or *didn't* into the gaps.

a Agatha Christie _____ educated at home. She _____ go to school.

b She _____ found in a hotel in Harrogate, after she _____ been missing for 11 days.

c She _____ stop writing while she _____ suffering from a nervous breakdown.

d Pablo Picasso _____ like going to school unless he _____ allowed to take one of his father's pigeons with him.

e His father _____ paint again after Pablo _____ completed the picture of the pigeons.

f Some paint _____ spilt on the French minister's trousers when he _____ visiting Picasso.

g Scott Joplin left home after his mother _____ died.

Note-taking and discussion

Choose *one* of the most famous writers, painters or musicians in your country and write some notes about him/her. Discuss your notes with a partner.

– Is he/she alive or dead?
– What is/was he/she?
– What works do you know?
– Do you like his/her work? Why? Why not?
– What do you know about his/her life?

● WRITING AND LISTENING

Adverbs in a narrative

Work in pairs.

1 Think about the worst holiday you ever had. Write some notes about it, then swap information with your partner.

2 Look at the top of page 33 and read about Jack and Liza's holiday. Put the words on the right into the correct place in each line, and make any necessary changes to the punctuation.

The *holiday*

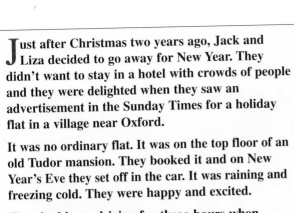

Just after Christmas two years ago, Jack and Liza decided to go away for New Year. They didn't want to stay in a hotel with crowds of people and they were delighted when they saw an advertisement in the Sunday Times for a holiday flat in a village near Oxford.

It was no ordinary flat. It was on the top floor of an old Tudor mansion. They booked it and on New Year's Eve they set off in the car. It was raining and freezing cold. They were happy and excited.

They had been driving for three hours when they saw the house in the distance. It looked magnificent with tall chimneys and a long, wide drive. They drove up to the huge front door, went up the steps, and knocked. Nothing happened. They knocked again. The door opened and a small, wild-looking, old lady stood there.

suddenly   somewhere

so   really

However
immediately
Although   heavily

nearly
finally
incredibly

loudly
more loudly   Eventually   slowly

3   **T.23**   Listen to Jack and Liza talking about what happened next and complete this part of the story.

The old lady was wearing …
She was carrying …
The house was …
When she was leading them upstairs …
When they saw the rooms they couldn't believe their eyes …

4   Read the end of the story. Put the words on the right into the correct place.

that wasn't

When they got outside again the rain had turned to snow. They ran to the car, laughing. They felt that they had been released from a prison and now they wanted to be with lots of people. They drove to the next village and as midnight was striking, they found a hotel with a room for the night. 'Happy New Year!' cried Jack, as he kissed the surprised receptionist on both cheeks. 'You have no idea how beautiful your hotel is!'

hysterically

desperately
fortunately   just

warmly

5   Write the story of your worst holiday in about 250 words.

– When was it?
– Where was it?
– Who were you with?
– Why was it bad?

Post Script

Giving opinions

1 What do the words in *italics* refer to in the sentences below?

a *It* was so boring I fell asleep in the first act.
b I didn't like his last *one*, but I couldn't put his latest *one* down until the last chapter.
c *It* was excellent. Have you seen *it* yet? *It* stars Anthony Hopkins and Emma Thompson.
d *She's* usually very good but I don't think *she* was right for this part.
e I think *they* spoil *them*. They always give *them* whatever they want.
f *It* was a good break, but the weather wasn't very good.
g *They* were delicious. John had tomato and mozzarella topping and I had ham and mozzarella.
h *It* was really exciting, especially when Smith scored in the closing minutes.

2 T.24 The following questions are all asking for opinions. Match them with the opinions given in Exercise 1.

Did you like the film? ☐
What did you think of the play? ☐
Did you enjoy your pizzas? ☐
Do you like Ben Brown's novels? ☐
What do you think of their children? ☐
What was your holiday like? ☐
What did you think of Hannah Smart? ☐
What was the match like? ☐

Listen and check your answers. Practise some of the questions and answers with a partner.

3 Write down some things you did, places you went to, and people you met last week.
Work with a partner and ask for and give opinions about them.

Example

Student A   **Student B**

I went to Peter's party.

Oh! What was it like?

Great! I really enjoyed it.

I met Maria's sister.

What did you think of her?

She's lovely. I liked her a lot.

4 Doing the right thing

Modal verbs (1)
Requests and offers

1 Look at the sentences.

You | can / must / should / have to | go.

2 Make the sentences negative.
Make them into questions.
Make them into the third person singular (*He/she ...*).

Which verb is different?

PRESENTATION (1)

can, *have to*, and *allowed to*

1 The teenage years can be difficult for both parents and children! What sort of problems can there be?

2 **T.25** Listen to Megan and Laura, aged 14 and 15. What are some of the things they like and don't like about being a teenager?

3 Complete the gaps.

a You _____ go out to work.

b You _____ pay bills.

c You _____ go out with your friends.

d I always _____ tell my Mum and Dad where I'm going.

e We _____ do the housework.

f You _____ buy what you want.

g Adults _____ worry about bills.

h We _____ wear a stupid school uniform.

i We _____ wear make-up.

j We _____ chew gum!

Listen again and check. Practise saying the sentences.

4 Laura's parents are called Malcolm and Barbara. What are some of the things they *have to* do, and some of the things they *don't have to* do?

Examples
Barbara doesn't have to work full-time.
Malcolm has to drive over a thousand miles a week.

- Who do you think has an easier life, Barbara or Malcolm?
- What about *your* family?
- Is there a division between what the men do and what the women do in your family?

● Grammar questions

– Put *have to* or *don't have to* into the gaps.

Children _____ go to school.

Adults _____ go to school, but they
_____ go to work.

Old people _____ go to work.

Teenagers _____ study for exams.

– Which sentence in each pair below is correct?

a You don't have to drive on the right in Britain.
   You mustn't drive on the right in Britain.

b You don't have to go to England to learn English.
   You mustn't go to England to learn English.

PRACTICE

1 Grammar and speaking

1 Put the sentences into the negative, the question, and
   the past.

   Example
   We can smoke.   *We can't smoke.*
                      Can we smoke?
                      We could smoke.

a I have to go.
b She has to work hard.
c He can do what he likes.
d We're allowed to wear what we want.

2 Look at the chart. Make true sentences about you and
   your family.

A	B	C
I		go out to work.
My parents		get up early in
My father		the morning.
My mother	has to	do the shopping.
My sister	have to	keep my room
My brother	doesn't have to	tidy.
My grandparents	don't have to	do the cooking.
My husband/wife	had to	take the dog for
My girlfriend/	didn't have to	a walk.
boyfriend		do the washing.
		do the washing-
		up.
		. . .
		. . .

Compare your sentences as a class.
Are/were your parents strict? Can/could you do what
you want/wanted?

3 Make questions using *have to* or *had to*.

   Example
   We had to get up very early to catch the bus.
   What time *did you have to get up*?

a My mother has to go abroad a lot.
   How often _____ ?

b I have to leave tomorrow morning.
   What time _____ ?

c We had to wait for ages.
   How long _____ ?

d I have to take my car to the garage.
   Why _____ ?

e Peter had to stay in bed for a week.
   Why _____ ?

2 Signs

What do the following signs mean?

Examples

You can't smoke in here.
You aren't allowed to smoke in here.

You have to show your passport.

a

b

c

d

e

f

g   h

3 Listening and speaking

1 **T.26** You will hear Bert Atkins, who was born in
1919, talking about his school days.
Check these words in your dictionary:

to knit   a cloth   a slate   chalk

What does he say about the following?

knitting	exams	
paper and pencils	walking to school	
chalk and a slate	a bike	
the 'Big Boys'	leaving school	writing lines
school	talking in class	homework

Listen again, and read the Tapescript on page 130 at
the same time.

2 Work in groups. Talk about *your* school rules.

– What aren't/weren't you allowed to do?
– What do/did you have to do?
– What punishments are/were there if you do/did
something wrong?

PRESENTATION (2)

must and should

1 **T.27a** Jim is going to backpack around the world for
a year, but his mother is worried. Listen to them.

Mum	You must write to us every week!
Jim	Yes, Mum! I will.
Mum	You mustn't lose your passport!
Jim	No, Mum! I won't.

Work in pairs. Make similar dialogues between Jim
and his mother. Use the cues and *must* or *mustn't*.

– look after your money	– talk to strangers
– go out when it's dark	– drink too much beer
– make sure you eat well	– have a bath regularly
– phone us if you're in	– go anywhere that's
trouble	dangerous

T.27b Listen and check your answers.

2 **T.28a** Jim is going to travel with his friend,
Anthony. Listen to them talking about their trip.

> I think we should take
> our travellers' cheques
> in American dollars.

> I don't think we should go to
> Thailand in September
> because it's the rainy season.

Use *I think ... should* or *I don't think ... should* to make
more suggestions. Take an idea in column **A**, and
match it with a line in column **B**.

A

a ... take plenty of suncream.
b ... buy a book called *See the World on $25 a Day*.
c ... put too much in our backpacks.
d ... take anything valuable.
e ... go to Australia first.
f ... go to Indonesia by boat.
g ... wait too long before we go.

B

☐ We might lose it.
☐ I've got some friends there who'll put us up.
☐ I want to get started.
☐ It'll have some good ideas about where to go and
where to stay.
☐ It'll be really hot.
☐ We won't be able to carry it all.
☐ It'll be cheaper than flying.

T.28b Listen and check your answers.

● Grammar questions

*You **must** look after your money.*
*We **should** take travellers' cheques.*

– Which sentence expresses strong obligation?
– Which sentence expresses a suggestion?
– Who is more forceful, Jim's mother or Anthony?

PRACTICE

1 Giving advice

Give advice in the following situations. Use
I think ... should or *I don't think ... should*.

Example
Peter's got a very bad cold.

I think he should go to bed.
I don't think he should go to work.

a I've lost my cheque book and credit cards.
b Tony wants to drive home, but he's had too
   much to drink.
c (In a restaurant) Ugh! My soup's cold!
d I never have any money!
e Jenny and Paul are only sixteen, but they say
   they want to get married.
f I'm really fed up with my job.

Do you have any problems? Ask the class for advice!

2 *must* or *have to*?

Read the Language Review on page 39 before you do this exercise.
Which sentence on the right goes with the sentence on the left?

Example
I must have a drink of water. 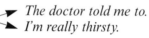 *The doctor told me to.*
I have to drink lots of water. *I'm really thirsty.*

1 a I must do my homework tonight.	I'm telling myself that it's important.
b I have to do my homework tonight.	This is why I can't come out with you. Sorry.
2 a We must go to Paris some time.	Another boring business trip. Yawn!
b We have to go to Paris next week.	It would be really nice!
3 a I must wear something nice to the disco.	It's the rule.
b Men have to wear a shirt and tie to go into a posh restaurant.	I want to look good.
4 a You must register for next term before Thursday.	It says on the noticeboard.
b You have to register for next term before Thursday.	One student is talking to another.
5 a I must water the plants today.	I haven't done them for ages.
b You have to water this plant daily.	It needs lots and lots of water.

3 Roleplay

Work in pairs.
Student A You are going to start a
            new job.
Student B You are a work colleague.

Decide what the job is. Ask and
answer questions about the
responsibilities, hours, breaks, etc.

> What time do I have to start?

> Do I have to wear a uniform?

> No, but you should look smart.

> When do we have a break?

4 Correcting mistakes

There is a grammar mistake in each
of the following sentences. Find it
and correct it!

a Do you can help me a minute?
b What time have you to start work?
c I must to go now. Bye-bye.
d We no allowed to wear jeans at
   school.
e We no can do what we want.
f I mustn't do the washing and
   ironing because my mother does it
   for me.
g You can't smoking in here. It's
   against the rules.
h My mother have to work very
   hard six days a week.

LANGUAGE REVIEW

Modals to express obligation

1 *Must* expresses a strong obligation.

   All visitors **must** *report to Reception.*
   You **mustn't** *steal things! It's naughty.*

2 *Have to* expresses a general obligation based on a law or a rule.

   Nurses **have to** *wear a uniform.*
   Malcolm **has to** *drive a thousand miles a week in his job.*

3 Sometimes *must* and *have to* are similar.

   I **must** *go now. Cheerio!*   *I* **have to** *go now. Cheerio!*

   Sometimes there is a difference. *Must* is personal. We use *must* when we express our personal feelings, and say what *we* think is important or necessary.

   You **must** *work harder.* (I am telling you what to do.)
   I **must** *wash my hair. It's dirty.*
   (I am telling myself that it's necessary.)

   Have to is impersonal. It expresses a general obligation based on what another person tells us to do.

   We **have to** *wear a stupid uniform.* (It's a school rule.)
   I **have to** *take this medicine three times a day.*
   (The doctor said.)

4 *Have to* is used to form the question, and the past and future.

   Do *you* **have to** *work full-time?*
   I **had to** *get up very early when I was at school.*
   You'll **have to** *work hard if you want to go to university.*

5 *Should* expresses what is right, or a good idea. It expresses advice, or a mild obligation.

   You **should** *get more exercise. Why don't you play tennis?*
   You **shouldn't** *eat so many sweets. They're bad for your teeth.*

Negatives

Mustn't and *don't have to* express very different ideas.

   You **mustn't** *take drugs.*
   (This is a strong obligation *not* to do something.)
   Teenagers **don't have to** *go out to work.*
   (There is *no* obligation, but they can if they want.)

Modals to express permission

Can, *can't*, and *be allowed to* are used to express permission. *Allowed to* is passive.

   We **can't** *smoke or chew gum.*
   We **aren't allowed to** *buy what we want.*

📖 **Grammar Reference: page 147.**

● READING AND SPEAKING

Pre-reading task

Work in pairs.

1 Look at the cartoons. What nationalities are the people? What makes it easy for you to identify them?

2 What is the stereotype English man or woman? What do you think is the stereotype for your nationality? Do you believe in stereotypes?

3 Which adjectives in the box do you think go with the nationalities below?
   Use your dictionary to check new words.

hard-working	easy-going	punctual	friendly
reserved	emotional	lazy	outgoing
hospitable	sociable	formal	casual
enthusiastic	quiet	tolerant	talkative
sophisticated	well-dressed	fun-loving	respectful
humorous	serious	nationalistic	romantic

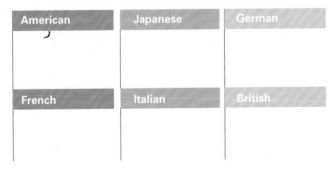

American	Japanese	German
French	Italian	British

Is your nationality one of those above? If so, which adjectives did you choose?
If not, choose some adjectives which you think go with your nationality.

Reading

Look at the title of the article. Do you think the article will be serious or light-hearted? Why?

First read the article quite quickly. All the nationalities on page 39 are mentioned.

1 Write down one thing about each nationality that you can remember.

2 Share what you have written with other students in the class.

A World Guide to Good Manners
How *not* to behave badly abroad

～ by Norman Ramshaw ～

Travelling to all corners of the world gets easier and easier. We live in a global village, but
5 how well do we know and understand each other? Here is a simple test. Imagine you have arranged a meeting at four o'clock. What time should you
10 expect your foreign business colleagues to arrive? If they're German, they'll be bang on time. If they're American, they'll probably be 15 minutes early. If they're British, they'll be 15 minutes late, and you should allow up to an hour for the Italians.

15 When the European Community began to increase in size, several guidebooks appeared giving advice on international etiquette. At first many people thought this was a joke, especially the British, who seemed to assume that the widespread
20 understanding of their language meant a corresponding understanding of English customs. Very soon they had to change their ideas, as they realized that they had a lot to learn about how to behave with their foreign business friends.

25 **For example:**

● The British are happy to have a business lunch and discuss business matters with a drink during the meal; the Japanese prefer not to work while eating. Lunch is a time to relax and get to know one
30 another, and they rarely drink at lunchtime.

● The Germans like to talk business *before* dinner; the French like to eat first and talk afterwards. They have to be well fed and watered before they discuss anything.

35 ● Taking off your jacket and rolling up your sleeves is a sign of getting down to work in Britain and Holland, but in Germany people regard it as taking it easy.

● American executives sometimes signal their
40 feelings of ease and importance in their offices by putting their feet on the desk whilst on the telephone. In Japan, people would be shocked. Showing the
45 soles of your feet is the height of bad manners. It is a social insult only exceeded by blowing your nose in public.

The Japanese have perhaps the strictest rules of social and
50 business behaviour. Seniority is very important, and a younger man should never be sent to complete a business deal with an older
55 Japanese man. The Japanese business card almost needs a rulebook of its own. You must exchange business cards immediately on meeting because it is
60 essential to establish everyone's status and position.

When it is handed to a person in a superior position, it must be given and received with both hands, and you must take time to read it carefully, and not just put it in your pocket! Also the bow is a very important part of greeting someone. You should
70 not expect the Japanese to shake hands. Bowing the head is a mark of respect and the first bow of the day should be lower than when you meet thereafter.

The Americans sometimes find it difficult to accept the more formal
75 Japanese manners. They prefer to be casual and more informal, as illustrated by the universal 'Have a nice day!' American waiters have a one-word imperative 'Enjoy!' The British, of course, are cool
80 and reserved. The great topic of conversation between strangers in Britain is the weather— unemotional and impersonal. In America, the main topic between strangers is the search to find a geographical link. 'Oh, really? You live in Ohio? I had an uncle who once worked there.'

'When in Rome, do as the Romans do.'
90 **Here are some final tips for travellers.**

● In France you shouldn't sit down in a café until you've shaken hands with everyone you know.

● In Afghanistan you should spend at least five minutes saying hello.

95 ● In Pakistan you mustn't wink. It is offensive.

● In the Middle East you must never use the left hand for greeting, eating, drinking, or smoking. Also, you should take care not to admire anything in your hosts' home. They will feel that they have to give it
100 to you.

● In Russia you must match your hosts drink for drink or they will think you are unfriendly.

● In Thailand you should clasp your hands together and lower your head and your eyes when you greet
105 someone.

● In America you should eat your hamburger with both hands and as quickly as possible. You shouldn't try to have a conversation until it is eaten.

Comprehension check

Read the article again and answer the questions. Discuss the questions in pairs.

1 Which nationalities are the most and least punctual?
2 Why did the British think that everyone understood their customs?
3 Which nationalities do *not* like to eat and do business at the same time?
4 'They (the French) have to be well fed and watered.' What or who do you normally have to feed and water?
5 Look at the pictures. What nationality are they? How do you know?
6 An American friend of yours is going to work in Japan. Give some advice about how he/she should and shouldn't behave.
7 Imagine you are at a party in (a) England (b) America. How could you begin a conversation with a stranger? Continue the conversations with your partner.
8 Which nationalities have rules of behaviour about hands? What are the rules?
9 Why is it *not* a good idea to ...
   ... say that you absolutely love your Egyptian friend's vase.
   ... go to Russia if you don't drink alcohol.
   ... say 'Hi! See you later!' when you're introduced to someone in Afghanistan.
   ... discuss politics with your American friend in a McDonald's.

Discussion

1 Do you agree with the saying 'When in Rome, do as the Romans do'? Do you have a similar saying in your language?

2 What are the 'rules' about greeting people in your country? When do you shake hands? When do you kiss? What about when you say goodbye?

3 Think of one or two examples of bad manners. For example, in Britain it is considered impolite to ask people how much they earn.

4 What advice would you give somebody coming to live and work in your country?

● VOCABULARY AND PRONUNCIATION

Word formation

1 Look at the entry for the word **photograph** in the *Oxford Wordpower Dictionary*.

☆**photograph** /ˈfəʊtəgrɑːf US -græf/ (also *informal* **photo**) *noun* [C] a picture that is taken with a camera: *to take a photo* o *a colour photograph* o *This photo is a bit out of focus.* o *to have a photo enlarged* o *That's a lovely photograph of you.* ☞ Look at **negative** and **slide**. **photograph** *verb* [T] to take a photograph of sb/sth.	**photographer** /fəˈtɒgrəfə(r)/ *noun* [C] a person who takes photographs. **photographic** /ˌfəʊtəˈgræfɪk/ *adj* connected with photographs or photography: *photographic equipment*. **photography** /fəˈtɒgrəfi/ *noun* [U] the skill or process of taking photographs: *wildlife photography*.

Notice how different parts of speech (noun and verb) and words formed from the headword (**photographer**, **photographic**, **photography**) are given in the same entry. Is this the same in your dictionary?

Look how the stress is shown: /ˈfəʊtəgrɑːf/. Practise saying the words in phonetic script.

2 Complete the charts with the different parts of speech. The missing words are all from the article *A World Guide to Good Manners*. Mark the stress. Use your dictionary to help you with the pronunciation.

Verb	Noun
_____	beˈhaviour
_____	arˈrangement
meet	
adˈvise	_____
_____	diˈscussion
feel	
deal	_____
_____	acˈceptance
tip	
_____	admiˈration

Noun	Adjective
ˈforeigner	_____
shock	_____
_____	high
_____	reˈspectful
ˈdifficulty	_____
reˈserve	_____
_____	strange
ofˈfence	_____

3 Rewrite the sentences, using the word in italics in a different word class.

Example
We had a long *discussion* about politics.
*We **discussed** politics for a long time.*

a She gave me some *advice* about which clothes to wear.
She _____ .

b How *high* is that wall?
What's the _____ ?

c Children should never speak to *strange* people.
Children _____ .

d I *felt* that there was someone watching me.
I had _____ .

e We had a lot of *difficulty* in finding the way here.
It was _____ .

f My son's *behaviour* at the party was very bad.
My son _____ .

g There are a lot of *foreign* people in town at the moment.
There are _____ .

h The *shock* made my hair turn white.
I was so _____ .

● LISTENING AND SPEAKING

Entertaining friends

1 Have you ever been a guest in someone's house in a foreign country? When? Why? What happened?

2 **T.29** You will hear three people describe how they entertain guests in their country. Sumie is from Japan, Rosa is from Spain, and Leslie is from the United States.

Listen and take notes under the following headings:
– the kind of invitation, formal or informal
– the time of day
– the preparations that the host or hostess makes
– the presents that people take
– the food and drink served

3 Work in small groups. Compare information. What similarities and differences are there?

4 What happens in your country? Is it usual to invite people to your home for a meal? What are such occasions like in your home?

● WRITING

Filling in a form

1 Most people hate filling in forms! What occasions can you think of when you have to fill in a form? What sort of information do you have to provide?

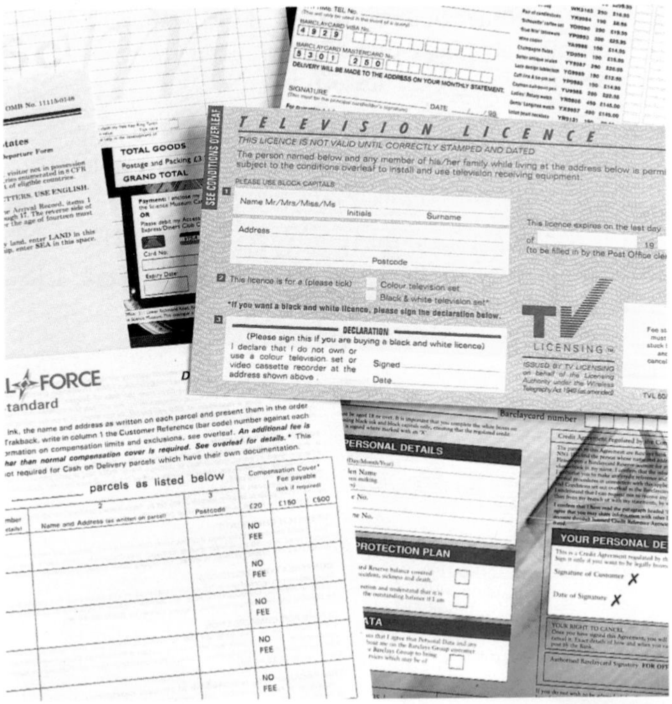

2 Forms do not usually ask questions, but they ask for information. Match a line in **A** with a question in **B**.

A	**B**
1 First name	a Where do you live?
2 Surname	b What do you do?
3 Date of birth	c Where are you living at the moment?
4 Country of origin	d Are you married or single?
5 Present address	e What's your first name?
6 Permanent address	f How much do you earn a year?
7 Marital status	g When were you born?
8 Occupation	h What's your surname?
9 Annual income	i Where were you born?

3 Forms ask you to do certain things. Do the following:

Write your name in block capitals.

_____

Sign your name. _____

Delete where not applicable.
I am a student / an employee / an employer.

Put a cross if you are male. ☐
Put a tick if you are female. ☐

4 Fill in the form. It is an application form to open a bank account.

CITY BANK ACCOUNT APPLICATION FORM

Applicant

Title   Mr ☐   Mrs ☐   Miss ☐   Ms ☐

Surname [   ]

First name(s) [   ]

Date of birth [/ / /]

Country of origin [   ]

Present address [   ]

[   ]

[   ] Post code [   ]

When did you move to this address? [/ / /]

Permanent address (if different from above)

[   ]

[   ]

[   ] Post code [   ]

Telephone no. (home) [   ]

Telephone no. (work) [   ]

Marital Status

Single ☐   Married ☐   Divorced ☐   Widowed ☐

No. of dependent children ☐

Residential details

Owned ☐   Rented ☐

Where do you reside?

With parents ☐   With a partner ☐   Alone ☐

Employment status

Employed full-time ☐   Employed part-time ☐

Self-employed ☐   Unemployed ☐   Retired ☐

Income details

Annual income [£   ]

Signature [   ]

Date [/ / /]

Requests and offers

1 Match a line in **A** with a line in **B**. Who is talking to who? Where are the dialogues taking place?

A

a Could you fill it up, please?

b Could I have the bill, please?

c It's a present. Do you think you could gift-wrap it for me?

d Two lagers, please.

e Can you tell me the code for Paris?

f I'll give you a lift if you like.

g Would you mind opening the window?

h Could I have extension 2387, please?

B

☐ Halves or pints?

☐ Not at all. It's very stuffy in here.

☐ One moment. I'll just look it up.

☐ Sure. Shall I check the oil as well?

☐ I'm afraid the line's engaged at the moment. Do you want to hold?

☐ Certainly, sir. I'll bring it straight away.

☐ Yes, indeed. I'll just take the price off.

☐ That's great. Would you drop me at the station?

2 **T.30** Listen and check your answers. Practise the dialogues, paying particular attention to intonation and voice range.

📖 **Grammar Reference: page 148.**

3 **T.31** Listen to the six dialogues. Answer the questions.

a Where are the people?

b What is the relationship between them? (parent and child; customer and shop assistant)

c What exactly are the words of the request?

Roleplay

Work in pairs. Make up a dialogue for one of these situations using the prompts given.

– **A** is a customer in a restaurant; **B** is a waiter. Prompts: table near the window; menu; wine list; ordering; clean fork; dessert; bill.

– **A** is going on holiday very soon; **B** offers to help. Prompts: pack; confirm flight; passport; travellers' cheques; look after cat; water plants.

– **A** is cooking a meal for twenty; **B** offers to help. Prompts: prepare the vegetables; check the meat; set the table; do the washing-up; open the wine.

On the move

Future forms
Travelling around

T.32 Read and listen to the joke. <u>Underline</u> the verb forms that refer to the future. What is the difference between them?

A Penguin Joke!

One day a man and his wife were walking down the street when they came across a penguin.

'Oh!' exclaimed the man. 'What a surprise! What shall we do with it?'
'I know,' said his wife. 'We'll ask a policeman.'
So they found a policeman and explained what had happened.
'Mmm,' said the policeman, 'I think the best thing is to take it to the zoo.'
'What a good idea!' said the woman. 'We'll go there straight away.'

The next morning the policeman was walking down the same street when he saw the couple again with the penguin. 'I thought I told you to take that penguin to the zoo,' the policeman said. 'Well, we did,' said the man. 'We took it to the zoo and we all had a really good time. So this afternoon we're taking it to the cinema, and this evening we're going to have a meal in a fish restaurant.'

PRESENTATION (1)

going to and *will*

1 John always writes himself a list at the beginning of every day. What's he going to do today? What's he going to buy?

Example
He's going to fill up the car with petrol.

> Things to do
> petrol
> electricity bill
> plane tickets from the travel agent
> the library
> a hair-cut
> the dog for a walk
>
> Things to buy
> sugar
> tea
> cheese
> yoghurt
> 2 avocados
> apples
> melon

2 T.33 Read and listen to the dialogue between John (J) and Anna (A).

J I'm going to the shops soon. Do you want anything?

A No, I don't think so. Oh, hang on. We haven't got any sugar left.

J It's all right. It's on my list. I'm going to buy some.

A What about bread? We haven't got any bread.

J OK. I'll go to the baker's and I'll buy a loaf.

A I'll be at work when you get back.

J I'll see you later, then. Don't forget Jo and Andy are coming round for a drink tonight.

A Ah, right. Bye.

J Bye, honey.

● Grammar questions

I'm going to buy some (sugar).
I'll buy a loaf.

– Why does John use different future forms?
What's the difference between *will* and *going to* to express a future intention?

– We don't usually say *going to go* or *going to come*. Find the examples in the dialogue where these forms are avoided.

PRACTICE

1 Dialogues

John said, *I'll go to the baker's and I'll buy a loaf.* Look at the list of items. What would Anna ask? What would John say?

Example
– some stamps

Anna   *Could you get some stamps?*
John   *OK. I'll go to the post office and buy some.*

– a newspaper   – some shampoo
– a bottle of wine   – a tin of white paint
– a joint of beef   – a video
– a film for her camera   – some felt-tip pens

2 Listening

T.34 Listen to the conversations. Say what's going to happen.

Example
A   Have you seen the air tickets?
B   Yes. They're with the travellers' cheques.
A   And do you have the address of the hotel?
B   No. I've just got the name. Do we need the address?
A   No. Maybe not. The taxi driver will know.
B   What about the milk? Have you cancelled the milk?
A   Yes. No milk for a fortnight. Right?
B   That's it. Well done.

> They're going to catch a plane.

> They're going to stay in a hotel.

> They're going to be away for two weeks.

3 *I think I'll …*

1 Use the prompts in **A** to make sentences with *I think … will*. Match them with a sentence in **B**.

Example
I think Jeremy will win the match. He's been playing really well recently.

A

a … Jeremy/win the match
b … it/be a nice day tomorrow
c … I/pass my exams
d … you/like the film
e … we/get to the airport in time
f … you/get the job

B

☐ But we'd better get a move on.
☑ He's been playing really well recently.
☐ The forecast is warm and dry.
☐ You've got all the right qualifications.
☐ It's a lovely story, and the acting is superb.
☐ I've been revising for weeks.

2 Now make sentences with *I don't think … will* with the words from **A** in Exercise 1. Match them with a sentence in **C**.

Example
I don't think Jeremy will win the match. He hasn't practised for ages.

C

☐ There's too much traffic.
☐ I haven't done any revision at all.
☐ The forecast said rain and wind.
☑ He hasn't practised for ages.
☐ You're too young and you've got no experience.
☐ It's not really your cup of tea.

3 Make true sentences about *you*.

Example
I/bath tonight
I think I'll have a bath tonight/I don't think I'll have a bath tonight.

– it/rain tomorrow
– I/go shopping this afternoon
– I/be a millionaire one day
– I/eat out tonight
– we/have a white Christmas
– the teacher/give us a lot of homework

4 Grammar

<u>Underline</u> the correct verb form in the sentences.

Example
'Oh, dear. I'm late for work.'
'Don't worry. *I'm going to give/I'll give* you a lift.'

a 'I've got a headache.'
  'Have you? Wait a minute. *I'll get/I'm going to get* you an aspirin.'

b 'It's Tony's birthday next week.'
  'Is it? I didn't know. *I'll send/I'm going to send* him a card.'

c 'Why are you putting on your coat?'
  'Because *I'll take/I'm going to take* the dog for a walk.'

d 'Are you and Alan still going out together?'
  'Oh, yes. *We'll get married/We're going to get married* next year.'

e (a telephone conversation)
  'Would you like to go out for a drink tonight?'
  '*I'll watch/I'm going to watch* the football on television.'
  'Oh! I didn't know it was on.'
  'Come and watch it with me!'
  'OK. *I'll come/I'm going to come* round at about 7.30.'

f 'Did you phone Peter about tonight?'
  'No, I forgot. *I'll do/I'm going to do* it now. What's his number?'

PRESENTATION (2)

Present Continuous

15 Friday

9.00 – 10.00
or 11.00? Visiting a factory

12.30 Having lunch with a designer

2.00 – 2.30 Seeing a customer in the office

2.30 – 5.30 In the office

1 Nina Kendle works in the fashion business.
Look at her diary for today. Imagine it is 9.30 in the morning.
– Where is she now?
– What's she doing?
– What are her plans for the rest of the day?

2 **T.35** Listen to a telephone conversation between a businessman, Alan Middleton, and Nina Kendle's secretary.

3 Look at the conversation between Nina Kendle's secretary (S) and Alan Middleton (A). Try to complete the gaps.

S   Hello. Nina Kendle's office.

A   Hello. Could I speak to Nina Kendle, please? This is Alan Middleton.

S   Oh, I'm afraid she's out at the moment. She (a) _____ a factory.

A   I see. What time (b) _____ she _____ back in the office?

S   I'm not sure. I don't know how long she's going to stay there.

A   All right. What about lunch-time? Is she free then?

S   Just one moment. I (c) _____ check. No, she (d) _____ lunch with a designer.

A   Till what time? Do you know?

S   Erm ... Well, she (e) _____ a customer here in her office at 2.00.

A   Ah! So when's a good time to try again?

S   Any time after 2.30.

A   Are you sure?

S   Definitely. She (f) _____ in her office for the rest of the afternoon.

A   OK. I (g) _____ phone back then. Thank you.

S   That's all right. Goodbye.

Look at the Tapescript on page 131 and check your answers.

● Grammar questions

– What tense are the verbs in a, d and e?

– Which refer to the present? Which refer to the future?

– Why are these sentences with *will*, not *going to*?

   I'll check.
   I'll phone back then.

▶ Read the Language Review on page 49.

PRACTICE

1 Roleplay

Work in pairs. Your teacher will give you a role card. Study the information on it carefully. Have telephone conversations similar to the one between Alan Middleton and Nina Kendle's secretary.

Remember the following expressions.

Could I speak to ... ?   I'm afraid ...

What time will ... be back?   At about ...

Is ... free at lunch-time?   I'll check. No, she's having/seeing/going ...

When's a good time to try again?   She'll be ...

I'll phone back ...   That's fine ...

2 Discussing grammar

Work in pairs and discuss your answers. Underline the correct verb form.

Example
I must hurry because *I'm going/I'll go* to the doctor's.

a   *Are you doing/Will you do* anything tonight? Would you like to come round for a game of cards?

b

The phone's ringing!

OK. *I answer/I'll answer* it.

c   'I've just booked our summer holiday.'
   'Really? Where *are you going/will you go*?'
   '*We go/We're going* to Spain.'

d   'There's a good film on at the cinema tonight. Are you interested?'
   'Yes, I am.'
   'Great! *I'll see/I'm seeing* you outside the cinema at 7.30.'

e   Do you think *it's raining/it'll rain* this afternoon?

f   '*We're having/We have* a party next Saturday.'
   'Who *are you going to invite/do you invite*?'
   'Just a few friends. Can you come?'
   'I'd love to, but *I'll go/I'm going* away for the weekend. Thanks, anyway.'

3 Arranging to meet

1 Imagine it is Friday morning. You need to arrange to meet someone over the weekend. First, fill in your diary. What are *you* doing this weekend? When are you free?

Friday

morning	afternoon	evening

Saturday

morning	afternoon	evening

Sunday

morning	afternoon	evening

2 Work in pairs. First decide *why* you want to meet. Is it for business, or to go out together somewhere? Consult your diary and try to find a time and a place to meet.

Future forms

will

1 *Will* expresses an intention or decision made at the moment of speaking.

*I'll **give** you my phone number. Ring me tonight.*
*I'll **check** her diary for you.*
*I'll **phone** back later.*

Many languages express this idea with a present tense, but *I give, *I check and *I phone are wrong.

2 The most common use of *will* is to refer to the future. It expresses a future fact or prediction.

*Tomorrow **will be** warm and sunny.*
*What time **will** she **be** back?*
*I'm sure you'**ll pass** your exam.*

going to

1 *Going to* expresses an intention or decision thought about *before* the moment of speaking. It expresses a plan.

*We're **going to have** a holiday in Sicily this summer.*
*My daughter's **going to study** modern languages at Bristol University.*

2 We use *going to* when we can see evidence now that something is certain to happen.

*Look at those clouds. It's **going to rain**.*

Present Continuous

The Present Continuous can be used to express a future arrangement between people. It is common with verbs such as *go, come, see, visit, meet, have* (a party), *leave.*

*Pat and Peter **are coming** for a meal tonight.*
*We're **having** salmon for supper.*

Sometimes there is little or no difference between a future intention (*going to*) and a future arrangement (Present Continuous).

*We're **going to see** a play tonight.*
*We're **seeing** a play tonight.*

📖 **Grammar Reference: page 148.**

LISTENING AND VOCABULARY

A weather forecast

1 Look at the map of the British Isles. Draw a line between the Bristol Channel and The Wash.

T.36a Listen to the description of the main geographical features of the British Isles.
– What can we find to the north of the line?
– What can we find to the south of the line?
– Match the numbers on the map to these places:

| | the Pennines | | the Welsh Mountains |
| | the Scottish Highlands |

2 **T.36b** Listen to the second part and take notes about the following areas and places.

the South West	the South East	East Anglia
the Midlands	the North West	Wales
the North East	Scotland	Ireland

Read the Tapescript on page 131. Check any new words.

3 Put the adjectives to do with temperature in the right order.

	(100°C)	freezing
		boiling
It's		cold
		warm
		chilly
	(0°C)	hot

4 Complete the chart with a word from the box.

snowing	windy	misty	wind	fog	stormy
snow	storm	blowing	snowy	cloud	foggy
shower	raining	sunny	rain	cloudy	

	Verb	Adjective	Noun
	The sun's shining.	It's _____.	sunshine
	It's _____.	It's rainy.	_____
	It's _____.	It's _____.	_____
	The wind is _____.	It's _____.	_____
		It's showery.	_____
		It's _____.	_____
		It's _____.	_____
FOG		It's _____.	_____
MIST		It's _____.	mist

5 **T.37** Listen to a weather forecast for the British Isles. Mark on the map what the weather will be like tomorrow. Use the symbols in Exercise 4. Write the temperature next to the symbol.

6 Work in pairs. Write a weather forecast for where *you* are. Read it to the rest of the class.

Map labels:
SCOTLAND · 3 · Forth · Glasgow · Clyde · Edinburgh · NORTHERN IRELAND · Belfast · North East · Lake District · REPUBLIC OF IRELAND · Dublin · North West · Liverpool · 2 · Manchester · Trent · The Wash · Midlands · Birmingham · East Anglia · ENGLAND · WALES · 1 · Thames · London · Cardiff · Bristol Channel · South East · South West · Brighton · Dartmoor

● LISTENING AND READING

Pre-listening task

1 Discuss the following questions.

– Do you get many foreign tourists in your country?
– What do they come to see? What do they come to do?
– What are the most popular towns for them to visit?
 What are the most popular places?
– Which countries do the tourists come from?

2 You are going to listen to, and then read, an interview
from a German newspaper. It is about some American
tourists in Europe. It's title is 'If it's Tuesday … we
must be in Munich'.
 What type of holiday does this describe?

Listening

1 Look at the pictures. Which do you recognize?
 Where can you find them?

2 **T.38** Read the introduction and then listen to the
American family. Put a tick (✓) in the box if they
mention what's in the picture.

> ### "If it's Tuesday …
> ## we must be in Munich"
>
> Americans do it faster. Käthe Faller, a
> German journalist, meets a family on the
> Express Tour: seven countries in twelve
> days. Breakfast in Paris, lunch in the Alps
> and dinner on the banks of the Rhine.

3 Why is the holiday called the Express Tour?
 Which countries have they already visited? Which are
 they going to visit?
 Where is the family now?

1

2

3

6

4

5

8

7

9

8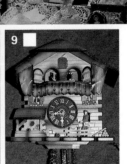

Reading

Now read the article and answer the questions.

– Who are the members of this American family?
– Who do you think is enjoying the holiday most?
– Who is not enjoying it so much? Why?
– How many Americanisms can you find in the article?

Example *Yup* = Yes

"If it's Tuesday … we must be in Munich"

Ruthie Schumacher, aged 68, and her husband Bob, 72, from Maryland have never been out of the US before. They are with their son, Gary, and his wife Gayle. I met them in Munich, in a café, two thirds of
5 *their way round a lightning cultural tour of Europe.*

Can I ask a few questions?
RUTHIE No problem. It's our pleasure. Isn't it, Bob?
BOB Yup.

10 **OK. What did you think of the Munich Glockenspiel? You always see tourists standing in front of it for hours, just watching and waiting.**
GAYLE The Glockenspiel?

Yes, you know, the clock with those little wooden figures that play music and
20 **dance round. Here in Munich, on the Marienplatz.**
RUTHIE Did we see that, Gary?
GARY Oh, yeah, this morning. It was real interesting. You Europeans probably can't understand it, but for us, something like that is real-life history.
30 GAYLE In America, if something is a hundred years old, that's pretty old. But in Europe everything is just so much older.
RUTHIE All those castles. Do you remember all those castles we saw when we went from Munich to Bonn in that boat?
40 GARY That was Heidelberg to Bonn.
RUTHIE You know, I can *feel* the history every time I look up from the sidewalks. I always say to Bob, 'Bob, if only the streets and stones could talk'. Well, I've gotten goose bumps now just thinking about it.

50 **Do you feel that it is possible to get to know the real Europe in such a short time?**
GAYLE Of course. We're seeing so much. Seven countries, 3,500 miles. So many towns, it's just wonderful. Best vacation ever!

60 **Yes, but sometimes you don't have time to get off the bus and walk round the town. You had to see Paris from the bus because you only had two hours. Isn't that frustrating?**

GARY Well no, it isn't a problem. You see, we have a bathroom on the bus.

70 **So what about the people? What do you think of Europeans?**
RUTHIE Well, everyone we've met has been real nice, real friendly.
BOB That's no surprise. They are all waiters and chambermaids. Everybody is friendly if they are waiting
80 for a tip.

Are the people you've met in Europe different from Americans?
GARY Yup. Americans are much more materialistic. Look at the store opening times. We wanted to buy a cuckoo clock in Lucerne, but we couldn't get one because
90 it was lunch-time and the store was closed for lunch. These people consider their break more important than just money, money, money.

So have you picked up any souvenirs?
RUTHIE Oh yeah. I bought some clothes in London and some lace from Brussels. And
100 I'm going to buy some crystal in Venice. I got a leather bag today in Munich. Did I forget anything?

GARY All your souvenir spoons. Mom collects these little coffee spoons which have a picture of the city on them.
BOB Please, don't remind
110 me of the stress we've had over those damn spoons. I can tell you: London, Paris, Lucerne, Bonn …
RUTHIE Now, now … don't get worked up about it, Bobby. I think it's real interesting to go shopping in all these countries. It's a cultural experience.

120 **So what's happening on the rest of the trip?**
GARY This afternoon we're driving through Austria, but not stopping, on our way to Venice.
GAYLE So tomorrow we're going on a gondola, and then doing a few museums and galleries. We're going to
130 have a few days in Italy. I'm really looking forward to seeing that tower in Pisa. What's it called?

The Leaning Tower of Pisa. Where else are you going in Italy?
RUTHIE The itinerary is Venice, Pisa, and a morning in Florence. We're going to
140 see that David thing—you know, the painting by Michelangelo.

It's a statue, actually. But tell me, where exactly have you been already? Which cities?

GARY Well, we started in London, then Brussels and on to Paris, ...

150 GAYLE The other way round, wasn't it?

GARY No. I'm sure it was Brussels first, then Paris. From there we went to Lucerne, then up to Bonn, and now we're in Munich.

I make that six countries. What's the seventh?

RUTHIE After Italy we're
160 going to Spain, to Madrid, and from there we're flying back to the States.

How will you feel when you get back?

RUTHIE Pretty exhilarated.

GARY Yeah, and exhausted.

GAYLE But excited, too.

BOB I'll just feel poor.

Comprehension check

Read the text again more carefully. Check any new words in your dictionary.

1 Are the following statements true (✓) or false (✗)? Correct the false ones.

a The Schumacher family often go abroad for their holidays.
b Munich is over half-way through their tour of Europe.
c They're going to see the Glockenspiel tomorrow.
d Ruthie gets a strange feeling when she walks through the streets of old towns and thinks about all their history.
e The interviewer asks a question about the toilets in Paris.
f They bought a cuckoo clock when they were in Lucerne.
g They think Swiss people are only interested in money.

h Bob is fed up with Ruthie because she is always looking for souvenir spoons.
i The next stop of the tour is Vienna.
j They're going to have just one afternoon in Italy.
k None of them knows very much about the places they are going to visit.
l They are catching the plane home from Florence.

2 Find three occasions when people correct each other in the interview. Who corrects who? About what?

Language work

Complete the following questions and answers.

Example
How long does the tour last?
Twelve days.

a _____ ever _____ before?
No, this is the first time they've visited another country.
b _____ interview take place?
In Munich.
c When _____?
They saw it this morning.
d _____?
Some clothes.
e _____ in Venice?
Some crystal.
f Why _____?
Because she thinks it is a cultural experience.
g What are they doing this afternoon?
_____
h How long _____ in Italy?
A few days.
i _____?
The Statue of David.
j Where _____ home from?
Madrid.
k How _____ Bob _____ when he gets back to the States?
Poor.

Class survey

Stand up and ask three students the following questions.

What sort of holidays do you like?

– relaxing in the sun?
– a holiday abroad/at home?
– a holiday like the Schumachers'?
– sightseeing?
– an activity holiday?

Compare answers with the rest of the class.

● WRITING

Sending a fax

1 Janet Cooper wants to go to Spain on holiday with her family. She decides to fax the receptionist at the Hotel Plaza in Alicante to see if they have the accommodation she requires.

Look at the information on this page, and fill in the first part of Janet's fax. She will get all the information on one page. The code for Spain from the UK is 00 34.

2 Write out the words of Janet's fax message in the correct order.

HOTEL PLAZA

This luxury hotel is situated on the water's edge of one of the most beautiful beaches in Spain.

For reservations and enquiries:
PHONE (6) 527 21 56
FAX (6) 527 15 02

Janet and Peter Cooper
8 Fast Lane
Chesswood
Herts WD5 8QR
tel 01923 284908
fax 01923 285446

7 June

Dear Lynette,
It was lovely to see…

Love,
Janet

FAX TRANSMISSION

From _____   Page 1 of _____

To _____   Date _____

For the attention of _____   To fax no _____

From fax no _____

Message

_____

_____

_____

_____

_____

_____

_____

_____

_____

Yours faithfully

Janet Cooper

a rooms hotel I to some would like reserve at your

b in 28 July We on Alicante are arriving

c ten hope stay to We for nights leaving 7 August on

d and husband like room I My double balcony a would with preferably a

e require Our a two teenage daughters twin room

f are all en-suite that We understand your bedrooms

g you this confirm Could?

h a sea view possible Is have it rooms to with ?

i available if me let you Please for know have these dates rooms

j grateful if I be would also me you could tell room each price the of

k from I forward look you to hearing

3 **T.39** Listen and check your answers.

4 You are the receptionist at the hotel. Write a reply to Janet, either by letter or fax.
– Thank her for her enquiry.
– Say you are pleased to confirm her reservation for the rooms she wants, and for the dates she wants.

– Tell her that all the rooms have an en-suite bathroom, and all the rooms have a sea view.
– The rooms are 21,000 pesetas per room per night.
– End the letter saying that you look forward to welcoming her and her family to your hotel.
– Finish with *Yours sincerely, Reception*.

Travelling around

1 Here are some lines from conversations on different kinds of transport.
Where does each conversation take place? Choose from the box.

car	bus	taxi	underground
train	plane	ferry	

> Do you think it'll be a rough crossing?

> Excuse me, I think you'll find those seats facing the front are ours.

> Two to the British Museum, please. And could you possibly tell us when it's our stop?

> Can you take us to Euston Station, please?

> I'll get a couple of coffees from the buffet car.

> That's all right, you can keep the change.

> No, no! He said turn left at the pub, not right!

> Excuse me, are we landing on time?

> Which line is it for Oxford Circus?

2 Match a line in Exercise 1 with a reply.

a Look! *You* drive and *I'll* navigate from now on! Right?
b Yes, of course. Hop in!
c Would you mind getting me a sandwich as well?
d I'm terribly sorry. We didn't notice that they were reserved.
e Yes. We're beginning our descent soon.
f Well, the forecast is good, so it should be very smooth.
g One pound eighty, please. Just sit near me and I'll give you a shout.
h The Jubilee Line to Green Park. Then change to the Victoria Line.
i Thanks a lot. Do you want a hand with those bags?

T.40 Listen and check your answers. Practise some of the conversations with a partner.

Roleplay
Work in pairs. You are in a hotel. **A** is the receptionist, and **B** is a guest. The guest has several requests, and phones Reception from his/her room. Change roles after 3 conversations.

Example
There are no towels.

A *Hello. Reception. Can I help you?*
B *Yes, please. There are no towels in my room. Could you send some up, please?*
A *Certainly. I'll see to it straight away.*
B *Thanks. Bye.*

Use these situations for **B**.

– You'd like some tea and a sandwich in your room.
– You want the telephone number of the railway station.
– You want Reception to recommend a good place to eat.
– You can't get the television to work.
– You want to be woken at 7.00 in the morning and have breakfast in your room.
– You want to order a taxi to take you to the airport.

Likes and dislikes

Like
Verb + *-ing* or infinitive?
Signs and soundbites

---

1 In the following sentences, is *like* used as a verb or a preposition?

a How do you *like* your coffee, black or white?

b I'm just *like* my father. We're both tall and thin with black hair and brown eyes.

c Don't you think that Pedro looks *like* Tom Cruise?

d What would you *like* to do tonight?

e 'We went to that new restaurant last night.'
'Really? What was it *like*?'

f 'How do you tie a tie?'
'Let me show you. *Like* this.'

g 'Shall we go home now?'
'If you *like*.'

2 Match a sentence with a picture.

☐ They stopped to talk to each other.

☐ They stopped talking to each other.

PRESENTATION (1)

Questions with *like*

1 In Britain, some school children go on exchanges to another country. They stay with a family for two weeks, and then the boy or girl of the family comes back to Britain for two weeks. Does this happen in your country?

2 Read the conversation between Anna and Nina, two schoolgirls. Put one of the questions from the box into each gap.

What does she like doing?   How is she?
What's she like?   What does she look like?
What would she like to do?

Anna   My French exchange visitor came yesterday.
Nina   What's her name?
Anna   Marie-Ange.
Nina   What a pretty name! (1) _____ ?

Anna	She's really nice. I'm sure we'll get on really well. We seem to have a lot in common.
Nina	Why do you say that? (2) _____ ?
Anna	Well, she likes dancing, and so do I. And we both like tennis and listening to music.
Nina	That sounds great. I saw you with someone this morning. Was it Marie-Ange? (3) _____ ?
Anna	She's quite tall, and she's got long, dark hair.
Nina	No, it wasn't her, then. Now, we're all going out tomorrow, aren't we? Shall we go for a pizza, or shall we go to the cinema? (4) _____ ?
Anna	I'll ask her tonight and tell you tomorrow. By the way, someone told me your mum's not very well. What's the matter? (5) _____ ?
Nina	Oh, she's OK. She's had a bad sore throat, that's all, but it's getting better now.
Anna	Oh, it's not too bad, then.

T.41 Listen and check your answers. In pairs, practise the conversation.

● Grammar question

– Match the questions from the box in Exercise 2 with the definitions below.

a Tell me about her physical appearance.
b Tell me about her interests and hobbies.
c Tell me about her because I don't know anything about her.
d Tell me about her health.
e Tell me about her preferences for tomorrow evening.

– In which questions is *like* used as a verb, and in which is it a preposition?

PRACTICE

1 Questions and answers

Match a question in **A** with an answer in **B**.

A
a What does he like?
b What's he like?
c What does he look like?
d How is he?

B

☐ He isn't very well, actually. He's got the 'flu.

☐ He's really nice. Very friendly and open, and good fun to be with.

☐ He likes swimming and skiing, and he's a keen football fan.

☐ He's quite tall, average build, with straight brown hair.

2 Listening

T.42 Listen to nine short descriptions of people or things. Write an appropriate question for each.

Example
Description
Gosh! Haven't you ever tried Indian food? It's absolutely delicious. Really rich! It can be hot, but it doesn't have to be.

Question

What's Indian food like?

3 Descriptions

In pairs, ask and answer the following questions.

a What sort of things do you like doing?
b How are your parents?
c Who do you look like in your family?
d Who are you like in terms of character?
e What are you like as a person?
f What's your school like?
g What does your teacher look like?

PRESENTATION (2)

Verb + -ing or infinitive?

1 Read the letter and <u>underline</u> the correct verb form.

Example
We've decided *going/to go/go* to Kenya for a holiday.

Dear Dennis

We just wanted (a) *say/to say/saying thank you for putting us up before we caught the plane last week. It was a lovely evening, and we enjoyed* (b) *meeting/to meet/meet your friends, Pete and Sarah. We managed* (c) *get/getting/to get to the airport with plenty of time to spare. We even tried* (d) *getting/to get/get an earlier flight, but it wasn't possible.*

We had a wonderful holiday in Spain. We just loved (e) *driving/to drive/drive through the countryside, and we often stopped* (f) *walk/walking/to walk round a mountain village. We met our friends, Bill and Sue, and they invited us* (g) *having/to have/have a meal with them. They wanted* (h) *that we stay/us to stay/we to stay with them, but we couldn't, as we had already booked a hotel.*

The weather was fantastic. The sun didn't stop (i) *shining/to shine/shine all the time we were there. Leaving Spain was very sad. It made me* (j) *want/wanting/to want to cry.*

Anyway, we're looking forward to hearing from you, and hope (k) *see/to see/seeing you soon. Let us* (l) *to know/knowing/know if you're ever in the area. You must call in.*

Best wishes
Sandra

2 **T.43** Listen and check your answers.

● Grammar question

Read the sentences.

Last night I was watching television when the phone rang.
*I stopped **watching** television.*
*I stopped **to answer** the phone.*

– What is the difference between *stop* + *-ing* and *stop* + the infinitive?

PRACTICE

1 Grammar and listening

1 When one verb is followed by another, different patterns are possible. Put the verbs from the Presentation text in the correct box.

1 **verb + -ing**	2 **verb + infinitive (with to)**
love doing	want to do

3 **verb + person + infinitive with to**	4 **verb + person + infinitive without to**
want someone to do	make someone do

2 **T.44** You will hear sentences with the verbs below. Add them to the correct box in Exercise 1.

Example
The teacher **told me to do** my homework. *Box 3*

I **promised to do** it carefully. *Box 2*

tell	promise	hate	agree
manage	need	forget	choose
like	refuse	can't stand	finish
ask	continue		

3 Look at the list of verb patterns on page 158 and check your answers.

2 Discussing grammar

Work in pairs and discuss your answers.

1 In the following sentences, two verbs are possible and one is not. <u>Underline</u> the verb that is *not* possible.

a My father _____ to mend my bike.
   1 promised   2 didn't mind   3 tried

b She _____ her son to turn down his music.
   1 asked   2 wanted   3 made

c I _____ going on long walks.
   1 refuse   2 can't stand   3 adore

d We _____ to go shopping.
   1 need   2 'd love   3 enjoy

e She _____ me do the cooking.
   1 wanted   2 made   3 helped

f I _____ working for the bank twenty years ago.
   1 started   2 stopped   3 decided

2 Change the sentences in Exercise 1 using the verbs you underlined.

LANGUAGE REVIEW

Asking for descriptions

1 *What's London like?* means 'Tell me about London because I don't know anything about it'. It is a very general question.
When it is asked about a person, the answer can refer to character or appearance or both.

What's Peter like?
He's quite tall, with short blond hair.
He's really nice. You'd like him.

2 *What does she look like?* asks for a physical description.

What does she look like?
She's very pretty. She's got long black hair, and dark, mysterious eyes.

3 *How are your parents?* asks about their health and general happiness. It does not ask for a description.

How are your parents?
They're fine, thanks. My mother had a cold, but she's better now.

Verb patterns

We use *-ing* after some verbs.

*I don't **mind cooking** but I **hate ironing**.*

We use the infinitive after some verbs.

*We **tried to save** some money because we **needed to buy** a new car.*
*My mother **asked me to tidy** up, and then **told me to go** to bed.*

Make and *let* are followed by the infinitive without *to*.

*She **made me go** to bed, but she **let me read** for a while.*

There is a list of verb patterns on page 158.

📖 **Grammar Reference: page 149.**

● VOCABULARY AND PRONUNCIATION

Words that go together

Use your dictionaries to look up any new words.

1 Look at the following groups of words. Which **four** of the surrounding words in each group **cannot** go with the noun in the centre?

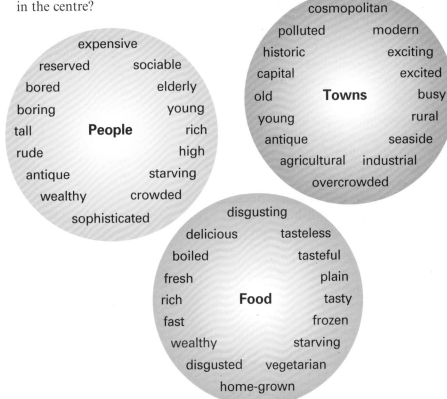

2 Put a suitable adjective from Exercise 1 into the gaps in the following conversations. If necessary, use their comparative or superlative forms.

Example
Billy's only two so he's ___the youngest___ in the family.

a 'What is Anna's brother like?'
'Well, he is certainly _____, dark and handsome, but I didn't enjoy meeting him at all. He is even _____ than she is!'

b 'What was your meal like?'
'Ugh! It was awful. The pizza was _____. We were absolutely _____, but we still couldn't eat it!'

c 'Did you have a good time in Amsterdam?'
'Excellent, thank you. There's so much to do. It's a really _____ city. And there are so many people from all over the world, it's even _____ than London.'

d 'Mmm! These courgettes are _____. Did you grow them yourselves?'
'Yes, we did. All our vegetables are _____.'

3 **T.45** Listen and check your answers. Work with a partner and practise saying some of the dialogues, paying particular attention to the intonation.

Pre-reading task

Work in pairs.

1 Do you know any typical meals from the
following countries?

France	Turkey	Italy	England
India	Spain	Mexico	
Switzerland	America	Greece	

What do you think influences a country's
food? What influences the food in your
country?

2 Read these quotations about English food.
Do all the people have the same opinion
about English food?

**'It takes some skill to spoil a breakfast—
even the English can't do it!'**
J K Galbraith, economist

**'On the Continent people have good
food; in England people have good
table manners.'**
George Mikes, writer and humorist

**'If the English can survive their food,
they can survive anything!'**
George Bernard Shaw, writer

**'Even today, well-brought up English
girls are taught to boil all vegetables
for at least a month and a half, just
in case one of the dinner guests
comes without his teeth!'**
Calvin Trillin, American writer

**'English cooking? You just put things
into boiling water and then take them
out again after a long while!'**
An anonymous French chef

Reading

Read the text quickly.
Match a paragraph 1–5 with a summary
below.

- Historical and climatic influences on
  British cooking
- There's everything except an English
  restaurant.
- The legacy of World War II
- Where there is hope for the future
- The British love affair with international
  cooking

In search of *good* ⋀

by Verona Paul and Jason Winner

1   How come it is so difficult to find English food in England?
In Greece you eat Greek food, in France French food, in
Italy Italian food, but in England, in any High Street in
the land, it is easier to find Indian and Chinese restaurants than
English ones. In London you can eat Thai, Portuguese, Turkish,
Lebanese, Japanese, Russian, Polish, Swiss, Swedish, Spanish, and
Italian—but where are the English restaurants?

2   It is not only in restaurants that foreign dishes are replacing
traditional British food. In every supermarket, sales of pasta, pizza
and poppadoms are booming. Why has this happened? What is
wrong with the cooks of Britain that they prefer
cooking pasta to potatoes? Why do the
British choose to eat lasagne
instead of shepherd's pie? Why
do they now like cooking in
wine and olive oil? But
perhaps it is a good thing.
After all, this is the end of
the 20th century and we
can get ingredients from all
over the world in just a few hours.
Anyway, wasn't English food always
disgusting and tasteless? Wasn't it
always boiled to death and swimming in fat?
The answer to these questions is a resounding 'No', but to
understand this, we have to go back to before World War II.

3   The British have in fact always imported food from abroad. From
the time of the Roman invasion foreign trade was a major influence
on British cooking. English kitchens, like the English language,
absorbed ingredients from all over the world—chickens, rabbits,
apples, and tea. All of these and more were successfully incorporated
into British dishes. Another important influence on British cooking
was of course the weather. The good old British rain gives us rich soil
and green grass, and means that we are able to
produce some of the finest varieties of meat,
fruit and vegetables, which don't need fancy
sauces or complicated recipes to disguise
their taste.

4   However, World War II changed
everything. Wartime women had to
forget 600 years of British cooking,
learn to do without foreign imports, and
ration their use of home-grown food. ▶

English food

The Ministry of Food published cheap, boring recipes. The joke of the war was a dish called Woolton Pie (named after the Minister for Food!). This consisted of a mixture of boiled vegetables covered in white sauce with mashed potato on the top. Britain never managed to recover from the wartime attitude to food. We were left with a loss of confidence in our cooking skills and after years of Ministry recipes we began to believe that British food was boring, and we searched the world for sophisticated, new dishes which gave hope of a better future. The British people became tourists at their own dining tables and in the restaurants of their land! This is a tragedy! Surely food is as much a part of our culture as our landscape, our language, and our literature. Nowadays, cooking British food is like speaking a dead language. It is almost as bizarre as having a conversation in Anglo-Saxon English!

5 However, there is still one small ray of hope. British pubs are often the best places to eat well and cheaply in Britain, and they also increasingly try to serve tasty British food. Can we recommend to you our two favourite places to eat in Britain? The Shepherd's Inn in Melmerby, Cumbria, and the Dolphin Inn in Kingston, Devon. Their steak and mushroom pie, Lancashire hotpot, and bread and butter pudding are three of the gastronomic wonders of the world!

Comprehension check

Read the article more carefully. Choose the best answer, a, b or c.

1 The writers believe that British cooking …
   a has always been very bad.
   b was good until World War II.
   c is good because it is so international.

2 They say that the British …
   a eat only traditional British food in their homes.
   b don't like cooking with foreign ingredients.
   c buy lots of foreign ingredients.

3 They say that the British weather …
   a enables the British to produce good quality food.
   b often ruins fruit and vegetables.
   c is not such an important influence on British food as foreign trade.

4 They say that World War II had a great influence on British cooking because …
   a traditional British cooking was rediscovered and some good cheap recipes were produced.
   b people had limitless supplies of home-grown food.
   c people started to believe that British food was boring, so after the war they wanted to cook more interesting and international dishes.

5 They say that …
   a British tourists try lots of new dishes when they are abroad.
   b nowadays it is very unusual for British people to cook British food.
   c literature and language are more culturally important than food.

6 The writers' final conclusion about British cooking is that …
   a there is no hope.
   b you will only be able to get British food in expensive restaurants.
   c you will be able to get more good traditional British dishes, especially in pubs.

Discussion

1 Do you agree that food is as much a part of a country's culture as its landscape, language, and literature?

2 Which are your favourite places to eat in your country? Why?

Language work

Work in pairs. Study the text and find the following.

1 One example of *like* used as a verb and two examples of *like* used as a preposition.

2 Two examples of the pattern, adjective + infinitive.
   *It's **impossible to learn** English.*

3 Examples of verbs that are followed by an *-ing* form.
   *I **love learning** English.*

4 Examples of verbs that are followed by an infinitive with *to*.
   *I **want to learn** Italian.*

New York and London

Pre-listening task

Look at the pictures of New York and London.
What do you know about the cities?
Have you been there? What did you do?
What did you think of these cities?

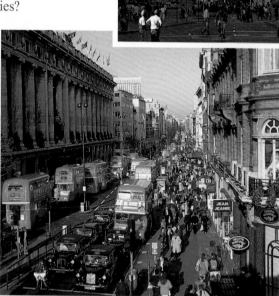

Listening

Work in two groups.

Group A

T.46a Listen to Sheila and Bob talking about when they lived in New York.

Bob and Sheila spent two years living in New York because of Bob's work as a banker. Neither of them had lived in a big city before. They now live back in England, in a small village outside London.

Group B

T.46b Listen to Terry. She is an American who lives in London.

Terry Tomscha talks about her experience of living and working in England, where she has been for the past eleven years.

Comprehension check

What do they/does she say about the following things?

	BOB AND SHEILA	TERRY
1 People		
– What are they like?		
– What is important to them?		
– What do they like doing?		
– Where do they live?		
2 Shops		
– What are they like?		
– Do they like them?		
– What time do they open?		
3 Work and holidays		
4 Transport		
– What do they mention?		
5 General opinions		
– Is it a good place to live? Why?		

Speaking

Find a partner from the other group. Compare your information.

Describing a room

1 Think of your favourite room. Draw a plan of it on a piece of paper.
Write down why you like it and some adjectives to describe it.

My favourite room is …   *I like it because it is …*

Show a partner your plan and talk about why you like the room.

2 **T.47** Read and listen to the description of a favourite room.
Use your dictionary to look up any new words.

3 There are four mistakes in the picture. What are they?

My favourite room

MY FAVOURITE room is our kitchen. Perhaps the kitchen is the most important room in many houses, but it is particularly so in our house
5 because it's not only where we cook and eat but it's also the main meeting place for family and friends. I have so many happy memories of times spent there: special occasions
10 such as homecomings or cooking Christmas dinner; troubled times, which lead to comforting cups of tea in the middle of the night; ordinary daily events such as making breakfast
15 on dark, cold winter mornings for cross, sleepy children before sending them off to school, then sitting down to read the newspaper with a steaming hot mug of coffee.
20 Whenever we have a party, people gravitate with their drinks to the kitchen. It always ends up the fullest and noisiest room in the house.

So WHAT does this special room look
25 like? It's quite big, but not huge. It's big enough to have a good-sized rectangular table in the centre, which is the focal point of the room. There is a large window above the sink,
30 which looks out onto two apple trees in the garden. The cooker is at one end, and above it is a wooden pulley, which is old-fashioned but very useful for drying clothes in wet
35 weather. At the other end is a wall with a large notice-board, which tells the story of our lives, past, present,

It always ends up the fullest and noisiest room in the house.

and future, in words and pictures: a school photo of Megan and Kate, a
40 postcard from Auntie Nancy in Australia, the menu from a take-away Chinese restaurant, a wedding invitation for next Saturday. All our world is there for everyone to read!

45 THE FRONT door is seldom used in our house, only by strangers. All our friends use the back door, which means they come straight into the kitchen and join in whatever is
50 happening there. The kettle goes on immediately and then we all sit round the table, drinking tea and putting the world to rights! Without doubt some of the happiest times of
55 my life have been spent in our kitchen. ■

4 The relative pronouns *which* and *where* are used in the text. Find them and <u>underline</u> them. What does each one refer to?

 Grammar Reference: page 149.

5 Link the following sentences with the correct relative pronoun: *who, which, that, where, whose.*

a The blonde lady is my wife. She's wearing a black dress.
b There's the hospital. My sister works there.
c The postcard arrived this morning. It's from Auntie Nancy.
d I passed all my exams. This made my father very proud.
e Did you meet the girl? Her mother teaches French.

6 Write a similar description of your favourite room in about 250 words.
Describe it and give reasons why you like it.

Post Script

Signs and soundbites

Where would you see or hear the following?

> *A table for four, please.*

DRY CLEAN ONLY

PAY AND DISPLAY

<u>Government health warning</u>
Tobacco seriously damages your health

The management accepts no responsibility.
Coats and other articles left at owner's risk.

VACANT

VISITORS ARE REQUESTED
TO KEEP TO THE PATHS

> Coming next on Capital—traffic news and the weather

> *No, I'm just looking, thank you.*

KEEP OUT OF REACH
OF CHILDREN

**SERVICES
20 MILES**

FOR EXTERNAL
USE ONLY

> *Is service included?*

*Yours faithfully,
Veronica Vazey*

> *Don't forget to give my love to everyone at home.*

The world of work

Present Perfect active and passive
On the telephone

1 Work in pairs. Ask and answer the questions.

a What do you do?
b How long have you had your present job?
c What did you do before that?
d

Do you live in a house or a flat?

e How long have you lived there?
f When did you move there?
g How long have you known your teacher?
h When did you first meet your teacher?
i Have you ever been to America?
j If so, when did you go?

2 Tell the rest of the class about your partner.

3 There are three tenses used in the questions. What are they?

PRESENTATION (1)

Present Perfect Simple

1 Read the job advertisement. Does this job interest you?
Do you have any of the necessary qualifications to apply?

WORLDWATCH

Business journalist   £35,000 p.a.

This international business magazine, with 23,000 readers worldwide, requires a journalist to help cover political news in Europe.

The successful applicant will be based in Geneva and should:

- ■ have at least two years' experience in business journalism
- ■ be fluent in French and German, and if possible have some knowledge of Spanish
- ■ have a degree in politics
- ■ have travelled widely.

Please write with full CV to
David Benton, *Worldwatch UK Ltd*,
357 Ferry Rd, Basingstoke RG2 5HP

WORLDWATCH

2   **T.48**   Nancy Mann has applied for the job and is being interviewed. Listen to the interview. Do you think she will get the job?

3 Read the first part of Nancy's interview. Put the correct auxiliary verb *do*, *did*, or *have* into each gap.

I Who _____ you work for at the moment, Ms Mann?

N I work for the BBC World Service.

I And how long _____ you worked for the BBC?

N I _____ been with the BBC for five years. Yes, exactly five years.

I And how long _____ you been their German correspondent?

N For two years.

I And what _____ you do before the BBC?

N I worked as an interpreter for the EU.

Listen to the first part again and check your answers.

● Grammar questions

– Does she still work for the BBC?
– Does she still work for the EU?
– Explain why Nancy says:

*I **work** for the BBC World Service.*
*I've **worked** for them for five years.*
*I **worked** as an interpreter for the EU.*

4 Read and complete the second part of Nancy's interview with *did*, *was*, or *have*.

I As you know, this job is based in Geneva. _____ you ever lived abroad before?

N Oh yes, yes I _____ .

I And when _____ you live abroad?

N Well, in fact I _____ born in Argentina and I lived there until I was eleven. Also, I lived and worked in Brussels for two years when I _____ working for the EU.

I That's interesting. _____ you travelled much?

N Oh yes, yes indeed. I _____ travelled all over western and eastern Europe, and I _____ also been to many parts of South America.

I And why _____ you go to these places?

N Well, mostly for pleasure, but three years ago I went back to Argentina to cover various political stories in Buenos Aires for the BBC.

Listen and check your answers.

● Grammar question

– The interviewer asks:

***Have** you ever **lived** abroad?*
*When **did** you **live** abroad?*

Nancy says:
*I've **been** to many parts of South America.*
*... three years ago I **went** back to Argentina ...*

Why are different tenses used?

PRACTICE

1 Biographies

1 Here are some more events from Nancy Mann's life. Match a line in **A** with a time expression in **B** to tell the story of her life. Put a letter a–k in the box.

A

a She was born
b She went to boarding school in England
c She studied French and German
d She hasn't spoken Spanish
e She's worked in both eastern and western Europe
f She worked in Brussels
g She's worked for the BBC
h She hasn't worked abroad
i She married for the first time
j She's been married
k She married for the third time

B

☐	for the last five years.
☐	three times.
☐	from 1970 to 1977.
e	at various times in her life.
☐	when she was twenty-one.
☐	when she was at Oxford University.
a	in Argentina in 1959.
☐	for two years, from 1989 to 1991.
☐	last year.
☐	since her son was born four years ago.
☐	since she was in Buenos Aires three years ago.

2 **T.49** Listen and check your answers.

3 Work in pairs. Write similar tables of your own life. Ask your partner to match the events and the times to tell the story of your life. Correct any wrong times.

2 Time expressions

Put *for*, *since*, *in*, or *ago* into each gap.

a I was born _____ 1961.
b I went to university _____ three years.
c I passed my driving test fifteen years _____ .
d I've had a car _____ 1983.
e Now I've got a BMW. I've had it _____ two years.
f I met my wife _____ 1985.
g We've been married _____ nine years.
h Our first daughter was born six years _____ .
i We've lived in the same house _____ 1990.

3 *Have you ever ...?*

1 The following verbs are *all* irregular. What is the past simple and past participle?

have	eat	win	forget	bring	make
be	drink	lose	sleep	find	give
meet	write	drive	hear	sing	
leave	read	ride	see	go (Careful!)	

2 Work with a partner. Choose from the list and make dialogues like the example.

Example
be/America?

A *Have you ever been to America?*
B *Yes, I have./No, I haven't. I've never been there.*
A *When did you go?*
B *Two years ago. I went to Disneyland with my family.*

have/an operation?	win/a competition?
be/on TV?	lose/your job?
write/a love letter?	hear/an opera?
ride/a motor bike?	see/a horror movie?
have/an English breakfast?	forget/an important birthday?
try/iced tea?	sleep/in the open air?
drive/a van?	sing/in a choir?
read/a book in a foreign language?	meet/anyone famous?

3 Tell the class as much as you can remember about your partner.

PRESENTATION (2)

Present Perfect active and passive

1 Read the newspaper headlines. Check any new words.

a **DANGEROUS PRISONER ESCAPES**

b **Floods bring road chaos**

c **Kidnapped baby found**

d **US CAR WORKERS MADE REDUNDANT**

2 ☐ **T.50a** Read and listen to the radio news headlines of the same stories. Fill in the gaps with the exact words you hear.

Here is the news...

RADIO NEWS HEADLINES

a The murderer Bruce Braden _____ from Parkhurst Prison on the Isle of Wight.
b After the heavy rain of the last few days, floods _____ chaos to drivers in the West Country.
c Amy Carter, the kidnapped baby from Leeds, _____ safe and well in a car park in Manchester.
d Two thousand car workers from a US car factory _____ redundant.

● Grammar questions

– Which of these questions can you answer? Which can't you answer?

Who has escaped from prison?
What has brought chaos to the West Country?
Who has found Amy Carter?
Who has made the car workers redundant?

– What is the difference between the verb forms in Exercise 2?

3 **T.50b** Listen to the news items and fill in the gaps to complete the stories. What other information do you learn about each one?

a Last night, the murderer Bruce Braden _____ from Parkhurst Prison. Prison officers _____ his cell empty at six o'clock this morning.

b Early this morning, floods _____ chaos to many roads in Devon. Drivers left their cars and _____ to work through the flood water.

c Late last night, the kidnapped baby Amy Carter, _____ safe and well in a car park in the centre of Manchester. The car park attendant _____ a noise coming from a rubbish bin and he _____ Amy wrapped in a warm blanket.

d Two thousand car workers from the General Motors factory in Detroit _____ redundant yesterday. The management _____ them no warning. The men were shocked and furious when they _____ the news yesterday evening.

● Grammar questions

– Which tense is used in the full stories in Exercise 3 above? Why?

– Which tense is used in the headlines in Exercise 2 on page 67? Why?

PRACTICE

1 Here is the news!

Work in pairs.

1 Here are some more headlines from newspapers. Make them into radio news headlines.

Examples

Plane crashes in Colombia

A Boeing 727 has crashed in the mountains of Colombia near Bogotá.

DANGEROUS PRISONER RECAPTURED

The murderer Bruce Braden has been recaptured near Parkhurst Prison.

a Famous film star leaves $3,000,000 to her favourite pet
b Priceless painting stolen from Louvre
c Seven people killed in train crash
d Princess runs away with gardener
e President forced to resign
f Sporting hero fails drug test

2 Choose two of the headlines and write the full stories. Read your news to the rest of the class.

3 What's in the news today? What national or international stories do you know?

2 Giving personal news

What about your personal news? What have you done today? This week? This year? Ask and answer questions with a partner.

Example
have/breakfast?

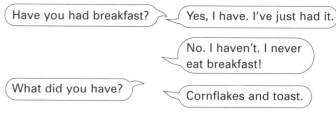

Today	This week	This year
travel/by bus?	go/cinema? (Careful!)	have/a holiday yet?
do/any work?	do/any exercise?	move/house?
have/a coffee break?	play/a sport?	have/your birthday yet?
have/lunch yet?	watch/TV?	take/any exams?
do/any exercise?	wash/your hair?	apply/for a new job?

3 Discussing grammar

Work in pairs.

1 Read the following sentences. Discuss where the words can go. Sometimes there are several possibilities.

just	yet	already	ever	never

a I've washed my hair.
b Have you played basketball?
c He hasn't learned to drive.
d They've finished the exercise.
e She's learned a foreign language.
f We've met your teacher.
g Have they finished doing the washing-up?
h Has it stopped raining?

2 Underline the correct verb form.

a The Prime Minister of Italy *has resigned/has been resigned* and a new prime minister *has elected/has been elected*.
b The Italian people *told/were told* of his resignation on television yesterday evening.
c I *lost/have lost* my glasses. *Did you see/Have you seen* them anywhere?
d 'Where *has* Liz *gone/did* Liz *go* on holiday?'
  'She's in Paris.'
e 'Where *has* Liz *gone/did* Liz *go* on holiday?'
  'She went to Paris.'
f '*Did* John ever *go/Has* John ever *been* to Paris?'
  'Oh, yes. Five times.'
g A huge earthquake *has hit/has been hit* central Japan. Nearly 1,000 people *have killed/have been killed*. It *happened/has happened* mid-afternoon yesterday.

LANGUAGE REVIEW

The Present Perfect

The Present Perfect relates past time to present time. It has three main uses.

1 To express unfinished past.

   I've lived here for five years. (I started living here five years ago and I still live here.)
   He's been a teacher since he was twenty-one.
   NOT * ~~He is a teacher since ...~~

2 To express an experience that happened some time in your life. It is the experience that is important, not when it happened.

   I've been to Australia. I went three years ago.
   'Have you ever lived in France?' 'Yes, I have. I lived there from 1993 to 1995.'

3 To express the present importance of a past event, usually a recent event. It is often used when giving news.

   The police have warned the public that the man is dangerous.
   I've lost my credit card. Have you seen it?

The Present Perfect passive

The uses of the Present Perfect are the same in the passive.

Two million cars have been produced so far this year. (Unfinished past)
'Have you ever been made redundant?' 'No, never, thank goodness!' (Past experience)
'Have you heard? I've been left £4,000 by my great aunt!' (Present importance)

📖 **Grammar Reference: page 150.**

● READING AND SPEAKING

Pre-reading task

1 Close your eyes for a few minutes. Imagine it is one hundred years ago and you are very rich.

– What is your life like?
– Where do you live? What do you do?
– Do you have any servants? How many? What do they do for you?
– What do you know about the lives of your servants? Where do they live?

2 Work in small groups and discuss your ideas in your group. Share your ideas with the rest of the class.

3 What about now? Do many people have servants?

Have you ever worked in anyone else's home? In what ways are servants today different from years ago?

Reading

The modern servant –
the nanny, the cook, and the gardener

1 You are going to read about three modern servants.
  Divide into three groups.

  Group A   Read about the nanny.
  Group B   Read about the cook.
  Group C   Read about the gardener.

  Read your article and answer the questions. Use your
  dictionary to help with new words. Discuss your
  answers with your group.

  a What and who influenced her/his choice of career?
  b What did her/his parents want her/him to do?
  c What was the parents' attitude to the choice of career
     at first?
  d Has the parents' attitude changed? If so, why?
  e In what ways do the parents think that times have
     changed since they were young?

2 Read your article again.
   Which of the following multi-word verbs can you find
   in your article? Underline them.

bring up (1)	look after, educate (a child)
bring up (2)	mention (in conversation)
carry on	continue
drop out	leave, not complete (a college course)
fall out	quarrel and no longer be friends
get on with	have a good relationship with
get over	recover from (an illness, a shock)
give up	stop (a job, a habit, e.g. smoking)
go through	experience
grow up	change from child to adult
look after	take care of
make up (1)	invent
make it up (2)	be friends again after an argument
pick up	learn unconsciously (e.g. a language)
put off	postpone
be taken aback	be surprised
take after	resemble
turn out	be in the end
take over	take control of

The nanny

Amanda Peniston-Bird, 21, is
the daughter of a judge and
has just completed a two-
year training course to be a nanny
5 at the Norland Nursery Training
College. She and her mother talk
about her choice of career.

Amanda

My sister Charlotte was born when I was
10 seven and my mother decided she needed
a nanny to look after us. So we got
Alison. She was very young, seventeen I
think, and wonderful. I adored her. She
only worked part-time with us before she
15 started her training at Norland College. She
had to dress us in the morning and take me
to school. After school she made us delicious
teas and read us stories in bed. On
Charlotte's birthday she organized a
20 fantastic party.

When Alison left, we had a trained nanny
who lived with us and worked full-time. She
was called Nanny Barnes by everyone,
including my parents. She was older and
25 quite traditional and wore a uniform. It was
then that I realized that I wanted to be a
nanny. I have always got on well with

**'My father wanted me to
be a solicitor.'**

children. I have always enjoyed taking care
of my sister and younger cousins. I told
30 Mummy very firmly that I wanted to be a
nanny when I grew up. At the time she
laughed. I know that she and Daddy

thought it was just a childish phase I was
going through, but it wasn't. They thought I
would follow in my father's footsteps and
35 study law. But I didn't. There were some
terrible rows but I didn't go to university.
I left school and spent a year working
at Ludgrove School, where Prince
William used to go. Then I started my
40 training course at Norland College. I
finished the course last month and I've
applied for the post of nanny to twins
aged six months. Mummy and Daddy
weren't angry for long, we made it up
45 before I went to college, and they have
encouraged me ever since.

Amanda's mother

*Her father is still a wee bit disappointed that she
didn't take after him and study law, but I think
50 we're both proud, and also pleased, that she has
made her own decisions in life and done so well.
We have brought her up to be an independent
thinker, so we can't complain. Everything has
turned out for the best. I had a nanny when I
55 was a child but I never thought of being one
myself, but times have changed and 'nannying'
has been socially acceptable for a long time. It
wasn't just Princess Diana who made it
fashionable!*

The cook

Giles Mildmay, 24, has been a professional cook for three years. His father, George, owns a two-hundred-acre farm in Devon. The family have farmed in Devon for over three hundred years. Giles' younger brother Tobias is studying farm management at Exeter University. Giles and his father talk about his choice of career.

Giles

I think I've always been interested in food. My grandparents (on my mother's side) lived in a huge old manor house in Lincolnshire and they had a wonderful cook. She made fantastic standard English food; her roast beef and Yorkshire pudding was out of this world. I used to love going down to the kitchen and watching her work, and I picked up a lot of cooking tips from her. I realized that I wanted to be a cook when I was about 12. I went to a boarding school and when other boys chose to do sport, I chose cookery. By the time I was

'My grandfather thinks I'm mad!'

15, I had taken over the cooking at home for my parents' dinner parties, and I had started to make up my own recipes. I knew my parents would not approve of cooking as a career, so I decided to introduce them slowly to the idea. I told them that I wanted to do a cookery course for fun, and I went for a month to a hotel in Torquay. I enjoyed it so much, I knew I couldn't put off telling my parents any longer, so I brought the subject up one night over dinner. At first there was silence, and then my father asked me why. I explained that cooking was like painting a picture or writing a book. Every meal was an act of creation. I could see that my father was not convinced, but he didn't get angry, he just patted me on the shoulder and smiled. My mother kissed me. And now that I have opened my own restaurant, I think they are very proud of me. However, my grandfather (on my father's side) is not so kind, he thinks I'm mad to have given up farming.

Giles' father

I know that times have changed, but I was brought up with a butler and a cook to look after me, and I never went near the kitchen. I was taken aback at first when Giles announced what he wanted to do. His grandfather still hasn't got over it, but his mother and I are delighted that he is doing something he enjoys. Nowadays anyone with a job that they enjoy is very lucky.

The gardener

Hugo Grantchester, 26, has been a gardener and a tree surgeon for four years. He went to Oxford University to study archaeology, but he dropped out after just one term. His father, Hector, is a surveyor and his mother, Geraldine, is an interior designer. Hugo and his mother talk about his choice of career.

Hugo

When I was 11, we moved to a large Tudor house in East Anglia which had three acres of garden. We had a gardener who lived in a little cottage at the end of our drive. I used to spend hours watching him work and talking to him. I think I picked up a lot about gardening without realizing it, because one summer, when I was still at school, I took a job at a garden centre and I knew all the names of the plants, and I could give people advice. Then I went to university and it was a disaster. After a term I told my parents that I was going to give it up and go back to work in the garden centre. They were furious, we had a terrible row, and they didn't speak to me for months. But I knew it was a waste of time to carry on studying archaeology, and the moment I started gardening again, I knew I'd made the right decision. I've enjoyed every moment of the last four years and my parents have learnt to accept what I do, not only because they can see how happy I am,

but also because a lot of my university friends have found it difficult to find good jobs or have been made redundant. Sometimes people are quite taken aback when they find out that their gardener went to university, but I think it makes them respect my opinion more when I'm helping them plan their gardens.

Hugo's mother

His father and I were so delighted when he went to Oxford, but when he gave it up so soon we were very, very angry. We thought manual labour was not the career for our only son. We fell out for months, Hector refused to allow Hugo into the house, and we all felt thoroughly miserable. But our daughter told us not to worry because Hugo would be a millionaire by the time he was forty. Anyway, we've made it up now we can see how happy he is, even though he hasn't become a millionaire yet! Times have changed and all kinds of people do all kinds of work, and I think the world's a better place for it!

'My parents were furious.'

Comprehension check

Find a partner from each of the other two groups.

1 Go through questions a–e in Exercise 1 on page 70 together. Compare and swap information about the people.

2 Read the other two articles quickly. Are the following statements true (✓) or false (✗)?

a Only Giles and Hugo were influenced by the servants in their families when they were children.

b Amanda wanted to be a nanny because she liked the uniform.

c Giles wanted to be a cook because the meals were so bad at boarding school.

d Hugo did well in his holiday job because he had learnt a lot about plants from the gardener.

e All of the parents were very angry when they were told about the choice of career.

f Hugo's parents were the least angry.

g All of the parents have become friends with their children again.

h Giles' grandfather has not forgiven him for becoming a cook.

i Some of the children have regretted their decision not to go to university.

j Hugo has already become a millionaire.

3 Show each other which multi-word verbs appear in your article. Discuss their meaning.
Which ones appear in more than one article?

Roleplay

Work in groups of three.

Students A and B

You are the parents of **C**. One of you is a doctor and the other a lawyer, and you would like **C** to follow one of these professions, but **C** has other ideas. Explain to **C** why yours are such good careers.

Student C

A and **B** are your parents. They want you to become a lawyer or a doctor, but you have different ideas! You want to be one of the following (or choose one of your own):

a dancer   a musician   a poet   an explorer
a model   a jockey   an astronaut   …

Talk together, and try to persuade each other to see your point of view.

● VOCABULARY

Multi-word verbs

There are many examples of multi-word verbs in the reading texts.

*She needed a nanny to **look after** us.*
*I told my parents that I was going to **give** it **up**.*
*I wanted to be a nanny when I **grew up**.*

📖 Grammar Reference: page 151.

Use your dictionary to do these exercises.

1 Meaning

In the following groups of sentences *one* meaning of the multi-word verb is literal and *two* are idiomatic. Say which is which.

1 a The plane to Hong Kong has just *taken off*.
b *Take* that vase *off* the table. It's going to fall.
c He's very famous now. His popularity really *took off* when he made that film.

2 a I'll *bring* you *up* some water when I come to bed.
b Have you *brought up* the question of borrowing the money?
c They *brought up* six children with very little money.

3 a Her health has really *picked up* since she moved to a sunny climate.
b Can you *pick up* my pen for me? It's under your chair.
c I *picked up* a little Italian when I was working in Rome.

Buongiorno! Come ti chiami?

4 a It took me a long time to *get over* the operation.
b Mario doesn't speak much English so it was difficult to *get over* to him what I wanted.
c Can you help me *get over* this wall? The gate is closed.

5 a I *looked up* Bob's number in the phone book.
b The new manager is very good. Sales have really *looked up* since he came.
c We *looked up* the tree and there was the cat on the top branch.

2 Verbs with two particles

Complete the pairs of sentences with one of the following multi-word verbs.

put up with   go out with   get on with   run out of   look forward to

a I don't _____ my sister's husband very well.
   Our teacher told us to _____ our work quietly.

b Has the photocopier _____ paper again?
   The children always _____ school immediately the bell goes.

c Why don't you ever _____ Christmas?
   We always _____ going on holiday.

d I must _____ the dog. She hasn't been for a walk yet.
   Tom and Flora used to _____ each other when they were teenagers.

e How do you manage to _____ the noise from your neighbours?
   Some parents _____ a lot of bad behaviour from their kids.

In which pairs of sentences is the meaning the same? In which is the meaning different?

3 Separable or inseparable?

Check whether the multi-word verb in the following sentences is separable or not.
Replace the word in *italics* with the pronoun.

Example
He turned on *the light*.   *He turned **it** on.*
She takes after *her father*.   *She takes after **him**.*

a I've just looked up *the word* in my dictionary.
b He's looking after *my cats* while I'm away.
c She has brought up *those children* really well.
d We picked up *Spanish* very quickly.
e I don't think they'll ever get over *the shock of her death*.
f He's taken up *golf* because he has a lot of free time since he retired.

● LISTENING AND SPEAKING

Pre-listening task

Work in groups and discuss the following questions.

– Is anyone in your family retired? Who?
– What job did they do before retiring?
– How old were they when they retired?
– How long have they been retired?
– What do they do now?

Thomas Wilson
– a retired man –

Listening

Look at the photograph of Thomas Wilson and his granddaughter, Philippa. Thomas used to be the managing director of a large textile company. He has now retired.

T.51 Listen to him talking to Philippa. Who do you think is happier, Thomas or Philippa? Why?

Comprehension check

1 Underline the correct question form and then answer it.

a How long *was he/has he been* retired?
b How long *did he work/has he worked* for the textile company?
c How long *was he/has he been* married?
d Who *did he go/has he gone* to Wales with?

2 Why does he like playing golf?
3 Which countries has he visited since he retired? Where did he go two years ago?
4 Why is he brown?
5 Who are the following: Rover, Keith, Miriam, Kylie, and Helen?
6 What are the two sad events in Thomas' life?
7 What does Philippa complain about?
8 What does Thomas mean when he says, 'You only get one go at it!'?

Discussion

- What is the usual retirement age for men and women in your country?
- What kind of thing do people like doing when they retire?
- Are attitudes to retirement changing?
- What do you think is the best age to retire?
- When would you like to retire?
- What would you like to do when you retire?

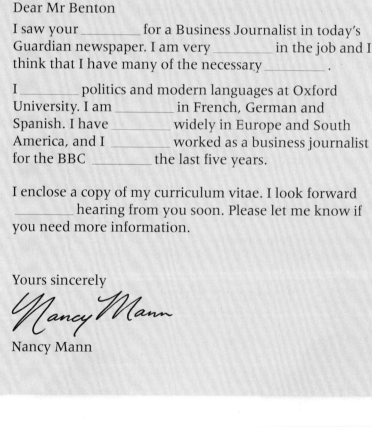

● WRITING

Formal letters

1 Read Nancy's letter of application to *Worldwatch*. Put *one* word into each gap.

Compare your answers with a partner.

2 Look at Nancy's letter again.

- In what other ways can you begin and end formal letters?
- In what ways can you begin and end informal letters?
- Where is Nancy's address written?
- Where is the address of the company she's writing to?
- In what other way you write the date?
- Where does Nancy sign her name? Where does she print her name?

There are three paragraphs. What is the aim of each one?

3 Write a letter of application for the following job in the *Daily News*.

---

17 Hillside Rd
Chesswood
Herts. WD3 5LB
Tel 01923 284171
Fax 01923 286622

Thursday 17 January

David Benton
Worldwatch UK Ltd
357 Ferry Rd
Basingstoke RG2 5HP

Dear Mr Benton

I saw your _____ for a Business Journalist in today's Guardian newspaper. I am very _____ in the job and I think that I have many of the necessary _____ .

I _____ politics and modern languages at Oxford University. I am _____ in French, German and Spanish. I have _____ widely in Europe and South America, and I _____ worked as a business journalist for the BBC _____ the last five years.

I enclose a copy of my curriculum vitae. I look forward _____ hearing from you soon. Please let me know if you need more information.

Yours sincerely

Nancy Mann

Nancy Mann

PostScript

On the telephone

1 All the phrases below are from typical telephone calls. Match a line in **A** with a line in **B**.

A

a Hello, this is Chesswood 285120. I'm afraid I'm not at home at the moment, but please leave your name and number after the tone and I'll get back to you as soon as I can.

b I'm afraid Mr Barrett's in a meeting. Can I take a message?

c Shall I ask Miss Jackson to give you a call when she gets back?

d Good morning. Payne and Stracey Advertising.

e Hello, Mrs Barrett … I'm afraid Mr Barrett's on another line at the moment. Do you want to hold or …? Oh, he's free now. I'm putting you through.

f Hello. Is that Sandra?

B

☐ Good morning. Can I have extension 321, please?

☐ No, I'm sorry, it isn't. She's just gone out. Can I take a message? She'll be back in a minute.

☐ Hi, Annie. This is er … Pete here. Pete Nealy. Er … I need to speak to you about next weekend. Can you give me a ring? Erm … I'm at home, by the way. It's ten o'clock now and I'll be here all morning, er … until two o'clock. Yes, thanks. Bye.

☐ Thank you very much. Frank? It's me, Diana.

☐ Yes, please. This is Pam Haddon. He rang me earlier and left a message on my answer phone and I'm returning his call. Can you tell him I'm back in my office now?

☐ Yes, please. I'm sure she's got my number but I'll give it to you again, just in case. It's 01924 561718.

2 T.52 Listen and check your answers. Which sound more like business calls?

3 Notice these common expressions on the telephone.

a A Hello!
  B Hello. Could I speak to Barry Perkins, please?
  A Speaking. (= I am Barry Perkins.)
  B Ah, hello. This is Jane Gardener. (NOT *I'm … or * Here is …)

b A Can I have extension 366, please?
  B Hold the line, please. I'm putting you through.

c A Can I speak to Mrs Barrett, please?
  B I'm afraid she's out at the moment. Can I take a message?
  A Yes. Can you ask her to give me a ring? I'll give you my number.

d A Can I speak to Mr Bray, please?
  B I'm afraid his line is busy at the moment. Would you like to hold?
  A No. I'll phone back later.

Leaving a message on an answer phone

1 It can be difficult to leave a message on an answer phone! You have to think quickly and speak clearly, and you have to pretend that you're talking to a person, but of course you're talking to a machine!

HOW to leave a message on an answer phone!

introduce yourself ▸▸▸	Hello. This is … / My name is …
give the day and time ▸▸	It's three o'clock on Monday afternoon.
reason for phoning ▸▸▸▸	I'm ringing … to let you know that … to find out if … because I need …
request action ▸▸▸▸▸▸	Could you ring me back? help me?
give your number ▸▸▸▸▸	My number is … You can get me on … I'm on 784 567 until five o'clock.
end ▸▸▸▸▸▸▸▸▸▸▸▸	Thanks a lot. Goodbye.

2 Work in pairs. Your teacher will give you role cards. Act out a telephone conversation!

Imagine!

Conditionals
Time clauses
would
Making suggestions

Test your grammar

1 Look at the pictures. Put the words under each picture in the right order to complete the sentences.

a I usually get the bus to school, but ...

get I if up late lift me Dad gives a my

if _____

b I've got my driving test next week, and ...

pass I test the if buy I'll car a new

if _____

c I don't have any money at all, but ...

million won I a if
round I'd the pounds
travel world

if _____

_____

2 Which situation ... is always true?
                      ... expresses a future possibility?
                      ... is possible but improbable?

PRESENTATION (1)

First conditional and time clauses

1 **T.53a** Jim is going to fly to Istanbul, and then he's going to backpack around the world with his friend, Anthony. His mother is very worried! Listen to their conversation. Put the words from the box in the gaps.

will you do	won't get	'll be	'll get
'll ask	won't do	get	'll be

Mum Oh, dear! I hope everything will be all right. You've never been abroad before.

Jim Don't worry, Mum. I _____ OK. I can look after myself. Anyway, I _____ with Anthony. We _____ anything stupid.

Mum But what _____ if you run out of money?

Jim We _____ a job of course!

Mum Oh. What about if you get lost?

Jim Mum! If we _____ lost, we _____ someone the way, but we _____ lost because we know where we're going!

Mum Oh. All right. But what if ...?

Practise the dialogue in pairs.

2 Make similar dialogues about other things that Jim's mother is worried about. Use *you* and *I*.

> Oh dear! What will you do if you get food poisoning?

> Don't worry, Mum. I'll ...

– get food poisoning
– lose your passport
– meet a girl who you fall in love with
– get sunburnt
– are homesick
– are mugged

– don't like the food
– don't understand the language
– don't get on with Anthony

3 **T.53b** Listen to the next part of their conversation. Put the verb into the correct tense.

Mum   But how will I know that you're all right?
Jim   When we _____ (get) to a big city, I _____ (send) you a postcard.
Mum   Oh. But Jim, it's such a long flight to Istanbul!
Jim   Mum! As soon as we _____ (arrive) in Turkey, I _____ (give) you a ring!
Mum   I _____ (be) so worried until I _____ (hear) from you.
Jim   It'll be OK, Mum. Honest!

● **Grammar questions**

– Which sentence expresses a future possibility, and which a future certainty?

   If *we run out of money, we'll get a job.*
   When *we get to a big city, I'll send you a postcard.*

– Tick (✓) the one that is right. Cross out (✗) the one that is wrong.

   ☐ *If we get lost, ...*
   ☐ *If we'll get lost, ...*

   ☐ *When we go ...*
   ☐ *When we'll go ...*

   ☐ *As soon as we arrive, ...*
   ☐ *As soon as we'll arrive, ...*

PRACTICE

1 Completing a conversation

1 Joe (**J**) is saying goodbye to his wife, Sue (**S**), who is going for a job interview. Put *if*, *when*, or *as soon as* into each box. Put the verb into the correct tense.

J   Goodbye, darling! Good luck with the interview!
S   Thanks. I'll need it. I hope the trains are running on time. ☐ the trains _____ (be) delayed, I _____ (get) a taxi. ☐ I _____ (be) late for the interview, I _____ (be) furious with myself!
J   Just keep calm! Phone me when you can.
S   I will. ☐ I _____ (come) out of the interview, I _____ (give) you a ring.
J   When _____ you _____ (know) ☐ you've got the job?
S   They _____ (send) me a letter in the next few days. ☐ they _____ (offer) me the job, I _____ (accept) it, and ☐ I accept it, we _____ (have to) move house. You know that, don't you?
J   Sure. But we'll worry about that later.
S   OK. What are you doing today?
J   I can't remember. ☐ I _____ (get) to the office, I _____ (look) in my diary. I don't think I'm doing much today.
S   Don't forget to pick up the children ☐ you _____ (get) back from work.
J   I won't. You'd better go now. ☐ you _____ (not hurry), you _____ (miss) the train.
S   OK. I _____ (see) you this evening. Bye!
J   Bye, my love. Take care, and good luck!

T.54   Listen and check your answers.

2 In pairs, ask and answer questions about Joe and Sue's conversation.

Example
What /Sue/do/if/trains/delayed?
What will Sue do if the trains are delayed?
She'll get a taxi.

a How/she/feel/if/late for the interview?
b When/Sue/phone/Joe?
c When/know/if/she's got the job?
d What/she/do/if/they/offer her the job?
e What/they/have to do/if/she/accept/job?
f What/Joe/do/when/get/office?
g What/happen/if/Sue/not hurry?

PRESENTATION (2)

Second conditional and *would*

1 Is there a national lottery in your country?
How much can you win?
In Britain you can win more than £10 million a week!

T.55 Look at the pictures and listen to some people saying what they would do if they won £2 million. Try to guess who says what and write a number in the box. Write notes on what they would do with it. Practise some of the sentences.

2 Complete these sentences from the interviews.

a 'I _____ on a boat trip around the world.'
'Oh, I _____ . I _____ so bored.
I _____ fly. It _____ so much quicker!'

b 'I _____ taking things easy for a bit, but then I _____ to just get on with my life, 'cos I'm very happy, really, with what I've got.'

Practise some of the sentences with *would*.
Notice the contraction *it'd* /ɪtəd/.

● Grammar questions

– Read the example below. Do we use the past tense forms *had* and *would* to refer to past time, or to show unreality?

If I had £2 million, I would go round the world.

– *I'd rather* (= I would rather) + infinitive means the same as *I'd prefer to* …

I don't like studying. I'd rather be outside playing tennis.

– *I wouldn't mind* + noun or *-ing* means *I would (quite) like* …

I wouldn't mind a cup of tea.
I wouldn't mind having a few weeks off work.

PRACTICE

1 Discussion

What would *you* do with two million pounds?
Work in groups. Ask and answer questions.

a What … buy?
b How much … give away? Who … give it to?
c … go on holiday? Where … to?
d What about your job? … carry on working or … give up your job?
e … go on a spending spree?
f How much … invest?
g … be happier than you are now?

2 Various conditional forms

1 Match a line in **A** with a line in **B** and a line in **C**.

	A	B	C
a	If Tony rings,	don't wait for me.	It would be really useful for work.
b	If you've finished your work,	I might do an evening class.	He can get hold of me there.
c	If I'm not back by 8.00,	you have to have a visa.	Keep warm and have plenty of fluids.
d	If you've got the 'flu,	you must give me a ring.	But you must be back here in fifteen minutes.
e	If you're ever in London,	tell him I'm at Andy's.	We could go out somewhere.
f	If you go to Australia,	you can have a break.	I'd love to be really good at photography.
g	I'd buy a word processor	you should go to bed.	You can get one from the Embassy.
h	If I had more time,	if I could afford it.	Go without me. I'll join you at the party.

T.56a Listen and check your answers. Practise some of the sentences. Look at the lines in **A** and **B**. What are the different possible verb forms?

Notice that when we have a conditional sentence with two present tenses, it expresses a situation that is always true. *If* means *when* or *whenever*. This is called the **zero conditional**.

If you boil water, it evaporates.

2 **T.56b** You will hear some questions. Say if they are examples of the first, second or zero conditional. In pairs, practise the questions and answer them.

3 Dialogues with *will* and *would*

Work in pairs.
Look at the following situations. Decide if they are …
… possible;
… imaginary and probably won't happen.

Ask and answer questions about what you *will do* or *would do* in each situation.

Example
There's a good film on TV tonight. (*Possible*)
What will you do if there's a good film on TV tonight?
I'll watch it.

You find burglars in your flat. (*Imaginary*)
What would you do if you found burglars in your flat?
I'd phone the police.

a You can't do this exercise.
b The weather's good this weekend.
c A good friend invites you out tonight.
d You are the president of your country.
e You don't have any homework tonight.
f Your teacher gives you extra homework tonight.
g You can speak perfect English.

LANGUAGE REVIEW

First conditional

First conditional sentences express real possibilities. Notice that we do not usually use *will* in the *if* clause.

*If I **see** a nice jumper in the shops, **I'll buy** it.*
*What **will** you **do** if you **don't have** enough money?*

Second conditional

Second conditional sentences express unreal or improbable situations. We use past tense forms to show 'unreality' and distance from the present.

*What **would** you **do** if you **saw** a ghost?*
*If I **were** Prime Minister, **I'd** increase income tax.*

Both first and second conditional sentences refer to the present and future. The difference is not about time but probability.

*If I **win** the tennis match, **I'll** …* (I think it's possible)
*If I **won** £5 million, **I'd** …* (but I don't think it'll happen)

Zero conditional

Zero conditional sentences refer to 'all time', not just the present or future. They express a situation that is always true. *If* means *when* or *whenever*.

If I read too much, I get a headache.
If you drop an egg, it breaks.

Time clauses

We do not usually use *will* in time clauses.

I'll give you a ring | *before I go.*
 | *as soon as I get back.*
 | *when I know the time of the train.*

📖 **Grammar Reference: page 152.**

● READING AND A SONG

Pre-reading task

1 Look at the title of the magazine article. It is based on a well-known song from a 1950s' American musical.

T.57 Listen to one or two verses of the song. What *don't* the singers of the song want to do? What *do* they want to do? The tapescript is on page 135.

2 The article is about people who win huge amounts of money in a lottery or on the football pools, and how this affects their lives. Which of the following do you think are good suggestions (✓) or bad suggestions (✗) for such people?

If you win a lot of money, …

… you should give up work. ☐

… you should buy a new house. ☐

. . . you mustn't let it change you. ☐

… it's a good idea to keep it a secret. ☐

… you should give money to everyone who asks for it. ☐

… you should go on a spending spree. ☐

What suggestions would *you* give to someone who has won a lot of money?

3 The words in **A** are in the article. Match a word in **A** with a definition in **B**.

A	B
envy	a sum of money you receive unexpectedly
to fantasize	an aim, a reason for doing something
a jigsaw	a feeling of discontent because someone has something that you want
a windfall	to spend money foolishly on small, useless things
a purpose	to imagine, to dream
to fritter away money	a picture cut into pieces that you have to put together again

Reading

Read the article. The following sentences have been taken out of the text. Where do you think they should go?

a They were furious!

b we feel at home

c It is tempting to move to a bigger house

d 'nothing but misery'

e what the money would do to us!

f it seems fantastic!

g most of their money will be frittered away

h if you lent him some money,

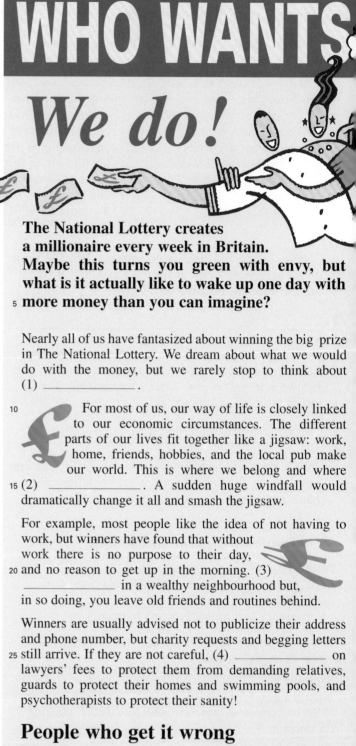

WHO WANTS
We do!

The National Lottery creates a millionaire every week in Britain. Maybe this turns you green with envy, but what is it actually like to wake up one day with
5 **more money than you can imagine?**

Nearly all of us have fantasized about winning the big prize in The National Lottery. We dream about what we would do with the money, but we rarely stop to think about (1) _____ .

10 For most of us, our way of life is closely linked to our economic circumstances. The different parts of our lives fit together like a jigsaw: work, home, friends, hobbies, and the local pub make our world. This is where we belong and where
15 (2) _____ . A sudden huge windfall would dramatically change it all and smash the jigsaw.

For example, most people like the idea of not having to work, but winners have found that without work there is no purpose to their day,
20 and no reason to get up in the morning. (3) _____ in a wealthy neighbourhood but, in so doing, you leave old friends and routines behind.

Winners are usually advised not to publicize their address and phone number, but charity requests and begging letters
25 still arrive. If they are not careful, (4) _____ on lawyers' fees to protect them from demanding relatives, guards to protect their homes and swimming pools, and psychotherapists to protect their sanity!

People who get it wrong

30 There are many stories about people who can't learn how to be rich. In 1989, Val Johnson won £850,000 on the pools. Immediately, she went on a spending spree that lasted for four years and five marriages. She is now penniless and alone. 'I'm not a happy person,' she says.
35 'Winning money was the most awful thing that happened to me.'

Then there is the story of Alice Hopper, who says that her £950,000 win four years ago brought her (5) _____ . She walked out of the factory where
40 she worked, and left a goodbye note for her husband on the

TO BE A MILLIONAIRE?

kitchen table. She bought herself a villa in Spain, and two bars (one a birthday present for her eighteen-year-old son). After three months, her son was killed while driving home from the bar on the motorbike which his mother had also
45 bought for him. She found the bars more and more difficult to run. She now sings in a local Karaoke bar to earn money for groceries. 'I wish I was still working in the factory,' she says.

'It won't change us!'

That's what all winners say when they talk to reporters and
50 television cameras as they accept the cheque and the kisses from a famous film star. And some winners, like Malcolm Price, really mean it. He refused to change his way of life when he won £2.5 million. The next Saturday night, he went to his local pub as
55 usual, and as usual he *didn't* buy his friends a drink. (6) _____ . He, too, is a lonely man now.

Imagine you are an average family and you have just won £1 million. At first (7) _____ . Just by picking up the phone you can get the toilet seat fixed, and the leak in
60 the roof repaired — all the problems that have been making your life miserable. 'But, it won't change us, darling,' you say to your wife. 'Yes, it will!' she insists. 'I want it to change us. It will make life better! It'll be brilliant!'

Already the children are changing. Just this morning they
65 were ordinary, contented kids. Now they are demanding computer games, CD players, motorbikes ... 'Hold on!' you shout. 'Let me answer the door.'

It is your neighbour, with a bunch of flowers and a loving smile on her face. 'Congratulations!' she shouts. 'I was
70 wondering if you could lend me ...' You shut the door.

In the first week you receive two thousand letters advising you how to spend your money, either by investing it or giving it to good causes. Your son comes home with a music system that is bigger than the
75 living-room, your sixteen-year-old daughter books a holiday to Barbados with her boyfriend, and your wife buys a Rolls-Royce.
'But darling,' you say, 'we haven't received one penny of this money yet! What about the broken toilet seat? What
80 about the leaking roof? What about me?'
'I haven't forgotten you,' says your wife. 'I've bought you a racehorse!'

The next day you get a begging letter from a man who won the lottery a year ago. He tells you how he spent £2,000,000
85 in three weeks. He says (8) _____ , he could start his life all over again. You begin to think that winning a fortune brings more problems than it solves! You realize that you are quite fond of the broken toilet seat and the leaking roof after all.

◀ Paul Maddison and Mark Gardiner celebrate with their wives

▼ David Caldwell splashes out with Joanna Lumley

£ A final thought

90 When you next buy your lottery ticket, or do the football pools, just stop for a minute and ask yourself why you're doing it. Do you actually want to win? Or are you doing it for the excitement of thinking about winning?

Comprehension check

1 Look back at the suggestions in the Pre-reading task. Have you changed your mind about any of them?

2 Answer the questions.
a Does the magazine article talk more about the positive side of winning a lot of money, or the negative side?
b How can a large amount of money affect …
  … our work?   … our home?   … our friends?
c How does the article say money can be 'frittered away'?
d The following groups are mentioned in the article: charities, relatives, lawyers, security guards, psychotherapists.
  Which of them is speaking in the following lines?

> 'Tell me about your relationship with your father.'
> 'Twenty pounds will feed a family for a month. Please give generously.'
> 'Now, John, you know you've always been my favourite nephew.'
> 'Sorry, sir. You can't go any further without permission.'
> 'I strongly advise you to take them to court.'

e Give three facts each about the lives of Val Johnson, Alice Hopper, and Malcolm Price.
  Why are they all mentioned?
f In the imaginary family that has won £1 million, who says, 'It won't change us'? Who says, 'I want it to change us'?
g What do the children want to have? What does the neighbour want?
h Who in the family doesn't buy anything? What do the others buy?

What do you think?

1 In what way is our life like a jigsaw?
2 How does winning a large amount of money smash the jigsaw?
3 Why do we need work in our lives?
4 In the story of the family that has won £1 million, what is the joke about the toilet seat?
5 What does he mean when he says, 'It won't change us'? What does his wife want to change?
6 What for you are the answers to the questions in the last paragraph of 'Who wants to be a millionaire?'?

Vocabulary

Find a word or words in the text that mean the same as the following definitions. They are in the same order as they appear in the text.

a not often
b very big
c break violently
d area around your house
e asking (for something) very strongly
f keep (something) safe, defend
g a time when you go to the shops and spend a lot of money
h having not a penny
i basic things to eat like bread, sugar, vegetables
j a hole through which water gets in

● SPEAKING

A maze

Work in groups and read the role card below.

Congratulations! Or is it? You have won five million pounds. What are you going to do with it? Talk together until you all agree on what to do next. Your teacher will then give you a card with more information, and another decision to make.

Carry on talking until you come to the end. The aim is to spend your money wisely without going mad!

Congratulations!
~
You have won
£5 MILLION!
~
Now you have to make some decisions.
Are you going to keep your win a secret,
or will you go to a big London hotel to receive
your cheque from a famous film star?
Of course the press will be there,
and your photo will be in all the newspapers.

If you want to
remain anonymous,
go to
10

If you want to go to
the hotel and the
press conference,
go to
15

● VOCABULARY

Base and strong adjectives

1 Some adjectives have the idea of *very*. Look at these examples from the article on pages 80–81.

a huge windfall	*huge* means *very big*
it seems fantastic	*fantastic* means *very good*
It'll be brilliant!	*brilliant* means *very good*

2 Put a base adjective from the box next to a strong adjective.

> good   bad   cold   frightened
> funny   tasty   angry   tired
> pretty/attractive   interesting   hot
> surprised   clever   dirty

Base adjective	Strong adjective
big	enormous, huge
_____	boiling
_____	exhausted
_____	freezing
_____	delicious
_____	fascinating
_____	horrid, horrible, awful, terrible, disgusting
_____	perfect, marvellous, superb, wonderful, fantastic, brilliant
_____	filthy
_____	astonished, amazed
_____	furious
_____	hilarious
_____	terrified
_____	beautiful
_____	brilliant

We can make adjectives more extreme by using adverbs such as *very* and *absolutely*.

Their house is very big.
But their garden is absolutely enormous.

Careful! We cannot say *absolutely big because *absolutely* only goes with strong adjectives, and we cannot say *very enormous because *enormous* already means *very big*.

The following adverbs can be used:

very tired	**absolutely** exhausted
quite good	**absolutely** freezing
really cold	**really** wonderful

3 **T.58** Listen to the dialogues. Complete them, using an adverb and an adjective.

Example

> What did you do last night?
>
> We went to the cinema.

> What did you see?
>
> *Murder in the Park.*

> Was it good?
>
> I thought it was *absolutely brilliant,* but Pete was *really terrified.* There was so much blood!

4 Make up similar dialogues. Talk about: a person, a meal, the weather, a book, an exam, the news.

● LISTENING

Pre-listening task

1 Have you ever given money to charity, or worked for a charity?

2 Look at the list of charities and charitable causes below. Which do you think are the most and least deserving?

– a charity that helps old people with food and housing
– a hospice for people who are dying of an incurable disease
– an organization that encourages people to sponsor a child in the Third World
– a charity that helps homeless people in cities
– cancer research
– a charity that helps people with HIV or AIDS
– a group that believes we should not exploit animals in any way at all

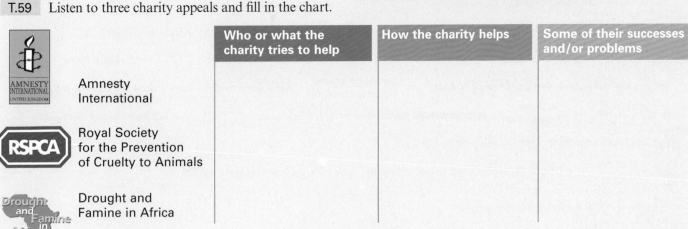

Listening

T.59 Listen to three charity appeals and fill in the chart.

	Who or what the charity tries to help	How the charity helps	Some of their successes and/or problems
Amnesty International			
Royal Society for the Prevention of Cruelty to Animals			
Drought and Famine in Africa			

What do you think?

Imagine that you have £5,000 that you want to give to charity.
Who would you give the money to? How would you divide it?
Think about what *you* would do, and then discuss your ideas with a partner.

Words that join ideas

1 Some words and expressions are used to make a comment on what is being expressed.

Examples
'Ah, now, Peter! Come over here!'
'My name's Jack, **actually**.' (Actually = I'm going to give you some extra information that you didn't know, or that you got wrong.)

What an awful journey you had! You must be exhausted! **Anyway**, you're here now so let's not worry any more. (Anyway = let's change the subject and talk about something else.)

2 Some words are used to join ideas and sentences.

Example
George was rich. He wasn't a happy man.
George was rich, **but** he wasn't a happy man.
Although George was rich, he wasn't a happy man.
George was rich. **However**, he wasn't a happy man.

3 In the letter, choose the words that fit best. Nearly all the words have appeared in this unit. The letter is written by Jacky, who is married to Joe and has two children, Samantha and Polly.

---

16 Cassandra Gardens, London N16

22 July

Dear Penny

I hope you're all well. We're all terribly busy, (a) | even / for example | Polly, who has finally managed to find some work. (b) | Unfortunately, / Generally, | it's not a very good job, but (c) | therefore / at least | it's a job, and maybe she will find something better in the future. She has (d) | especially / also | found somewhere else to live – a small flat about five miles away, (e) | so / because | now there's (f) | nearly / only | Joe and me left at home. After 24 years of having children to look after, it's very strange to have the house to ourselves, (g) | although / so | I do appreciate coming home to a tidy house at the end of a day. By the way, Polly has broken up with her boyfriend, Peter. We were very sorry, (h) | because / but | we got on well with him, and they seemed to be well-suited.

Samantha has some interesting news, (i) | either. / as well. | She passed her final exams. We heard last week, so (j) | of course, / however, | we had a small family celebration. She doesn't know what she wants to do yet, (k) | so / but | she has plenty of time to decide. She doesn't have a boyfriend at the moment, (l) | either. / too. | I don't know what's the matter with them! They're both (m) | enough pretty! / pretty enough! | Joe's fine, but he hasn't been able to do much in the garden (n) | because / because of | the weather, which has been terrible. (o) | Actually / Meanwhile | it has rained every day for the past fortnight. It's unbelievable, isn't it?

(p) | After all, / Anyway, | that's enough of my news. How are you all? What are you up to?

Do write soon and tell me everything!

Love

Jacky

Making suggestions

1 Maggie's bored and Paul's broke. Look at the suggestions made by their friends. Are they talking to Maggie or Paul? Which suggestions include the speaker?

> Let's go to the cinema!

> Why don't we go for a walk?

> If I were you, I'd get a better-paid job.

> I don't think you should go out so much.

> Why don't you ask your parents?

> Shall we have a game of cards?

> You ought to save some money every month!

> You'd better get a loan from the bank!

> I'm broke!

> I'm bored!

2 **T.60** Listen to Maggie and Paul and their friends. How can we make suggestions in English?

3 Listen again and read the tapescript on page 136. Notice how we accept and reject suggestions.

Work in pairs. Practise the dialogues. Take it in turns to cover the page.

4 Change the sentence using the prompts.

Example

Let's go to the cinema.

a Why don't we …?

> Why don't we go to the cinema?

b eat out tonight?

> Why don't we eat out tonight?

c I think we should

> I think we should eat out tonight.

Let's go to the cinema.	Why don't you phone Pat?
a Why don't we …?	a You'd better
b eat out tonight?	b the police
c I think we should	c tell the truth
d invite Pete to dinner tomorrow	d If I were you, I'd
e redecorate the house	e look for a different job
f If I were you, I'd	f You should
g You ought to	g She
h buy some new clothes	h ought to
i go shopping	i have a break
j Shall we …?	j Let's

5 Work in pairs. Make dialogues for the situations, using ways of making suggestions.

Example
You have got a terrible cold.

A *My head's killing me! And my nose is so sore!*
B *I think you should go to bed with a hot drink.*
A *That's a good idea. I'll go right now.*
B *I'll make you a hot lemon drink.*
A *Oh, that would be lovely!*

a You've just got a job in Moscow, so you need to learn the Russian language, and find out about Russian people and culture as quickly as possible.

b You both have the evening free, and there's nothing on TV.

c Your flat's a mess, it hasn't been decorated for ages, and the furniture is ancient. Suddenly you inherit some money!

d You can't decide whether to go to university (but you don't know what to study) or have a year off and go round the world.

e It's Christmas time! What can you buy for the teacher and the different members of the class?

f You've been invited to the Queen's garden party at Buckingham Palace in June. What are you going to wear? The weather in June is very unpredictable.

Relationships

Modal verbs (2) probability
So do I! Neither do I!

---

9

1 Read the pairs of sentences. Which sentence in each pair expresses a fact? Put a ✓. Which sentence expresses a possibility? Put a ?.

Example
I'm in love!   ✓
I must be in love!   ?

a She's having a shower.
   She could be having a shower.

b That pen's mine.
   That pen might be mine.

c He doesn't own a Rolls Royce.
   He can't own a Rolls Royce.

d You must have met my brother.
   You've met my brother.

e They haven't met the Queen.
   They can't have met the Queen.

f Shakespeare might have lived there.
   Shakespeare lived there.

2 Which of the sentences in Exercise 1 are about the present? Which are about the past?

PRESENTATION (1)

Modal verbs of probability in the present

1 Do you ever read the Problem Page in magazines or newspapers? What kinds of problems do people often write about?

2 Here are the replies to letters from two people who wrote to Susie's Problem Page in *Metropolitan Magazine*. Read them and discuss with a partner what you think the problem is. Use your dictionary to check any new words.

Susie's Problem page

Lucy has a problem:
"I live in Scotland and he lives in California! ..."

Dear Lucy

Everyone has daydreams and there is nothing wrong with this. There is only a problem when you forget where dreams end and the real world begins. Don't write any more letters to him. It's a waste of time and money, and you know really that a relationship with him is impossible. For one thing he lives in California and you live in Scotland. Try to get out more and find some friends in the real world; sitting at home crying over his records won't help you. You need to find other interests and other people of your own age to talk to. Your parents clearly don't have enough time to listen. Study hard and good luck next June!

Yours Susie

3 Look at the texts. Say who *she*, *he*, or *they* refer to in the following sentences.

a She must be exhausted.

b She must be in love with a pop star.

c She could be a doctor or a nurse.

d She can't have many friends.

e He might be an alcoholic.

f He must be unemployed.

g They can't have a very good relationship with their daughter.

h They might not have any children.

i She can't get on very well with her daughter-in-law.

j She must be studying for exams next June.

k They might live near a busy road.

l He must snore.

4 Give reasons for each statement.

Example
Pam must be exhausted … because she works hard, she does everything in the house and she can't sleep.

**Pam has a problem:
"He spends all his time at his mother's! …"**

Dear Pam

If all you say is true, it is remarkable that you are still together. But you are not helping your relationship by saying nothing and doing everything. He doesn't seem to notice how you feel. I know he's worried about his mother but he seems to spend more time at her house than his own. You have a tiring and stressful job, caring for sick people all day, and it is unfair that he is always at his mother's and leaves you to do all the housework. The empty whisky bottles under the bed are also worrying. Perhaps he will feel better about himself when he finds work. In the meantime, you must try to talk openly to each other about your feelings, otherwise anger and resentment will grow. Also, buy some earplugs—you need a good night's sleep!

Yours Susie

● **Grammar questions**

– Which statement is the most sure? Which are less sure?

*She **must be** in love.*
*She **could be** in love.*
*She **might be** in love.*

– The above sentences all express *I think it's probable/possible that she is in love.*
How do you express *I don't think it's probable/possible that she is in love?*

PRACTICE

1 Controlled speaking

Work in pairs.

Student A Talk to Student B about Lucy.
Student B Talk to Student A about Pam.

Put *one* suitable verb form into each gap.

Student A

Lucy _____ in Scotland so she must _____ Scottish. She _____ a lot of letters to a pop star in California, so she must _____ a lot of money on stamps. She _____ in her room and _____ to his music all of the time so she can't _____ many friends or hobbies. She should _____ out more and _____ some friends and then she might _____ the pop star. She could _____ to talk to her parents again, but they might not _____ because they _____ very busy.

Student B

Pam must _____ very tired at the end of the day because she _____ a stressful job. She must _____ sorry for her husband because he _____ unemployed but she must also _____ very angry with him because he never _____ any housework. She could _____ her mother-in-law to help but she can't _____ a very good relationship with her because her husband _____ too much time at her house. Things might _____ better if he could _____ a job and if they could _____ to each other.

2 Grammar and pronunciation

Respond to the statements or questions using the word or words in brackets.

Example
I haven't eaten anything since breakfast.
(must, very)
You must be very hungry!

a Mr and Mrs Brown never go on holiday.
   (can't, much money)
b The phone's ringing! (might, Jane)
c Paul's taking his umbrella. (must, rain)
d There are three fire engines!
   (must, fire somewhere)
e I don't know where Hannah is.
   (could, her bedroom)
f My aunt isn't in the kitchen.
   (can't, cook dinner)
g Whose coat is this? (might, John's)
h We've won the lottery! (must, joke!)

T.61 Listen and check your answers.
Practise the stress and intonation in pairs.

3 What are they talking about?

Work in small groups.

1 **T.62** Listen to five short conversations and guess the answer to the questions.

   Example
   A It's Father's Day next Sunday.
   B I know. Shall we buy Dad a present or just send him a card?

   Who do you think they are?
   *They **must be** related. They **can't be** just friends. They **could be** husband and wife but they're **probably** brother and sister.*

a Where do you think the people are? At home? In a restaurant? In a pub? In a hotel?
b What do you think his job is? A sales manager? A bus driver? An actor? A taxi driver?
c What do you think she's talking about? Visiting her parents? A first day in a new job? Meeting her boyfriend's parents? Her wedding day?
d Who or what do you think they are talking about? A dog? The au pair? A horse? A baby?
e What do you think they are doing? Swimming? Fishing? Rowing? Water-skiing?

2 Look at the photos. They are all of Verity and her family. Which is Verity? Who do you think the others are? Your teacher will tell you which group is closest.

PRESENTATION (2)

Modal verbs of probability in the past

1 **T.63a** Poor Carl has had an accident. He is speaking to his friend, Andy, on the phone. In pairs, read and listen to Andy's side of the conversation. What do you think they are talking about? Use a dictionary to check any new words.

- Hi! Carl? It's Andy. Yeah. How are you? Feeling better?

- Really? Still using a crutch, eh? So you're not back at work yet?

- Two more weeks! That's when the plaster comes off, is it?

- No, I'm fine. The suntan's fading, though. Josie's is, too. She sends love, by the way.

- Yes, yes, I have. I got them back today. They're good. I didn't realize we'd taken so many.

- Yes, the sunset. It's a good one. All of us together on Bob and Marcia's balcony, with the mountains and the snow in the background. It's beautiful. Brings back memories, doesn't it?

- Yes, I know. I'm sorry. At least it was towards the end; it could have been the first day. You only came home two days early.

- Yes, we have. Yesterday, in fact. Bob wrote it and we all signed it. I don't know if it'll do any good, but it's worth a try.

- Yeah. They found it. It arrived on the next flight. Marcia was delighted.

- Sure. Some ups and downs, but generally I think we all got on well and had a great time. Shall we go again next year?

- Good! Great! It's a date. Next time look out for the trees! I'll ring again soon, Carl. Take care!

2 Tick (✓) the two sentences which you think are possible. Cross (✗) the one you think is not possible.

Example
What is the relationship between Andy and Carl?
- They must be friends. ✓
- They could be father and son. ✗
- They can't be business colleagues. ✓

a Where have they been?
- They must have been on holiday. ☐
- They can't have been somewhere sunny. ☐
- They might have been to Switzerland. ☐

b What happened to Carl?
- He must have broken his leg. ☐
- He could have broken his arm. ☐
- He must have come home early. ☐

c How many people went on holiday?
- There must have been at least five. ☐
- There might have been more than five. ☐
- There must have been three. ☐

d Where did they stay?
- They could have stayed on a campsite. ☐
- They must have stayed in a hotel. ☐
- They might have stayed with friends. ☐

e What did they do on holiday?
- They must have taken a lot of photos. ☐
- They could have been sunbathing. ☐
- They can't have been skiing. ☐

f What did Bob write?
- He might have written a letter to his wife. ☐
- He could have written a letter of complaint to the hotel. ☐
- He could have written a letter to the tour operator. ☐

g How did they travel?
- They must have flown. ☐
- They must have gone by train. ☐
- They might have hired a car. ☐

h What arrived on the next flight?
- It could have been Marcia's skis. ☐
- It must have been Marcia's suitcase. ☐
- It might have been Marcia's coat. ☐

3 Use some of the ideas in sentences a–h to say what you think happened to Andy and Carl.

Example
Andy and Carl must be friends and they must have been on holiday together. They might…

4 **T.63b** Listen to the full conversation between Andy and Carl. Which of your ideas were correct?

● Grammar questions

- What is the past of the following sentences?

He	*must* *can't* *could* *might*	*be on holiday.*

- What is the past of these sentences?

*I **must** buy some sunglasses.*
*I **have to** go home early.*
*I **can** see the sea from my room.*

PRACTICE

1 Pronunciation and speaking

1 Work in pairs. Respond to the following situations using the word or words in brackets and the perfect infinitive (*have* + past participle). Take it in turns to read aloud and respond.

Example
Student A   I can't find my ticket. (must, drop)
Student B   *You must have dropped it.*

a John didn't come to school yesterday. (must, ill)
b Look at my new gold watch! (can't, buy yourself)
c Why is Isabel late for class? (might, oversleep)
d I can't find my homework. (must, forget)
e The teacher's checking Maria's work. (can't, finish already)
f Did you know that Charles got top marks in the exam? (must, cheat)
g Where's my umbrella? (could, leave it on the train)

2 **T.64**   Listen and check your answers. Do the exercise again paying particular attention to stress and intonation.

2 Discussing grammar

1 Fill in the gap in the second sentence with the modal verb in the past. Discuss your answers with a partner. (This exercise includes modal verbs of obligation and ability.)

a The pond is frozen. It *must* be very cold outside. (present probability)
You _____ very cold when you were out skiing. (past probability)

b You *must* do your homework tonight. (present obligation)
When I was at school we _____ homework every night. (past obligation)

c He *can't* be a member of the football team. He's hopeless at all sports! (present probability)
He _____ a member of his school football team. He was hopeless at all sports. (past probability)

d Jane *can* swim really well. (present ability)
She _____ really well when she was just eighteen months old. (past ability)

2 Work in pairs. Look at the list of modal auxiliary verbs. How many can you fit *naturally* into each gap? Discuss with your partner the differences in meaning.

can	can't	could	must	might	shall	should

a He _____ have been born during World War II.
b _____ you help me with the washing up, please?
c You _____ see the doctor immediately.
d It _____ be raining.
e _____ we go out for a meal tonight?
f I _____ stop smoking.
g It _____ have been Bill that you met at the party.
h I _____ learn to speak English.

LANGUAGE REVIEW

must, could, might, can't

1 *Must, could, might,* and *can't* are used to express degrees of probability about the present.

He **must be** *in love.* = very probable that he is in love	95% sure
He **could be** *in love.* He **might be** *in love.* = possible, but less probable	45% sure
He **can't be** *in love.* = very probable that he is *not* in love	95% sure

2 They are used to express degrees of probability about the past (using the perfect infinitive).

He **must have been** *in love.*
= very probable that he was in love

He **could have been** *in love.*
He **might have been** *in love.*
= possible, but less probable

He **can't have been** *in love.*
= very probable that he was *not* in love

3 They can also be used with the continuous infinitive.

You *must* **be joking!**
She *could* **be having** *a shower.*
It *may/might* **have been raining.**

4 *May* can be used instead of *might* and *could.*

📖 **Grammar Reference: page 153.**

VOCABULARY AND SPEAKING

Character adjectives

What sort of person *are* You?

1 Are you usually smiling and happy? ❑
2 Do you enjoy the company of other people? ❑
3 Do you find it difficult to meet new people? ❑
4 Is it important to you to succeed in your career? ❑
5 Does your mood change often and suddenly for no reason? ❑
6 Do you notice other people's feelings? ❑
7 Do you think the future will be good? ❑
8 Can your friends depend on you? ❑
9 Is your room often in a mess? ❑
10 Do you get annoyed if you have to wait for anyone or anything? ❑
11 Do you put off until tomorrow what you could do today? ❑
12 Do you work hard? ❑
13 Do you keep your feelings and ideas to yourself? ❑
14 Do you often give presents? ❑
15 Do you talk a lot? ❑
16 Are you usually calm and not worried by things? ❑

Work in pairs.

1 Do the personality quiz above to discover what type of person you are. Use a dictionary to check any new words. Write **Y** for Yes, **N** for No, and **S** for Sometimes.

2 Ask your partner to do the quiz about you.
Look at your ideas and your partner's ideas about you. Are they the same?

3 Match these adjectives with the questions in the quiz.

a	untidy	9	i	lazy
b	optimistic		j	generous
c	sociable		k	moody
d	talkative		l	hard-working
e	reserved		m	easy-going
f	shy		n	reliable
g	impatient		o	cheerful
h	ambitious		p	sensitive

Which are *positive* qualities and which are *negative*? Which could be both?

4 What is the opposite of each of the sixteen adjectives in Exercise 3?
Remember that the prefixes *in-* and *un-* can sometimes be used to make negatives. Which of the adjectives above can use these?

5 Describe someone in the class to your partner but don't say who it is. Can your partner guess who it is?

LISTENING AND SPEAKING

Brothers and sisters

Pre-listening task

Do a class survey.

Find out who has any brothers and/or sisters. How many? Who has the most? Do they like having lots of brothers and sisters? Does anyone have a twin?
How many only children are there in the class? Do they like being an only child?

Listening and note-taking

T.65   Listen to two people talking about their families. First listen to Jillie, and answer the questions.

– How many brothers and sisters does she have?
– Was she happy as a child? Why? Why not?
– Is she happy now? Why? Why not?
– How has the family changed over the years?
– What do you learn about other members of her family and friends?

Now listen to Philippa and answer the same questions.

Discussion

– How many children do you have/would you like to have?
– What size is the perfect family?
– Would you like to have twins?

READING AND SPEAKING

Pre-reading task

Read the following quotation.

'Only when the last tree has died and the last river has been poisoned and the last fish has been caught will we realize that we can't eat money.'

Work in small groups. Who do you think said it?

a A political leader.
b A member of *Greenpeace*.
c An American Indian.
d An African fisherman.
e A Greek philosopher.
f A French farmer.

When do you think it was said?

a In the 5th century BC.
b In the 19th century.
c In the 20th century.

Your teacher will give you the correct answer.

Reading

You are going to read some extracts from a story by the French writer, Jean Giono (1895–1971), called *The Man Who Planted Trees*. In it Giono describes the world of a solitary shepherd who plants trees, while in the background there are two world wars.

T.66a Read and listen to the extracts and answer the questions after each one.

THE MAN WHO PLANTED TREES

Extract 1

About forty years ago, I was taking a long trip on foot over mountain heights quite unknown to tourists. All around was barren and colourless land. Nothing grew there but wild lavender.

5 After five hours' walking I had still not found water. All about me was the same dryness, the same coarse grasses. I thought I saw in the distance a small black silhouette. It was a shepherd. Thirty sheep were lying about him on the baking earth. He gave me a
10 drink and took me to his cottage on the plain.

I felt peace in the presence of this man. I asked if I might rest here for a day. He found it quite natural—or, to be more exact, he gave me the impression that nothing could surprise me. I didn't
15 actually need to rest, but I was interested and wished to know more about him.

1 Giono wrote the story in 1953. In which year does the actual story begin?
2 The story takes place in France. Which part of France do you think it is? Why? What is the countryside like?
3 Why do you think the writer is interested in the shepherd? What do you think he likes about his lifestyle?

The shepherd puts a large sack of acorns onto the table. He inspects each acorn and carefully chooses one hundred perfect ones before going to bed. The writer is curious. The next day when he goes out with the shepherd into the hills, he discovers what the acorns are for.

T.66b Extract 2

I noticed that he carried for a stick an iron rod as thick as my thumb and about a metre and a half long. He began thrusting his iron rod into the earth, making a hole in which he planted an acorn; then he refilled the hole. He was planting oak trees. 5

After the midday meal he resumed his planting. I suppose I must have been fairly insistent in my questioning, for he answered me. For three years he had been planting trees in this wilderness. He had planted one hundred thousand. Of the 10 hundred thousand, twenty thousand had sprouted. Of the twenty thousand he still expected to lose half. There remained ten thousand oak trees to grow where nothing had grown before. 15

That was when I began to wonder about the age of this man. He was obviously over fifty. Fifty-five he told me. His name was Elzéard Bouffier. I told him that in thirty 20 years his ten thousand oaks would be magnificent. He answered that if God granted him life, in another thirty years he would have planted so many more that these ten 25 thousand would be like a drop of water in the ocean.

The next day we parted.

4 How old do you think the writer was at the time of the story? A boy in his teens? In his twenties? Middle-aged? Older? Why?
5 How old will Elzéard be in thirty years time? What year will it be?
6 What do you think Elzéard's ambition is? What is his vision of the future?

For the next five years the writer is a soldier and fights in World War I. The war ends in 1918 and his thoughts turn again to the tree-planter in the mountains. He returns to look for him.

T.66c **Extract 3**

I had seen too many men die during those five years not to imagine easily that Elzéard Bouffier was dead, especially since, at twenty, one regards men of fifty as old men with nothing left to do but die. He
5 was not dead. As a matter of fact, he was extremely well. He had changed jobs. He had got rid of the sheep because they threatened his young trees. For, he told me, the war had disturbed him not at all. He had imperturbably continued to plant.

10 The oaks were then ten years old and taller than both of us. It was an impressive spectacle. I was literally speechless, and as he did not talk, we spent the whole day walking in silence through his forest. It measured eleven kilometres in length and
15 three kilometres at its greatest width. When you remembered that all this had come from the hands and the soul of this one man, you understood that men could be as effective as God in ways other than destruction.

7 Why did the writer think that Elzéard might have died?
8 How had the war affected Elzéard?
9 Why is the writer speechless?
10 What thoughts about human behaviour does he have in the last sentence?

The writer returns for a final visit in 1945 after World War II. Elzéard is still alive. The writer is amazed at what he sees. Not only is there the forest, but many villages have been rebuilt, and by 1953 more than ten thousand people in the area owe their happiness to Elzéard Bouffier.

T.66d **Extract 4**

The bus put me down in Vergons. In 1913 this village of ten or twelve houses had three inhabitants. All about them nettles were feeding upon the remains of abandoned houses. Now everything had changed.
5 Even the air. Instead of the harsh dry winds, a gentle breeze was blowing, laden with scents. A sound like water came from the mountains: it was the wind in the forest. Most amazing of all, I heard the actual sound of water falling into a pool. I saw a fountain
10 had been built. Ruins had been cleared away, and five houses restored. Now there were twenty-eight inhabitants, four of them young married couples. It was now a village where one would like to live.

When I think that one man was able to cause
15 this land of Canaan to grow from wasteland, I am convinced that in spite of everything, humanity is good.

Elzéard Bouffier died peacefully in his sleep in 1947.

11 What has happened in the writer's life that could have made him pessimistic?
Is he in fact pessimistic about the world? Give a reason for your answer.
12 How is it that so many people owe their happiness to one man? What are the results of his tree-planting?
13 How old is Elzéard when he dies? Why is it so important that he had a long life?

What do you think?

Work in groups.

1 Do you think the story about Elzéard is true?
Do you think Elzéard was ever married?

Give reasons for your opinions. Your teacher will tell you if you are correct.

2 How would you describe the personality of Elzéard Bouffier? Do you know any people like him in your life?

3 In the context of the twentieth century and its two world wars, what message is Giono trying to make about nature and the importance of individual human beings?

(This little book has been translated into over a dozen languages. Perhaps you could read the whole book in your own language, or better still, read it in English.)

● WRITING

Sentence combination

1 Read the sentences about Elzéard Bouffier and then compare them with the paragraph below. Note the ways in which the sentences are combined.

Elzéard Bouffier was a shepherd.
He was poor.
He was solitary.
He lived in the mountains.
The mountains were barren.
They were in southern France.
Elzéard had a love of nature.
He had an incredible idea.
During his life he planted thousands of acorns.
The acorns grew into a forest of oak trees.
The forest made the countryside rich and fertile again.
He died when he was 89.

Elzéard Bouffier was a poor, solitary shepherd, who lived in the barren mountains of southern France. His love of nature gave him an incredible idea. During his life he planted thousands of acorns. These grew into a forest of oak trees, which made the countryside rich and fertile again. Elzéard died when he was 89.

2 Rewrite each group of sentences to form a more natural sounding paragraph.

a **A person**

Alan Higgins is a writer.
He is famous.
He is a millionaire.
He comes from the north of England.
He has gone to live in the USA.
He has written twenty-five novels.
His novels have been translated into five languages.
Hollywood is going to make a film of his latest novel.
The film will star Sunny Shaw.
Sunny Shaw's last film was a big box office hit. The film was called *Hot Night in the Snow*.

b **A place**

Oxford is a city.
It is a city in the south of England.
It is on the River Thames.
It has a population of about 100,000.
The city is famous.
It has one of the oldest universities in the world.
It has lots of other old buildings.
It has the Bodleian Library.
It has the Ashmolean Museum.
The Ashmolean was built in 1683.
Oxford was once the capital of England.
Not many people know this about Oxford.
Charles I made it the capital.
It was the capital from 1642–1645.

3 Write a short profile of a person (it could be you) and a place that are important to you.

PostScript

So do I! Neither do I!

1 Read the statements in the chart below. Complete the **You** column by putting (✓) if it is the same for you and (✗) if it isn't.

	You	Polly	Polly's words
I want to travel the world.			
I don't want to have lots of children.			
I can speak four languages.			
I can't drive.			
I'm not going to marry until I'm 35.			
I went to America last year.			
I have never been to Australia.			
I don't like politicians.			
I am bored with the British Royal Family.			
I love going to parties.			

2 **T.67** Listen to Polly. She is at a party and lots of friends are talking to her about themselves. Complete the **Polly** column by putting (✓) for what is the same and (✗) for what is not the same for Polly.

3 Listen again and write on the chart the *exact* words that Polly uses. Choose from the lists below.

So am I.	So do I.	So can I.	So did I.	So have I.
Neither am I.	Neither do I.	Neither can I.	Neither did I.	Neither have I.
I am.	I do.	I can.	I did.	I have.
I'm not.	I don't.	I can't.	I didn't.	I haven't.

What does she say when it is the same for her?
What does she say when it is different?

📖 **Grammar Reference: page 153.**

4 Work in pairs.
Read out the statements in Exercise 1 to each other and give the correct response for you.

5 Go round the class.
Everyone must make a statement about themselves or give an opinion about something. The others in the class must respond.

Examples

Student 1	*I love chocolate ice cream!*
Other students	*So do I./Me too.* *I don't!*
Student 2	*I didn't do my homework.*
Other students	*Neither did I./Me neither.* *I did!*

Obsessions

Present Perfect Continuous
Time expressions
Complaining

10

Test your grammar

1 For each pair, match a line in **A** with a line or picture in **B**.

A	B
a What do you do What are you doing	on your hands and knees? for a living?
b She smokes She's smoking	twenty cigarettes a day. a Russian cigarette.
c He has He's having	a bath. He can't come to the phone. a lot of money.
d You're stupid. You're being stupid.	You always are. You aren't usually.
e Someone fired a gun. Someone was firing a gun.	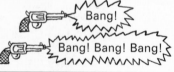
f The cat drowned. The cat was drowning	so I jumped into the water and saved it. It was terribly sad.
g What have you done with my headphones? What have you been doing	I can't find them. since I last saw you?
h Who has drunk my beer? Who has been drinking my beer?	

2 Look at the second sentence of each pair. What do the verbs have in common?

PRESENTATION (1)

Present Perfect Continuous

1 Look at the newspaper headline and the picture of Peter.
- What's Peter's job?
- What has he passed?
- 'L' stands for *Learner*. What are L-plates on a car for?
- What is he tearing up? Why?
- Can you explain the play on words in the headline?

Here endeth

Young vicar passes driving test after 632 lessons over 17 years

VICAR Peter Newman is celebrating success — he has finally passed his driving test. He has been learning to drive for the past 17 years, and he
5 **has had a total of 632 lessons.**

Peter, 34, has spent over £9,000 on tuition, he has had eight different instructors, and he has crashed his car five times. Then, one week ago
10 he changed to an automatic car — and he passed his test immediately. He said last night, 'I've been praying for a driving-licence for over half my life, and at last my prayers have
15 been answered.'

2 | **T.68** | Read and listen to the article. Then answer the questions.

- Why is Peter celebrating?
- Was it easy?
- What helped him to pass his test?
- What was his first accident?
- What was his big problem with driving?
- What has happened to his instructors? Why?
- Why hasn't he seen some of his relatives for so long?

3 Here are the answers to some questions. Write the questions using *he*. They all contain either the Present Perfect Simple or Continuous.

a Seventeen years. (How long has he …?)
b 632. (How many …?)
c Over £9,000. (How much …?)
d Eight. (How many …?)
e Five times. (How many times …?)
f For over half his life. (How long …?)
g That he would never pass. (What …?)
h Fifty-six times. (How many …?)
i By visiting relatives and people in the remote villages. (How …?)

| **T.69** | Listen and check your answers.

the Lessons

Peter, of St Andrew's Church, Repton in Nottinghamshire, began driving at the age of 17.

'It was in the country,' he said, 'and I was doing quite well until one morning, in a narrow lane, I saw a tractor coming towards 20 me. I panicked and drove into a ten-foot hedge.'

Peter said, 'My big problem was confusing the clutch and the brake. I was absolutely hopeless. My instructors have been telling me 25 for years that I would never pass, but I was determined to prove them wrong. Many of them have turned grey because of me!'

The turning-point came when Peter tried an automatic, and took his test again — for the 30 fifty-sixth time.

He said, 'When I was told I'd passed, I went down on my knees and thanked God.'

So how has he been celebrating? 'I've been visiting all my relatives and people who live in 35 the remote villages around here. I haven't seen some of them for years because I haven't been able to get to them. Now I can go anywhere!'

● **Grammar questions**

- Find the examples of the Present Perfect Simple and Continuous in the text.

- What is the difference between the Present Perfect Simple and Continuous?

  He **has been learning** to drive for 17 years.
  He **has had** 632 lessons.

- Which describes a *completed action*?
- Which describes an *activity over a period of time*?

PRACTICE

1 Questions and answers

1 | **T.70** | Listen to two people talking about driving and cars. Complete the questions.

a _____ drive?
b How long _____ ?
c _____ a car?
d How long _____ ?
e How much _____ pay _____ ?
f How many kilometres _____ ?
g _____ ever _____ ?
h Whose fault _____ ?

Ask and answer the same questions across the class.

2 Write a question with *How long …?* Use either the Present Perfect Simple or Continuous. If both are possible, use the Continuous.

a I live in the country. How long _____ ?
b I play a lot of tennis. How long _____ ?
c I know Jack well. How long _____ ?
d I work in Prague. How long _____ ?
e I have an American car. How long _____ ?

3 Make statements about yourself using the same verbs. In pairs, ask and answer questions with *How long …?*

4 For each of the sentences in Exercise 2, write another question in the Past Simple.

a When _____ move there?
b How old _____ when _____ started _____ ?
c Where _____ meet _____ ?
d Why _____ decide _____ ?
e How much _____ pay _____ ?

2 Dialogues

T.71   Work in pairs and make dialogues. Listen to the example.

Example
A   tired – what ... doing?
B   exhausted – getting ready to go on holiday
A   done everything?
B   packed cases ... been to the bank ... haven't booked the taxi yet

A   *You look tired. What have you been doing?*
B   *I'm exhausted! I've been getting ready to go on holiday.*
A   *Have you done everything?*
B   *Well, I've packed the cases and I've been to the bank, but I haven't booked the taxi yet.*

a   A   covered in paint – what ... doing?
     B   decorating the bathroom
     A   finished yet?
     B   painted the door ... haven't put the wallpaper up yet

b   A   oil on your face – what ... doing?
     B   servicing the car
     A   done it yet?
     B   mended the lights ... haven't changed the oil yet

c   A   dirty hands – what ... doing?
     B   filthy – working in the garden
     A   finished now?
     B   cut the grass ... haven't watered the flowers yet

d   A   your eyes are red – what ... doing?
     B   exhausted – revising for my exams
     A   finished yet?
     B   done my chemistry and history ... haven't done any English yet

3 Discussing grammar

There is something wrong with the following sentences! Talk to a partner. Why are they strange? What would be better?

a Ouch! I've been cutting my finger.
b I've read Tolstoy's *War and Peace* this afternoon. It was a nice little read.
c 'Why is your hair wet?' 'I've swum.'
d I'm terribly sorry, but I've been crashing into the back of your car.
e You've got tears in your eyes. Why have you cried?

PRESENTATION (2)

Time expressions

1 Joanna Hardy is a writer. Look at the chart of events in her life. Answer the questions.

Age	Events
0	Born 1950
5	Started school
6	Wrote short stories about animals
8	Collection of poems published April 1958; visit to France and Germany
11	16 Sept. 1961 mother died; visit to Italy
15	Wrote a novel (unpublished)
18	Went to Cambridge University for three years to read English literature
19	Met her first husband
20	Got married spring 1970
21	Graduated 20 June 1971 First novel, *Chains*, published autumn 1971
22	Daughter born 14 June 1972
25	Novel *Strangers in the Night* published; won *The Times Literary Award* for best fiction
29	Divorce; visit to India and the Far East
31	Bought a house in north London
33	Novel *The Cry at Dawn* published
35–37	Made a series of TV programmes over a two-year period; met Jack, a BBC producer
38	Got married 10.30, 3 August 1988 to Jack; moved to her present address in Paris
40	Won *The Whitbread Trophy* for literary merit
46	Began her autobiography 1996
Now	Still writing her autobiography

a Joanna has had an interesting life. What are some of the things she has done?
b How long has she been writing?
c What sort of things has she written?
d How many novels has she written?
e Has she won any prizes for her writing?
f How long has she been married to Jack?
g How many times has she been married?
h How long has she been writing her autobiography?

2 Complete the sentences with words from the box.

> while she was at university
> since she married Jack
> After the publication
> two years after she
>   got married
>
> at the age of six
> until she married Jack
> between 1968 and 1971
> while she was making

a She wrote her first stories _____ .
b _____ of a collection of poems in 1958, she went to France and Germany.
c She was at Cambridge University _____ .
d She met her first husband _____ .
e Her daughter was born _____ .
f She met Jack _____ a series of TV programmes.
g She lived in north London _____ .
h She has been living in Paris _____ .

PRACTICE

1 Questions and answers

Ask and answer the questions about Joanna Hardy.

a When ... born?
b When ... collection of poems published?
c When ... mother die?
d When ... get married for the first time?
e When ... graduate?
f When ... daughter born?
g When ... India and the Far East?
h When ... for the second time?
i How long ... first marriage last?
j How long ... in Paris?

> T.72 Listen and check your answers.

2 *How long are you here for?*

1 Joanna is on a two-week tour of the United States. Look at her itinerary.

	Week 1	Week 2
Sun	New York	Kansas City
Mon	New York	Kansas City
Tues	Boston	Dallas
Wed	Boston	Denver
Thurs	Cleveland	Los Angeles
Fri	Chicago	Los Angeles
Sat	Chicago	Fly home

2 It is Monday of the second week, and she is at a press conference. How does she answer these questions?

> How long are you in the States for?

> How long have you been in the States?

> When do you go back to England?

> Where were you the day before yesterday?

> Where were you this time last week?

> Where will you be the day after tomorrow?

> T.73 Listen and check your answers.

3 Imagine you are on tour for two weeks. Write your itinerary. Decide what day it is and where you are. In pairs, ask and answer the same questions.

3 Discussing grammar

Work in pairs.

1 Correct the mistakes in the questions.

a What time did you go to bed at last night?
b What did you do the last weekend?
c What are you doing this night?
d When this lesson begin?
e When ends this lesson?
f Are you going to study English the next month?
g When you born?
h What's today date?

2 Ask and answer the questions above.

LANGUAGE REVIEW

Present Perfect Continuous

The Present Perfect Continuous relates past activities to the present. It has two main uses.

1 To express unfinished past.
I've been working here for fifteen years.
How long have you been learning English?

Remember the verbs that rarely take the continuous.
I've known Jack for years and years.
How long have you had your car?

2 To express the present result of past activities.
You look tired. What have you been doing?
I've been doing my homework.

Time expressions

See the Grammar Reference section, page 154.

📖 **Grammar Reference: page 153.**

● READING

Pre-reading task

1 Work in pairs. Which of the following do you think is the riskiest?

playing Russian roulette	hang-gliding
taking cocaine	smoking tobacco
riding a motorbike at 200 kph	
crossing the road with your eyes closed	

2 Read the quotations about smoking. What view of smoking does each quotation express?

a 'Out of a thousand smokers of 20 cigarettes a day, one will be murdered, six will be killed on the roads, and about three hundred and thirty will die prematurely because of their smoking.'

b 'If you decide to give up smoking and drinking, you don't actually live longer; it just seems longer.'

c 'Teenagers begin to smoke because they think it's cool and because they think they look grown-up. The cigarette is a symbol of defiance and an attack on authority.'

d 'I have every sympathy with the American who was so horrified by what he had read about the effects of smoking that he gave up reading.'

e 'The world spends $150 billion a year on smoking-related illnesses.'

3 Have attitudes to smoking changed in your country over the past few years? How? Do as many people smoke?

4 You are going to read an interview with a man called B J Cunningham. Look at the pictures and read these facts about him.

> He's a chain smoker.
> He wears black leather cowboy clothes.
> He rides a Harley-Davidson motorbike.
> He has a weak chest.
> He returned to his true love after six months.
> He has started his own tobacco company.
> His company is not very successful.
> He smoked fifteen cigarettes during the interview.

– How old do you think he is?
– What do you know about his way of life?
– What kind of a man do you think he is?
– What nationality do you think he is?
– Would you like to meet him?

Reading

Read the text.
Were your ideas about B J Cunningham correct?
Did you learn anything about him that surprised you?

'Here! Have one of mine!'
'Death cigarettes? You must be joking!'

David Andrews meets B J Cunningham, a dedicated smoker who loyally puffs his own cigarettes called Death.

OK. So here are the facts. There's an Englishman called B J Cunningham who has been smoking since he was eleven. He's a chain smoker who's in love with smoking. He smokes between two and three packets a day, and already, at the age of 30, has a weak chest. He was in hospital for six days when his lungs collapsed. 'It was at that point that I did actually give up cigarettes for six months.' But then he returned to his true love. He wears black leather cowboy clothes and has a fondness for classic Harley-Davidson motorbikes, which he has been riding for the past fifteen years. 'I've had about ten of them,' he says coolly.

So far, not a very remarkable life. But then, B J Cunningham (no one actually knows what B J stands for) had an idea one night in a bar in LA. 'Let's market a cigarette called *Death*,' he said to a business partner. 'Why?' said the partner.

'It's obvious,' he explains to me. 'When you take a packet of cigarettes out of your top pocket and put it on the bar in front of you, you're making a statement about yourself, exactly as you do with the clothes you wear, the music you like, and the newspaper you read. You're saying, "These cigarettes are a part of me."'

'So, if you take out a packet of Benson and Hedges, you're saying, "I'm classy — gold packet — part of high society." If you take out a packet of Marlboro, you're saying, "I'm an outdoor type, I like wearing a cowboy hat and riding horses …"'

'Now, if you produce a packet of *Death* cigarettes,' he continues, producing a packet of *Death* cigarettes to illustrate his point, 'what you're saying is …'

He looks at me to make sure that I'm going to write down what you're saying about yourself if you smoke *Death* cigarettes. But do I need to? We all know what *Death* cigarettes are about. B J Cunningham has been telling us about them since he started his Enlightened Tobacco Company (ETC) in 1991.

Everyone has now got the joke, thank you very much. We've seen the black packets with their death's head on the front and the white packets which are called *Death Lights*; and we've heard about the coffin-shaped vending machines in pubs and clubs.

However, for anyone who has managed to avoid B J's publicity, here goes. *Death* cigarettes are for the smoker who wants to say, 'Yes, I'm killing myself, but at least I know it, and I smoke a brand which doesn't try to hide the fact.' '*Death* cigarettes,' concludes B J, 'say, "Don't you dare tell me to stop!"'

B J Cunningham, now on his ninth cigarette of the interview, says he wants to expose the hypocrisy behind the tobacco industry. Governments can't afford to ban smoking because they receive huge amounts of money in tax. Tobacco companies try to improve their image by sponsoring sports events such as motor racing, rugby, football, cricket, and tennis, at vast expense. 'What everybody wants to forget is that smoking kills. That's why I'm here, to remind people that smoking and death are linked.'

The ETC hoped to win a good share of the UK market. 'Cigarettes in Britain are a £12 billion industry in which four companies control 95% of the market. The question is: How do we get a share?' He knows the question but he can't afford the answer. The ETC can't afford to advertise like the big companies. It has been losing about £1 million a year.

Personally, I have a very different opinion as to why so few people choose to smoke a brand of cigarette called *Death*. B J Cunningham has misunderstood human psychology. Of course smokers *know* that their habit is probably going to kill them, but they prefer not to think about it. The only people who are going to smoke his cigarettes are people like himself. When I offered one to a friend recently, his reaction was, 'You must be joking.' And this is what *Death* cigarettes are all about. It's a joke that was funny, but isn't funny any more.

But B J is still obsessed by fags. 'Do you know the main reason I love my job?' he says. 'It's because it gives me a chance to attack the anti-smoking killjoys! Those puritans who try to control our lives. I've met many people who don't smoke, but who tell me that if smoking were made illegal, they would fight it. You just can't have laws which control every aspect of the way people live.'

I finally started to warm to this character B J Cunningham. It was the end of the interview, and the number of fag ends in the ashtray had increased to fifteen. Perhaps he had something important to say after all. Not just, 'Hey, everybody! Look at me! I'm weird, and I'm killing myself!'

Comprehension check

Read the text more carefully. Complete the sentences with the best ending, a, b, or c.

1 B J Cunningham smokes two or three packets of cigarettes a day …
a even though he has a weak chest.
b because he has to for his job.
c to prove that smoking is safe.

2 He wears cowboy clothes and rides a Harley-Davidson motorbike because …
a he plays in a rock 'n' roll band.
b he likes everything that comes from the States.
c it is part of the image he wants to create for himself.

3 B J Cunningham says that smokers choose a certain brand of cigarettes …
a because it shows the kind of person they are.
b to go with the clothes they are wearing.
c because they want to be sporty or part of high society.

4 We get the impression that the interviewer …
a likes and admires B J Cunningham.
b is bored and irritated by B J Cunningham.
c is very angry with B J Cunningham.

5 B J Cunningham says *Death* cigarettes are for people …
a who want to be honest and aggressive.
b who want to prove that smoking cigarettes doesn't kill.
c who want to expose the hypocrisy of governments and the tobacco industry.

6 B J Cunningham says that his job …
a is to get sponsorship for sports events.
b is to sell as many cigarettes as he can.
c is to be honest about the dangers of smoking.

7 The interviewer thinks that the ETC hasn't been successful because …
a the big tobacco companies spend £12 billion on advertising.
b everybody thinks that *Death* cigarettes are just a joke.
c smokers don't want to be reminded that smoking kills.

8 B J Cunningham …
a wants to defend people's right to smoke.
b wants to control the lives of smokers.
c thinks that smoking will one day be made illegal.

9 The interviewer warms to B J Cunningham at the end of the interview …
a when B J Cunningham gives his main reason for selling *Death* cigarettes.
b because he realizes that he is just a weird eccentric.
c when he finally puts out his last cigarette.

Language work

Here are the answers to some questions. Write the questions.

1 _____ ?
Since he was eleven.

2 _____ ?
Between forty and sixty.

3 _____ ?
Yes, he has. He gave up for six months after his lungs collapsed.

4 _____ ?
For fifteen years.

5 _____ ?
About ten.

6 _____ ?
In 1991.

7 _____ ?
About £1 million a year.

8 _____ ?
Fifteen.

Discussion

Discuss the following in small groups. Then report back to the whole class.

1 How much is a packet of cigarettes in your country?
How much of that is tax?
What sort of health warnings are there?
Do tobacco companies sponsor any sports events?

2 Why is it that drugs such as nicotine and alcohol are legal in many countries, while other drugs are illegal?

3 Do you think smoking should be banned in all public places? Or, should smokers be allowed to smoke when and where they want?

● VOCABULARY AND PRONUNCIATION

Compound nouns

1 The following are definitions of words from Unit 10. What are the words?

Example
What you wear if you want to listen to your Walkman.
Headphones.

a The piece of paper that means you can drive a car.
b What you have to pass to get the piece of paper!
c What you put on the walls of your house when you decorate a room.
d An interview given to a lot of journalists to make an announcement.
e Someone who smokes one cigarette after another.
f Someone that you run a business with.
g Where smokers put out their cigarettes.

What do you notice about these words?

2 Nouns can be combined to make a new word. These are called **compound nouns**. They are written in different ways.

postcard *postbox* *postman* *postcode*	One word.

post office	Two words.

Occasionally the words are hyphenated (*window-shopping*). There are no rules, and English people themselves often have to go to a dictionary to check the spelling.

T.74 Listen to the words. Where is the stress?

3 Put one word in each box to form three compound nouns. Look at the example. Check the spelling in a dictionary.

a	*tooth* _____	ache brush paste	i	_____	conditioning mail port
b	dining living changing	_____	j	_____	cup spoon pot
c	_____	lights warden jam	k	_____	glasses bathing set
d	_____	way racing bike	l	news travel estate	_____
e	cookery telephone note	_____	m	wrapping writing toilet	_____
f	_____	engine place works	n	chair fire dust	_____
g	birthday credit get-well	_____	o	_____	centre basket spree
h	_____	dresser brush cut	p	_____	case shop worm

4 Work in pairs.
Look up the words below in your dictionary and find more compound nouns. Write some sentences like those in Exercise 1 to test the other students in the class.

hand   head   night   snow   eye   back   land

Collectors

Pre-listening task

1 What kinds of things do people often collect?

2 Do you collect anything? Did you use to when you were younger?

Listening

You are going to listen to two people who are both keen collectors. Divide into two groups.

Look at the picture about your person. What can you see? What does she/he collect? What questions would you like to ask her/him? Listen and answer the questions.

Group A

T.75a Listen to Margaret Tyler. She lives in Wembley, north London. Her children have now grown up and left home, and so she lives alone with her incredible collection.

Group B

T.75b Listen to Ted Hewitt. He lives with his wife and three small children in Chorleywood, a village between London and Oxford. He owns a coach business.

Comprehension check

1 Where does she/he live? Who with?
2 What does she/he do for a living?
3 How big is her/his collection?
4 How long has she/he been collecting?
5 How many rooms of the house are taken up with the collection?
6 What's her/his favourite piece?
7 How much has the collection cost?
8 Where do the pieces come from?
9 Is she/he in touch with other people who share the same hobby?
10 What ambitions does she/he have?

When you have answered the questions, find a partner from the other group. Compare and swap information.

Guessing game

Your teacher will tell one student what he or she collects. The others must ask questions to find out what it is.

> How big are they?

> Can you buy them?

When you've guessed what it is, ask some of the questions in the Comprehension check above.

> How long have you been collecting?

● WRITING

Beginning and ending letters

1 Match the correct beginning and ending for the five letters on the right. Which letter …

… asks for information? … accepts an invitation?
… invites? … gives news?
… says that money has been received?

2 Which of these sentences continues each letter?

a Could you please send me your brochure and a price list? I would be most grateful.
b I've changed my job a few times since I last spoke to you, and as you know, I've moved, too.
c Unfortunately this amount did not include packing and postage, which is £7.50.
d June and I are having a barbecue with all our friends, and we were wondering if you could come.
e We'd love to come. I haven't been to your part of the country for ages.

3 Note the following points about formal and informal letters.

• We can write contractions (*I've, we're, I'll*) in an informal letter, but not in a formal one.
• All letters begin with *Dear* …
• You can end an informal letter with *Best wishes* or *Love*.

Here are some useful phrases for informal letters:

Beginning
It was lovely to hear from you. I was pleased to hear that …
Thank you for your letter. I was sorry to hear that …
I'm sorry I haven't written before, but …
This is just a note to say …

Giving news
We're having a lovely time in …
I've been very busy recently. Last week I … and next week I'm going to …

Ending
I'm looking forward to seeing you …/to hearing from you soon.
Give my regards to Robert …
Write to me soon …
I hope to hear from you soon …
Write and tell me when …

4 Write a letter to a friend who you haven't been in touch with for a long time. Give your news, describe some things that you have done recently, and say what your future plans are. Ask about his/her news and family. Try to arrange to meet somewhere. Remember to put your address and the date in the top right-hand corner of your letter.

Beginnings

a Dear Mary

This is just a note to ask if you and Dave are free on the evening of July 11.

b Dear Jane

Many thanks for your letter. It was lovely to hear from you after such a long time. You asked me what I've been doing. Well, …

c Dear Sir/Madam

I saw an advertisement in the Daily Telegraph for weekend breaks at your hotel.

d Dear Peter

Thank you so much for inviting Dave and me to your summer party.

e Dear Mr Smith

We received your order for the *World Encyclopaedia* on CD ROM, and your cheque for £75.

Endings

1 Many thanks. I look forward to hearing from you in the near future.
Yours faithfully
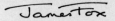
James Fox

2 We will have pleasure in meeting your order as soon as we can.
Yours sincerely
Thames Valley Computer Software

3 It would be lovely to meet some time. Do you ever come to London? You must let me know.
Love

4 Do get in touch soon and tell me if you can make it.
Regards to you all.
Best wishes

5 We're really looking forward to seeing you again, and to meeting your friends.
Best wishes

Complaining

1 Choose a word or words from the box to complete the sentences. Some are used more than once.

too much	a few	any	How many
as much as	How much	some	too many
as many as	enough	a little	

a '_____ cigarettes do you smoke a day?'
'Forty.'
'That's _____ . You shouldn't smoke _____ at all.'

b '_____ alcohol do you drink?'
'About a bottle of wine a day.'
'That's _____ . You shouldn't drink _____ that.'

c '_____ do you weigh?'
'Sixteen and a half stone.'
'That's _____ . You should try to lose _____ weight.'

d '_____ do you earn?'
'Not _____ money to pay all my bills!'

e '_____ people are there in your class?'
'Forty.'
'I think that's _____ .'

f '_____ aspirins do you take when you have a headache?'
'About ten or twelve.'
'That's _____ . You mustn't take _____ that!'

g 'How old are you?'
'Seventeen. I'm old _____ to get married, but I'm not old _____ to vote!'

h 'When did you last go to the cinema?'
'Quite recently. Just _____ days ago.'

i 'Do you take sugar in your coffee?'
'Just _____ .'

2 In pairs, ask and answer the same questions.

3 Write a dialogue of complaint, either in a restaurant, a hotel, or a clothes shop. Act it out to the rest of the class.

Example

Waiter	Lady
How was your meal, madam?	*It was terrible. The soup was too salty, the steak wasn't cooked enough, and there weren't enough vegetables. The table was too noisy and the waiters were slow.*
But apart from that?	*It was fine, thanks.*

11 Tell me about it!

Indirect questions
Question tags
Informal language

1 T.76 Look at the picture. Read and listen to the story.

The Tramp

A tramp was sleeping on a park bench late at night. A man and woman were walking past. One of them tapped him on the shoulder and asked, 'Excuse me! What's the time?' The tramp was very annoyed at being woken up. 'I don't know!' he said angrily. 'I haven't got a watch.' And he went back to sleep.

Some time later another man was passing. He woke the tramp up and said, 'I'm sorry to bother you, but I wonder if you could tell me what time it is.'

Again the tramp said that he didn't know. By now he was very fed up, so he got a pen and a piece of paper and wrote I DON'T KNOW WHAT THE TIME IS on it, and went back to sleep.

Half an hour later, a policeman was passing. He read the sign, woke the tramp up and said, 'It's 2.30, sir.'

2 Correct these sentences.

*I wonder if you could tell me ~~what time is it.~~
*I don't know ~~what's the time.~~

PRESENTATION (1)

Indirect questions

1 T.77 Rosie has just arrived at the railway station of a strange town. She goes to the tourist office to get some information.

Look at the information she wants, then listen to the dialogue. Complete her sentences.

What Rosie wants to know	What Rosie says
a Could you help me?	I wonder _____
b What time do the banks close?	I don't know _____
c How old is this town?	Have you any idea _____ ?
d Are we near the centre of town?	I'm not sure _____
e Which hotel did you suggest?	I can't remember _____

● **Grammar questions**

– How does the word order change in indirect questions?
– What happens to *do/does/did* in indirect questions?
– What do we use if there is no question word (*where? how old? what time?*)?

2 In pairs, practise the conversation. How much can you remember?

3 Here is some more information that Rosie wants. Use the prompts to ask indirect questions.

a When was the town founded? (Could you tell me …?)

b What's the population of the town? (Do you know …?)

c Where can I change some money? (I'd like to know …)

d What's the exchange rate today? (Do you happen to know …?)

e Is there a dry cleaner's near here? (I wonder …)

f Where is there a cheap place to eat? (Have you any idea …?)

g How long does it take to get to the centre of town from here? (Can you tell me …?)

h Did it rain here yesterday? (Do you remember …?)

4 In pairs, ask and answer similar indirect questions about the town where you are now.

PRACTICE

1 *We can't hear what she's saying!*

1 T.78 Listen to the radio news. Unfortunately the reception is bad, and there are some things you can't hear. What don't you know?

Example
We don't know
We've no idea | *what time the*
I couldn't hear | *train crash*
I'm not sure | *happened.*

2 Your teacher has the information. Ask the direct questions.

2 Speaking

1 *Madame Tussaud's Waxworks* is London's most popular tourist attraction. What do you know about it?

Make statements about *Madame Tussaud's* using the prompts.

I wonder …   I haven't a clue …
I'd love to know …   Does anybody know …

Example
where … born
I wonder where she was born.

a where Madame Tussaud … (come) from
b when … alive
c how … (learn) to make things in wax
d which countries … (live) in
e … married
f … children
g why … (go) to England
h when the Waxworks … (open) in London
i how many people a year … (visit) the Waxworks

2 Work in pairs. Your teacher will give you some information about Madame Tussaud, but you will not have the same information. Ask and answer questions to complete the information. Use both direct and indirect questions.

Example

Student A
Marie Tussaud was born in Strasbourg in 1761. Her father died … (*When?*), and her family moved to Switzerland.

Student B
Marie Tussaud was born in Strasbourg in 1761. Her father died two months before she was born, and her family moved to … (*Where?*)

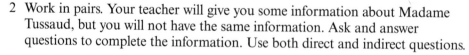

Do you know when her father died?

He died two months before she was born.

Where did her family move to?

To Switzerland.

3 Asking polite questions

1 Match a word in **A** with a line in **B** and a line in **C**.

A	B	C
What	football team newspaper colour long	times have you been on a plane? does it take you to get ready in the morning? do you support? shoes do you take?
Which	size flavour far	of car have you got? do you read? ice-cream is your favourite?
How	sort many much	is it to the station from here? time do you spend watching TV? eyes have you got?

2 Indirect questions can be more polite than direct questions. In pairs, ask and answer indirect questions using the ideas in Exercise 1.

Example

> Could you tell me which football team you support?

> Would you mind telling me what size shoes you take?

PRESENTATION (2)

Question tags

1 **T.79** Look at the picture and listen to Jessie (J), aged 3, talking to her mother, Sarah (S).

J Mummy?
S Yes, Jessie?
J I've got ten fingers, haven't I?
S Yes, that's right, my darling. Ten lovely little fingers.
J And my brother's called Joe, isn't he?
S Yes, he is. He's at school at the moment.
J And Daddy went to work this morning, didn't he?
S Yes, he went in his big blue car.
J And we don't like tigers, do we, Mummy?
S Well, they're beautiful, but they're dangerous, it's true.
J Can I have a biscuit now, Mummy?

● Grammar questions

– Jessie *knows* that she has ten fingers, and she *knows* that her brother's called Joe. So she's not really asking questions. What *is* she doing?

– How do we make question tags?

2 Look at the dialogue between Caroline Bailey (C) and her secretary, Norma (N). Fill each gap with the correct question tag. Choose from the box.

didn't I?	aren't I?	isn't it?
am I?	haven't I?	does it?

C Now, what's happening today? I've got a meeting this afternoon, _____ ?
N Yes, that's right. With Henry and Ted.
C And the meeting's here, _____ ?
N No, it isn't. It's in Ted's office, at 3.00.
C Oh! I'm not having lunch with anyone, _____ ?
N No, you're free all morning.
C Phew! I'll start on that report, then. Er ... I signed all my letters, _____ ?
N No, you didn't, actually. They're on your desk, waiting for you.
C Ah, right! And tomorrow I'm going to Scotland, _____ ?
N Yes. You're booked on the early morning shuttle.
C OK. It doesn't leave until 8.00, _____ ?
N 8.15, to be precise.
C Gosh, Norma! Where would I be without you?

T.80 Listen and check your answers.

● Grammar questions

– Did the intonation of Jessie's question tags go up or down? What about Caroline's?

– Whose use of question tags means, 'I'm not sure so I'm checking'? Whose use of question tags means, 'Please talk to me'?

PRACTICE

1 Grammar and intonation

1 Look at the sentences and complete the question tags.

a	It isn't very warm today,	*is it?* ▼
b	The weather forecast was wrong again,	
c	You can cook,	
d	You don't eat snails,	
e	You've got a CD,	
f	Sally's very clever,	
g	There are a lot of people here,	
h	The film wasn't very good,	
i	I am a silly person,	
j	You aren't going out dressed like that,	

2 **T.81a** Listen and check your answers. Put ▼ if the tag falls and ▲ if it rises.

3 Match one of the following responses with a sentence in Exercise 1.

- ☐ Yes. She's as bright as a button.
- ☐ Believe it or not, I haven't. I've got a tape recorder, though.
- ☐ Why? What's wrong with it? I thought I looked really smart.
- ☐ Yuk! No, I don't! They're disgusting!
- ☐ No, it's freezing.
- ☐ No, you're not. Just because you made one mistake doesn't mean you're silly.
- ☐ Me? No! I can't even boil an egg.
- ☐ Yes! It always is, though, isn't it?
- ☐ I know! It's absolutely packed! I can't move!
- ☐ Terrible! The worst I've seen for ages.

T.81b Listen and check your answers. In pairs, practise the dialogues.

2 Conversations

Work in pairs.

1 Your teacher will give you a dialogue. Decide where you think question tags could go, what they are, and whether they fall or rise.

2 Learn the dialogue by heart. Act it out to the rest of the class.

3 **T.82** Listen and check your answers. Are your ideas the same?

LANGUAGE REVIEW

Indirect questions

1 Indirect questions are introduced with expressions such as the following.

I don't know …
I wonder …
Could you tell me …?
I'm not sure …

2 Indirect questions have the same word order as the positive, and there is no *do/does/did*.

*I don't know **where he went**.*
*I wonder **if she's arrived** yet.*
*Could you tell me **what the answer is**?*
*I'm not sure **how much it costs**.*

Question tags

The meaning of a question tag depends on how you say it.

1 A question tag with a falling intonation isn't really a question at all. It is a way of making conversation by asking the listener to agree with the speaker.

*It's a lovely day, **isn't it**?*
*We didn't play very well today, **did we**?*

2 A question tag with a rising intonation is more like a real question. It means 'I think I'm right, but can you confirm it for me?'

*Our train leaves at 7.00, **doesn't it**?*
*You haven't lost the keys, **have you**?*

📖 **Grammar Reference: page 155.**

● VOCABULARY AND IDIOMS

Do you know what your body can do?

Use your dictionary to check any new words.

1 As a class, brainstorm all the parts of the body that you know. Fill the board with all that you can think of.

2 Work in pairs and say which parts of the body you use to do the following things.

kick	bite	hit	climb	chew	drop
hold	hug	kiss	lick	point	scratch
tie	kneel	think	pat	blow	clap
stare	whistle				

3 Which verbs go with which nouns and phrases? Match a line in **A** with a line in **B**.

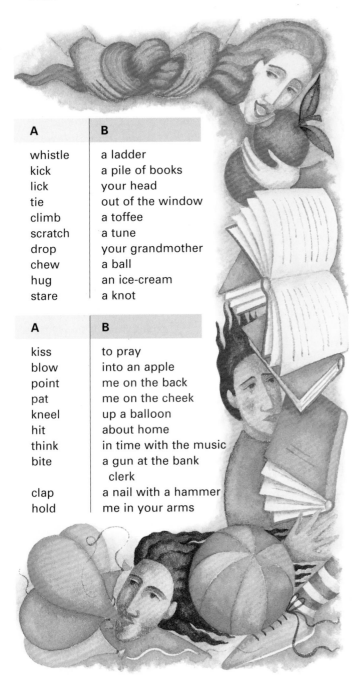

A	B
whistle	a ladder
kick	a pile of books
lick	your head
tie	out of the window
climb	a toffee
scratch	a tune
drop	your grandmother
chew	a ball
hug	an ice-cream
stare	a knot

A	B
kiss	to pray
blow	into an apple
point	me on the back
pat	me on the cheek
kneel	up a balloon
hit	about home
think	in time with the music
bite	a gun at the bank clerk
clap	a nail with a hammer
hold	me in your arms

4 Many of the verbs above form interesting idioms. How many of the following do you know or can you guess? Check the others in your dictionary.

to drop someone a line
to kick the habit
to think the world of someone
to kiss something goodbye
to blow your own trumpet
to hit the roof
to hold your breath

5 Complete the gaps with one of the idioms in Exercise 4. If necessary, change the form of the verb. The first letter of each missing word is given.

a The best way to stop hiccups is to h_____ your b_____ and count to ten.

b My parents h_____ the r_____ when I said I'd been to an all-night party.

c I've tried so many times to stop biting my nails, but I just can't k_____ the h_____ .

d I've never seen a couple so in love. They clearly t_____ the w_____ of each other.

e When my teenage daughter learnt to drive, I had to buy her a car or k_____ my own car g_____!

f Tell your brother to stop b_____ his own t_____. We don't want to hear how wonderful he thinks he is!

g D_____ me a l_____ when you know what time you're coming, and I'll meet you at the station.

● READING AND SPEAKING

How well do you know your world?

Pre-reading task

1 Work in small groups. How many of the following questions can you answer?

– Why do women live longer than men?
– What man-made things on Earth can be seen from space?
– How many new words enter the English language every year?
– Why is walking under ladders thought to be unlucky?
– Why are horseshoes believed to be lucky?
– Why is the expression 'Mayday' used as a distress call?
– Why do they drive on the left in Britain and on the right in other countries?
– What is the biggest office in the world?
– How clever are dolphins?

2 Preface each question above with one of the following according to what is true for you. Remember the word order for making indirect questions.

I think I know ...   I'm not sure ...   I don't know ...
I've no idea ...   I wonder ...

3 Discuss your answers as a class. Which of the questions interest you most? Why?

Reading

The questions in the Pre-reading task were all sent in to a science magazine. Read the answers to the questions. How much of the information did your class already know?

You ask
. . . we answer!

Q Why do women live longer than men?

A Women generally live about six years longer than men. Evidence suggests that boys are the weaker sex at birth, which means that more die in infancy. Also women do not have as much heart disease as men. In terms of lifestyle, men smoke more than women and thus more die of smoking-related diseases. They drink more and are more aggressive in behaviour, particularly when driving cars, so they are more likely to die in accidents. Also, they generally have more dangerous occupations, such as building work.

Historically, women died in childbirth and men in wars. Hence nuns and philosophers often lived to great ages. Now, childbearing is less risky and there are fewer wars. The country with the highest life expectancy is Japan, where the average age for men is 76 and for women 82.

Morimoto, the oldest living man in the world (1877 –)

Q What man-made things on Earth can be seen from space?

A 'When men first flew in space, they were amazed to discover that the only man-made object visible from orbit was the Great Wall of China.' This is a nice idea, but it's not true. The Great Wall is mostly grey stone in a grey landscape and, in fact, is very difficult to see even from an aeroplane flying at a mere 15 kilometres above. What can be seen when orbiting the earth (from about 200 kilometres up) are the fires of African desert people, and the lights of fishing boats off Japan; also, a very long wire fence in Western Australia which marks farmland on one side and desert on the other.

Q Why is walking under ladders believed to be unlucky?

A *There are a few explanations for this. The most common is that someone on the ladder might be holding a pot of paint or a bucket of water which could drop on you if you walked underneath. Another explanation relates to the Tyburn gallows at what is now Marble Arch in London. Until 1783 criminals climbed a ladder to the gallows with a rope round their neck and this was then kicked from under them. The belief grew that walking under a ladder invited death.*

Q Why is the expression 'Mayday' used as a distress call?

A The term 'Mayday' is the internationally recognized radio telephone signal of distress. It is only used when a ship is in great danger and needs help immediately. The signal is transmitted on a wavelength of 2,182 kHz, which is permanently monitored by rescue services on the shore. The use of the expression has a very straightforward explanation. It simply came from the French phrase 'm'aidez', which means 'help me'. It was officially adopted internationally in 1927.

Q How many new words enter the English language every year?

A Unfortunately no list is kept. In France there is the Académie Française which approves new words but in England there are only dictionaries. The most authoritative of these is the *Oxford English Dictionary* (OED) which has 20 volumes, but this does not make rules about the language. It simply records the development of English worldwide as best it can. It accepts about 4000 new words (or new meanings) every year. The OED has readers in all English-speaking parts of the world, who record repeated uses of new words, including numerous technical terms. Some words take a surprisingly long time to enter the OED. For example 'acid rain' was first used in 1859, but its usage was rare for over 100 years and it didn't appear in the dictionary until the 1980s.

Q What is the world's biggest office?

A The Pentagon is the largest office in the world. This famous five-sided building, which is the US Department of Defense, was built in just 16 months during World War II, in Arlington, Virginia. It is designed to hold up to 40,000 people. It has 28 kilometres of corridors, 7,754 windows, 284 bathrooms, and parking space for 8,770 cars. 17,000 meals a day are served in its restaurants.

Q Why are horseshoes believed to be lucky?

A *In 1700, Henri Misson, a Frenchman visiting Britain, asked villagers why they had horseshoes nailed above their doors. They said that it was to keep witches away. Horseshoes are made of iron and the strength of the iron was thought to protect from evil. Still today they are thought to bring good luck and many brides carry silver ones at their wedding. The position of the horseshoe is very important. It must point upwards like a cup so that the luck cannot fall out.*

Q Why do they drive on the left in Britain and on the right in other countries?

A The reason for this goes back to the days when people travelled by horse. Most people are right-handed, and thus the left is the natural side to ride on if you are on horseback and need your right hand to hold a sword in case of trouble. So why didn't the rest of the world do the same? Because of Napoleon Bonaparte. He insisted that his armies marched on the right, and as he marched through Europe, he imposed this rule wherever he went. In the twentieth century Adolf Hitler did the same. Signs reading 'Rechts fahren' were put up whenever he took over a country.

The question suggests that only the British drive on the left, but in fact, out of 178 countries in the world, there are about 50 that drive on the left, including Japan. However, most of them are former British colonies.

Q How clever are dolphins?

A Dolphins do have fairly large brains. There are many stories, ancient and modern, about dolphins saving sailors from drowning. Ever since the film *Flipper*, we have all seen how clever they are at learning how to do tricks. However, the truth is that dolphins are no more intelligent than rats, which can also be trained to do tricks. The stories about them rescuing people are true, but they automatically rescue anything which is about the same size as themselves. Sometimes they kill sharks and then immediately try to rescue them.

Comprehension check

Work in groups.

1 Here are nine questions, one for each text.
  Which question goes with which text?
  What do the words underlined refer to?

a When was <u>it</u> built?
b <u>What</u> is a nice idea but not true?
c Do <u>they</u> rescue people because they are highly intelligent?
d Why is <u>its</u> position important?
e Why don't the majority of countries do <u>this</u> like the British?
f What is the most common explanation for <u>this superstition</u>?
g Why isn't it possible to provide an exact list of <u>these</u>?
h Where did <u>the expression</u> come from?
i Why are <u>they</u> more likely to have accidents?

  Now answer the questions a–i.

2 Find the following numbers in the texts. What do they refer to? Make a sentence about each number.

  4,000   40,000   50   200   1783
  1927   1700   17,000   82   76   16

Producing a class poster

Work in small groups.

1 Make a list of some questions about the world that you would like to ask. Think of such things as places (countries, cities, buildings), people (famous people, languages, customs, superstitions), plants and animals, or things (machines, transport, etc.).

2 Check round the class to see if anyone can answer your questions.

3 Choose at least two questions and research the answers. You could go to an encyclopaedia. Write the answers in a similar style to the ones in the article.

4 Compile them into a poster for your classroom wall.

● LISTENING AND SPEAKING

The forgetful generation

Pre-listening task

You are going to listen to an item from a radio magazine programme called *Worldly Wise*. It is about the problem of forgetfulness in modern society.

1 **T.83a** Read and listen to the introduction to the programme.

> 'Hello and welcome to *Worldly Wise*. How's your day been so far? Have you done all the things you planned? Kept all your appointments? Collected that parcel from the Post Office? Oh — and have you remembered to send your mother a birthday card? If so, well done! If not — you're not alone. Many of us are finding it more and more difficult to remember everything. Once upon a time we just blamed getting older for our absent-mindedness, but now experts are blaming our modern lifestyle. They say that we have become "the forgetful generation" and that day after day we try to do too much!'

2 Discuss the following in small groups.

– Does *your* lifestyle mean that you have a lot to remember to do each day? What kind of things fill your day?
– In what ways do you think modern society is busier and more stressful than a hundred years ago?
– In what ways do you help yourself remember all that you have to do each day? Or, have you got such a good memory that you don't have to do anything?

Listening

1 **T.83b** Listen to the stories of Ellen, Josh and Fiona, and take notes about them.

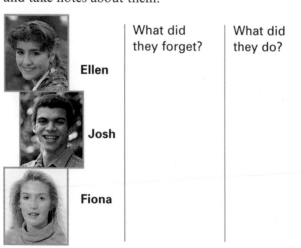

	What did they forget?	What did they do?
Ellen		
Josh		
Fiona		

2 **T.83c** Listen to the rest of the programme and answer the questions.

a What is Professor Alan Buchan's job?
b What is it about some modern day working practices that causes forgetfulness?
c Why did the lady think that she was going mad?
d In what ways was her lifestyle stressful?
e What helped the lady feel more relaxed?
f Does Professor Buchan advise using a personal computer to help remember things?
g What does he advise? Why does he advise this?
h How does the presenter try to be funny at the end of the interview?

What do you think?

Have a class discussion.

Do you think Professor Buchan's explanation for forgetfulness is true?
Have you got any stories of forgetfulness, either your own or somebody else's?

● WRITING

For and against

1 Do you live and/or work in a city? Is it very big? How many advantages and disadvantages of city life can you think of?
Write them down and compare them with a partner.

2 Read the text on the next page about the advantages and disadvantages of living in a city.

3 Answer the questions about the text.

a There are three paragraphs. What is the purpose of each one?

b Replace the words underlined with one of the following.

in spite of	pros and cons
another point is that	one advantage is that
all things considered	for instance
to sum up	in my opinion
one disadvantage is that	especially
moreover	finally

Living in the City

● Living in a city has both <u>advantages and disadvantages</u>. <u>On the plus side</u>, it is often easier to find work, and there is usually a choice of public
5 transport, so you don't need to own a car. Also, there are a lot of interesting things to do and places to see. <u>For example</u>, you can eat in good restaurants, visit museums, and go to the theatre and to concerts. <u>What is more</u>, when you want to relax, you can usually find a park where you
10 can feed the ducks or just sit on a park bench and read a book. <u>All in all</u>, city life is full of bustle and variety and you need never feel bored.

● However, for every plus there is a minus. <u>For one thing</u>, you might have a job, but unless it is very well-paid, you
15 will not be able to afford many of the things that there are to do, because living in a city is often very expensive. It is <u>particularly</u> difficult to find good, cheap accommodation. What is more, public transport is sometimes crowded and dirty, particularly in the rush hour, and even the parks can
20 become very crowded, especially on Sundays when it seems that every city-dweller is looking for some open space and green grass. <u>Last of all</u>, <u>despite</u> all the crowds, it is still possible to feel very lonely in a city.

● <u>In conclusion</u>, <u>I think that</u> city life can be particularly
25 appealing to young people, who like the excitement of the city and don't mind the noise and pollution. However, many people, when they get older, and particularly when they have young children, often prefer the peace and fresh air of the countryside.

4 Write rough notes about the pros and cons of living in the country. Compare them with your partner.

5 Write three paragraphs called 'The Pros and Cons of Living in the Country'.
In the conclusion give your own opinion. Write about 250 words.

Informal language

1 When we speak, we use a lot of informal language, depending on who we're speaking to!

Example
These shoes cost ninety quid.

In the dialogues, choose the informal words that fit best.

a A Let's have a break, shall we?
   B All right. | I'm dying for a cuppa.
      I see. |

b A My old man isn't at work today.
   B Why? | What's he on about?
           | What's up with him?
   A He was walking to work yesterday when this guy in a car knocked him over.
   B Really! | Is he OK?
      Yuk! |
   A Well, | he was very lucky. He just got a few
      Right, | cuts and grazes.

c A Can I have one of your fags?
   B Sure. | Help yourself. I've got loads.
      Damn. |
   A Oh! | Do *you* want one?
      Ta! |
   B No. I've just put one out.

d A Gimme your homework so I can copy it.
   B What a pity! | You can do it yourself!
      No way! |

e A Did you manage to fix the telly?
   B Kind of. | The picture's OK, but the sound
      All right. | isn't quite right.
   A What's on tonight?
   B Dunno. Look in the paper.

f A What's that stuff called that you use to clean between your teeth?
   B What do you mean?
   A You see! | It's like string. White.
      You know! |
   B Oh! | You mean dental floss.
      Wow! |
   A That's it!

T.84 Listen and check your answers.

2 There are lots of other examples of informal language in the dialogues. How do we say them more formally? Be careful if you try to use them!

12 Two weddings, a birth and a funeral!

Reported speech
Saying sorry

Test your grammar

1 Read the story in **a** and write the actual words of the conversation in **b**.

The Marriage Proposal

a John greeted Moira and asked how she was. She told him she was fine and asked about him. He said he felt wonderful because they were together again. He added that it had been a long time since their holiday in Paris. She said she had loved every minute in Paris and that she would never forget it. She asked if they could go back there next spring. He said that he loved her. He asked if she would marry him and come to Paris with him for their honeymoon. She said that she would and that she loved him, too.

b John   'Hello, Moira. How _____ ?'
  Moira   'I'm _____ .'
  John   'I feel _____ because
    we _____ .
    It's been _____ .'
  Moira   'I loved _____ .
    I'll never _____ .
    Can we _____ ?'
  John   'I _____ .
    Will you _____ ?'
  Moira   'Oh yes, yes, I _____ .'

2 Which is direct speech and which is reported speech?

3 T.85   Listen to the conversation. Are there any differences with yours?

PRESENTATION (1)

Reported statements and questions

1 Match a line in **A** with a line in **B** to make a natural sounding conversation. Put the letters a–j in the right box. Where is the conversation taking place? Who are Adam and Beatrice?

A (Adam)
a Are you on your own?
b How do you know John and Moira, then?
c Do you like big weddings?
d Where did you meet your husband, then?
e Why aren't you drinking?
f Have you travelled far to get here?
g Why aren't you wearing a hat?
h Where are you staying tonight?
i Can you give me a lift there?
j Yes, I am. Will there be enough room in your car?

B (Beatrice)
☐ I never wear hats.
☐ Oh, yes, lots. There won't be a problem.
☐ We're at the *Red Lion*.
☐ Because I'm driving.
☐ No, I'm not. I'm with my husband.
☐ I prefer smaller ones.
☐ Actually, I met him at a wedding.
☐ Yes, we have. We flew in from New York yesterday.
☐ I was at university with Moira.
☐ Yes, we can. Are you staying at the *Red Lion*, too?

2 **T.86a** Listen and check your answers.

3 Beatrice is telling her husband about the conversation with Adam. Read what she says.

> 'I've just met this really friendly young man. Do you know what he said to me?
> First he asked me if I was on my own, and of course I said that I wasn't, I was with you.
> Then he asked me how I knew John and Moira, and I told him I had been at university with Moira ...'

● **Grammar questions**

Read the sentences and answer the questions.

*'**I'm** with my husband,' she said.*
*She said (that) **she was** with her husband.*

*'**I was** at university with Moira,' she told him.*
*She told him (that) **she had been** at university with Moira.*

– What is the basic rule about the use of tenses in reported speech?
– What is the difference in the way *say* and *tell* are used?

*'**Are** you on your own?' he asked.*
*He asked **if I was** on my own.*

*'How **do you know** John and Moira?' he asked.*
*He asked how **I knew** John and Moira.*

– What differences are there between direct questions and indirect questions?
– When is *if* used?

PRACTICE

1 Reporting a conversation

You are Beatrice. Continue reporting the conversation to a partner.

Example
Then he asked if I liked ... and I said that I ...

T.86b Listen and check your answer.

2 Grammar

1 Put the following direct speech into reported speech.

a 'I'm exhausted!' he said.
b 'Are you leaving on Friday?' she asked me.
c 'We haven't seen Jack for a long time,' they said.
d 'We flew to Madrid,' they said.

e 'Which airport did you fly from?' I asked them.
f 'The flight has been cancelled,' the announcement said.
g 'Our plane was delayed by five hours,' they told us.
h 'What time did it take off?' she asked.
i 'I'll help you unpack,' he said.
j 'I can't do this exercise,' he told the teacher.

2 What's the difference in meaning in the following examples of reported speech? Discuss with a partner.

a Beatrice said she lived in New York.
  Beatrice said she'd lived in New York.

b Moira told her mother that she'd love John.
  Moira told her mother that she loved John.

c Adam asked them how they'd travel to Paris.
  Adam asked them how they'd travelled to Paris.

What did the people actually say in direct speech?

3 Stress and intonation

1 Work in pairs and complete the conversation.
A is talking to B about a friend, George. B has not heard the same as A.

Example

George doesn't like his new job.

But he told me *he loved it*! (love)

a A He loves living in London.
  B But he told me _____! (hate)

b A He's moving to Canada.
  B But he told me _____! (Australia)

c A His girlfriend has left him.
  B But he told me _____! (he/leave/her)

d A He'll be thirty next week.
  B But he told me _____! (twenty-one)

e · A He went to Amsterdam for his last holiday.
  B But he told me _____! (Barbados)

f A He can't give up smoking.
  B But he told me _____! (three years ago)

g A He was given the sack last week.
  B But he told me _____! (promotion)

h A He's fallen in love with a French girl.
  B But he told me _____! (with me)

2 **T.87** Listen and check your answers. Pay particular attention to the stress and intonation.
Practise the dialogues with a partner.

PRESENTATION (2)

Reported commands

1 Read the newspaper article.

'A marriage made in hell!'

'We can get a good night's sleep now!' say Mr and Mrs Fish

This is how Judge Margaret Pickles described the marriage of Patrick and Pauline Peters as she ordered them to spend fourteen days in prison for rowing.

THE COUPLE only married six months ago and already they are famous for their rows. Neighbours complained that they could hear them shouting from the bus stop six hundred yards away. Mrs Iris Fish, who lives opposite, said, 'First I asked them nicely to stop because my baby couldn't get to sleep, but they didn't. Then my husband knocked at their door and told them to stop, but still they didn't. They threw a chair at him out of the window. It just missed him! So that was it! We rang the police and asked them to come immediately.'

Mr and Mrs Peters admitted they had been arguing. Mrs Peters said that she had accused Mr Peters of wasting their money on drink and gambling. However, they denied throwing the chair.

The judge clearly did not believe them. She reminded them that they had already had two previous warnings from the police and she told them that they would soon cool down in prison, especially as they would be in separate prisons. She advised them to talk to a marriage guidance counsellor.

Mr and Mrs Fish and their baby are looking forward to some sleep! ■

2 Who is speaking? Find the lines in the text that report the following.

a 'You must go to prison for a fortnight.'
b 'It's terrible. We can hear them shouting from the bus stop.'
c 'Please, will you stop making that noise? My baby can't get to sleep.'
d 'Stop making that noise!'
e 'Please, can you come immediately?'
f 'OK. OK. It's true. We were arguing.'
g 'You've been wasting our money on drink and gambling again!'
h 'We didn't throw the chair.'
i 'Remember that you have already had two warnings from the police.'
j 'You'll soon cool down in prison.'
k 'I think you should see a marriage guidance counsellor.'

Compare the direct and reported speech.

● Grammar questions

– Four of the sentences a–k are commands or requests. Which are they? How are they reported in the text? Which verbs are used to report them?

– Underline the two sentences with *told* in the article. Which is a reported statement and which is a reported command?

– Which of the sentences below is a reported question? Which is a reported request?

I asked them to stop making a noise.
She asked me if I knew the time.

– *Say* and *tell* are both used to report statements. How many other reporting verbs can you find in the article?

PRACTICE

1 Other reporting verbs

1 Which verb can be used to report the direct speech in the sentences below? Put a letter a – j in the box.

tell [c]   order [ ]   remind [ ]   beg [ ]   advise [ ]

ask [ ]   invite [ ]   warn [ ]   refuse [ ]   offer [ ]

a 'Please can you translate this sentence for me?' Maria said to Mark.
b 'Don't forget to send Aunt Maud a birthday card,' Mary said to her son.
c 'Sign on the dotted line,' the postman said to me.
d 'Please, please, please marry me. I can't live without you,' John said to Moira.
e 'Please come to our wedding,' John said to his boss.
f 'I'll pay for the next round,' Mark said.
g 'Don't run round the edge of the swimming pool or you'll fall in,' Mary said to her children.
h 'I won't go to bed!' Bobby said.
i 'You should talk to your solicitor,' Ben said to Bill.
j 'Take that chewing gum out of your mouth immediately!' the teacher said to Jo.

2 Change the sentences in Exercise 1 into indirect speech using the appropriate verbs.

2 Listening and speaking

You are policemen or policewomen taking statements.

1 Divide into two groups.

Group A

T.88a Listen to Pauline Peters and take notes about what she says happened.

Group B

T.88b Listen to Iris Fish and take notes about what she says happened.

2 Find a partner from the other group and report what you heard. Find the differences. Begin like this.

A *Pauline admitted that they sometimes argued. She said that …*
B *Iris complained that they argued every night. She said that …*

3 Write the reports for the police records.

LANGUAGE REVIEW

Reported statements

The usual rule for reported statements is that the verb form moves back one tense when the reporting verb is in the past tense.
The verbs *say* and *tell* are used to report statements but other verbs can also be used.

'He's **having** a shower.'
*She said/told me (that) he **was having** a shower.*

'I've **lost** my wallet!'
*He said/complained (that) he **had lost** his wallet.*

'They **took** a taxi.'
*I said/thought (that) they **had taken** a taxi.*

'I'll **ring you** tomorrow.'
*He said (that) he **would ring** me the next day./He promised to ring me the next day.*

The Past Simple and the Present Perfect both change to the Past Perfect.

Reported questions

In reported questions the word order is like a statement. Verbs other than *ask* can be used.

When are you leaving?
*He asked (me)/He wondered **when I was leaving**.*

Where does John live?
*She inquired **where John lived**.*

Have you met Moira?
*He asked (me) **if I had met Moira**.*

When there is no question word, *if* is used, and there is no question mark.

Reported commands

These are formed with the infinitive with *to*. The verbs *ask* and *tell* are used to report commands but other verbs can be used as well according to the meaning.

Sit down and be quiet!
*He told/ordered them **to sit** down and be quiet.*

Please can you give me a lift?
*She asked him **to give** her a lift.*

If I were you I'd see a doctor.
*She advised me **to see** a doctor.*

📖 **Grammar Reference: page 155.**

● VOCABULARY AND PRONUNCIATION

Birth, marriage and death

1 Use your dictionary to sort the following words and phrases into the categories below.

cot	bouquet	funeral	to get engaged
grave	pregnant	godmother	to have a baby
nappy	reception	cemetery	best man
grief	to bury	widow	maternity leave
wedding	bonnet	christening	bridegroom
pram	mourners	honeymoon	to get divorced
wreath	coffin	sympathy	to exchange rings

Birth	Marriage	Death

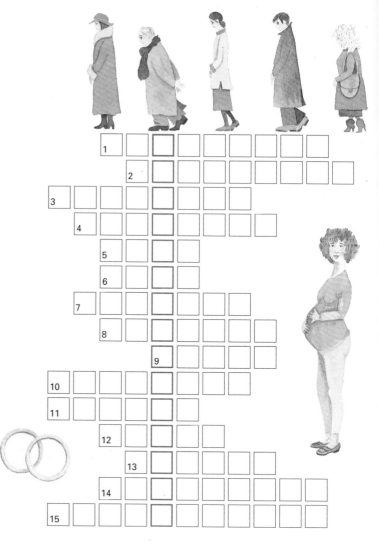

2 Decipher the phonetic script to complete the puzzle. Find out the vertical word.

1 Three hundred people came to our /rɪ'sepʃn/ after the wedding.
2 I am my niece's /'gɒdmʌðə/.
3 Thousands of /'mɔːnəz/ attended the king's funeral.
4 My sister is four months /'pregnənt/.
5 Our dog likes to /'berɪ/ his bone.
6 My daughter loves playing with her dolls' /præm/.
7 His brother was his /bes'mæn/.
8 The bridesmaid caught the /bʊ'keɪ/.
9 In Britain you get eleven weeks' maternity /liːv/.
10 You haven't shown me very much /'sɪmpəθɪ/ for my toothache.
11 The Queen laid a /riːθ/ at the grave of the Unknown Soldier.
12 They say that old Bill died of /griːf/ after his wife died.
13 The emperor was buried in a gold /'kɒfɪn/.
14 Where did John and Liz go on their /'hʌnɪmuːn/?
15 The baby screamed throughout the /'krɪsnɪŋ/.

3 What happens at births, weddings and funerals in your country?

● READING AND LISTENING

A birth and a death

Pre-reading task

Work in small groups.

1 Obviously you can't *remember* anything about the day you were born, but what have you been *told* about it? Who told you? What did they say?

Discuss what you have learnt with others in your group. Are there any interesting stories? Tell the whole class.

2 You are going to read an extract from Chapter one of *David Copperfield*, a very famous novel by the English writer, Charles Dickens.

– Do you know anything about the kind of novels Dickens wrote?
– Do you know any of their names?
– When did he write?
– What kind of people did he write about?

Reading and listening (1)

A birth

T.89a Read and listen to Part I. It is the day of David Copperfield's birth and his young, widowed mother meets her dead husband's aunt, Betsey Trotwood.

What impression do you form of the characters of the two women? Have they met before?

David Copperfield

CHAPTER 1

I AM BORN (PART I)

I was born at Blunderstone, in Suffolk. I was a posthumous child. My father's eyes had closed upon the light of this world six months when mine opened on it.

5 On the afternoon of that eventful and important Friday, my mother was sitting by the fire, very timid and sad, and very doubtful of ever coming alive out of the trial that was before her, when, lifting her eyes to the window opposite, she saw a strange lady coming 10 up the garden. When she reached the house, instead of ringing the bell, she came and looked in at that window, pressing her nose against the glass. She gave my mother such a turn, that I have always been convinced I am indebted to Miss Betsey for having 15 been born on a Friday. Then she made a frown and a gesture to my mother, like one who was accustomed to being obeyed, to come and open the door. My mother went.

'Mrs David Copperfield, I *think*,' said Miss Betsey.
20 'Yes,' said my mother faintly.
'Miss Trotwood,' said the visitor. 'You have heard of me, I dare say?'

My mother answered that she had had the pleasure. 'Take off your cap, child,' said Miss Betsey, 'and let 25 me see you. Why, bless my heart! You are a very baby!'

My mother was, no doubt, unusually youthful in appearance; she hung her head, as if it was her fault, poor thing, and said sobbing, that indeed she was afraid she was but a childish widow, and would be a 30 childish mother *if* she lived.

'Well?' said Miss Betsey. 'And when do you expect?'
'I am all in a tremble,' faltered my mother. 'I don't know what's the matter. I shall die, I am sure!'
'No, no, no,' said Miss Betsey. 'Have some tea. I 35 have no doubt it will be a girl. I have a presentiment that it must be a girl. Now, child, from the moment of the birth of this girl ...'
'Perhaps boy ...,'
'Don't contradict. From the moment of this girl's 40 birth, child, I intend to be her friend. I intend to be her godmother, and I beg you'll call her Betsey Trotwood Copperfield. There must be no mistakes in life with *this* Betsey Trotwood. She must be well brought up. I must make that *my* care.'

Comprehension check

Read the passage again and answer the questions. Use your dictionary to check new words.

1 Which of the following adjectives describe David's mother and which describe Betsey Trotwood? Which word describes neither of them?

> forceful shy confident frightened weak
> strong miserable impatient bossy meek
> insensitive motherly severe flustered

2 Why was David a 'posthumous child'? (l.2) When had his father died? What was his father's name?
3 Why is that Friday called 'eventful and important'? (l.5)
4 What is 'the trial'? (l.8)
5 Why is David 'indebted to Miss Betsey for having been born on a Friday'? (l.14)
6 Why does Miss Betsey call David's mother 'child'? (l.24)
7 How many reasons can you find as to why David's mother is sad and frightened?
8 What is Betsey Trotwood absolutely certain about?

What do you think?

1 What 'mistakes in life' might have happened to Miss Betsey Trotwood?

2 What do you think will happen next?

T.89b Read and listen to Part II. Who do you think Mr Chillip is?

I AM BORN (PART II)

The mild Mr Chillip sidled into the parlour and said to my aunt in his meekest manner: 'Well, ma'am, I'm happy to congratulate you.'

'What upon?' said my aunt sharply.

5 Mr Chillip was flustered again by the extreme severity of my aunt's manner, so he made her a little bow and gave her a smile.

'Mercy on the man, what's he doing?' cried my aunt, impatiently. 'Can't he speak?'

10 'Be calm, my dear ma'am,' said Mr Chillip, in his softest accents. 'Be calm. I am happy to congratulate you. All is now over, ma'am, and well over.'

'How is she?' said my aunt, folding her arms.

'Well, ma'am, she will soon be quite comfortable,
15 I hope,' replied Mr Chillip. 'Quite as comfortable as we can expect a young mother to be. There cannot be any objection to your seeing her presently, ma'am. It may do her good.'

'And *she*. How is *she*?' said my aunt, sharply.

20 Mr Chillip laid his head a little more on one side, and looked at my aunt.

'The baby,' said my aunt. 'How is she?'

'Ma'am,' replied Mr Chillip, 'it's a boy.'

My aunt said never a word, but took her bonnet
25 by the strings, aimed a blow at Mr Chillip's head with it, put it on, and walked out. She vanished and never came back any more.

Comprehension check

1 What is Betsey Trotwood's opinion of Mr Chillip? What does he think of her?
2 What is the misunderstanding between them?
3 Does Betsey go to see the baby?
4 What does Betsey Trotwood hit Mr Chillip with? Why does she hit him?
5 Why does she leave?

What do you think?

– What do you think of Betsey Trotwood's behaviour?
– Do you think David Copperfield ever meets his aunt?

Vocabulary

1 Find words in Part I that mean the same as the following.

shy	uncertain	was used to	hat	crying

2 Find words in Part II that mean the same as the following.

gentle	most humble	strictness	hat	hit
disappeared				

Language work

Read the account of Betsey Trotwood's conversation with David Copperfield's mother. Fill each gap with a suitable word from the box. Use each word once only.

> said   asked   begged   told (x 2)
> invited   expressed   suggested   added
> didn't answer   exclaimed   introduced

Miss Betsey Trotwood (1) _____ herself to David's mother, who (2) _____ that she had heard of her. Then Miss Betsey (3) _____ her to take off her cap so that she could see her properly. She was very surprised and (4) _____ that David's mother looked *very* young indeed! Next she (5) _____ when the baby was due, but David's poor mother (6) _____ the question, she just (7) _____ the fear that she would die having the baby. Miss Betsey dismissed these fears and (8) _____ her to have some tea. She (9) _____ that she had no doubt that the baby would be a girl. David's mother tentatively (10) _____ that it might be a boy but Miss Betsey (11) _____ her not to contradict, and (12) _____ her to call the baby Betsey Trotwood Copperfield.

Reading and listening (2)

A death

Pre-reading task

1   T.90   Close your books and close your eyes. Listen to a poem by W H Auden (1907–1973). The poem is called *Funeral Blues*. Don't worry about understanding every word but try to understand the overall 'message'.
It is a love poem.
What has happened? How does the writer feel about the world now?

2   What words or lines can you remember? Share what you can remember with the rest of the class.

Reading

Read the poem and answer the questions. Use your dictionary to check new words.

FUNERAL BLUES

STOP ALL the clocks, cut off the telephone,
  Prevent the dog from barking with a juicy bone,
Silence the pianos and with muffled drum
  Bring out the coffin, let the mourners come.

Let aeroplanes circle moaning overhead
  Scribbling on the sky the message *He Is Dead*,
Put crêpe bows round the white necks of the public doves,
  Let the traffic policemen wear black cotton gloves.

He was my North, my South, my East and West,
  My working week and my Sunday rest,
My noon, my midnight, my talk, my song;
  I thought that love would last forever: I was wrong.

The stars are not wanted now; put out every one;
  Pack up the moon and dismantle the sun;
Pour away the ocean and sweep up the wood;
  For nothing now can ever come to any good.

W H Auden (1907–1973)

1   A loved one has died. What in general does the poet want the rest of the world to do? Why does the poet feel like this?
2   Which lines describe things that could possibly happen? Which describe impossible things?
3   Which verse describes the closeness of the relationship?
4   When you fall in love it is said that you see the world through 'rose-coloured spectacles'. What does this mean? In what ways is this poem the opposite of this?

Learning by heart

1   Choose one verse and learn it by heart.

2   Recite the poem round the class.

● WRITING

Correcting mistakes

1 Kati was a student of English in London, where she stayed with the Bennett family. She has now returned home. Read the letter she has written to Mr and Mrs Bennett. Her English has improved but there are still over 25 mistakes. How many can you find?

Szerens u. 43
Budapest 1125
Hungary
Friday 6 September

Dear Mr and Mrs Bennett

I am home now since two weeks, but I have to start work immediately, so this is the first time is possible for me to write. How are you all? Are you busy as usual? Does Andrew still work hard for his exam next month? I am miss you a lot and also all my friends from my English class. Yesterday I've received a letter from my greece friend, Christina, and she told about some of the other students. She say that Etsuko and Yukiko will write me from Japan. I am lucky because I made so many good friends during I was in England. It was really interesting for me to meet people from so many differents countries. I think that we not only improved our English (I hope this!) but we also knew people from all over the world and this is important.

My family are fine. They had a good summer hollyday by the lake. We are all very exciting because my brother will get married just before Christmas and we like very much his girlfriend. They have looked for a flat near the city centre but it is no easy to find one. If they won't find one soon they will have to stay here with us.

Please can you check something for me? I can't find my red scarf. I think maybe I have forgotten it in the cuboard in my bedroom.

Please write soon. My family send best wishes to you all. I hope I can come back next year. Stay with you was a very wonderful experience for me. Thank you for all things and excuse my mistakes. I already forget so much words.

Love

Kati

PS I hope you like the photo. It's nice, isn't it?

2 Compare the mistakes you have found with a partner. Correct the letter.

3 Write a thank-you letter to someone you have stayed with.

Saying sorry

1 Read the conversations and put the correct expression from the box into the gap.

| (I'm) sorry   I *am* sorry   Pardon   Excuse me   What |

a '_____, can you tell me where the post office is?'
  '_____, I'm a stranger here myself.'

b

'Ouch! That's my foot!'
'_____. I wasn't looking where I was going.'

c
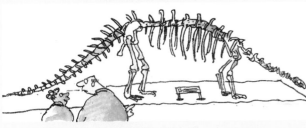

'_____, what's that creature called?'
'It's a Diplodocus.'
'_____?'
'A Diplodocus. D-I-P-L-O-D-O-C-U-S.'
'Thank you very much.'

d 'I failed my driving test for the sixth time!'
  '_____.'

e '_____! We need to get past. My little boy isn't feeling well.'

f 'Do you want your hearing aid, Grandma?'
  '_____?'
  'I said: *Do you want your hearing aid?*'
  '_____?'
  'DO YOU WANT YOUR HEARING AID?!'
  '_____, I can't hear you. I need my hearing aid.'

2 **T.91a** Listen and check your answers. Act out the conversations, paying particular attention to stress and intonation.

3 What *exactly* would you say in the following situations? Respond in one or two sentences.

a You were cut off in the middle of an important phone call to a business colleague. You think there is a problem with the switchboard in your office. You ring your colleague back.

b You want the attention of the waiter in a very crowded restaurant. You want another large bottle of fizzy mineral water for your table.

c A friend tells you that she can't meet you for lunch as planned next Thursday because she suddenly has to go to an aunt's funeral.

d Your daughter, aged fourteen, tells you that she wants to go to an all-night party and take a bottle of your whisky with her.

e You thought you had bought a *medium* jumper, but when you get it home you see it's the wrong size. You take it back to the shop.

f You ask for directions in a foreign country, but you don't understand the reply. Ask the person to say it again.

g You want to get off a very crowded train at the next stop. You have a huge suitcase.

h Your dinner guest reminds you that he is vegetarian. You have just put a huge steak on his plate.

4 **T.91b** Listen to the sample answers. Were your answers similar?

Tapescripts

UNIT 1

Tapescript 1

1 The modern Olympic Games started in 1896.
2 It takes eight minutes for the sun's rays to reach Earth.
3 He was stepping down onto the moon.
4 A vegan doesn't eat any animal products at all.
5 If you are buying things with rupees, you are in India.
6 The first books were printed in China before 800 AD.
7 The gods Brahma, Vishnu, and Siva are worshipped in Hinduism.
8 Michael Jackson's *Thriller* has sold more copies than any other.
9 VIP stands for Very Important Person.
10 Ben Johnson didn't get the gold medal because he failed a drug test.
11 Abraham Lincoln was watching a play in the theatre when he was assassinated.
12 Brazil has won the World Cup four times.
13 A butterfly has four wings.
14 If you are eating *sushi*, you are eating raw fish and rice.

Tapescript 2a

The sun rises in the west.
It doesn't rise in the west! It rises in the east!

Tapescript 2b

(* means sample answer)

*a He doesn't come from Australia! He comes from Italy!
*b She isn't wearing a swimming costume! She's wearing a dress!
c They don't drive on the right! They drive on the left!
*d She hasn't got ten sisters and brothers! She's got two!
*e We didn't go to Iceland! We went to Spain!
*f I didn't have a huge breakfast! I just had a cup of coffee!
*g It won't snow tomorrow! It'll be sunny!
h We aren't learning Chinese! We're learning English!
*i I don't live in a palace! I live in a flat!
*j It isn't made in Scotland! It's made in France!
k Cats can't swim, but dogs can!

Tapescript 3

1 My sister's a teacher.
2 She's on holiday at the moment.
3 She's just come back from Greece.
4 She's been there for two weeks.
5 She's going back to work next week.
6 She's got three children.
7 Her husband's a builder.
8 He's building a house.
9 It's made of stone.
10 It's got three bedrooms.

Tapescript 4a   See page 8

Tapescript 4b

Dad   Morning! Did you sleep well?
Emma   Yes, I did.
Dad   Do you want any breakfast?
Emma   No, I don't. I'm not hungry.
Dad   Oh. Have you fed the cat?
Emma   Yes, I have.
Dad   Has the post come?
Emma   No, it hasn't.
Dad   OK. Are you going to be late tonight?
Emma   No, I'm not. I'll be back at the usual time.

Tapescript 5

1 Is it hot today?
2 Is it raining?
3 Are you in class?
4 Are you wearing a suit?
5 Do you usually come to school by bus?
6 Does your teacher smoke?
7 Are you going out tonight?
8 Did you go out last night?
9 Can you swim?
10 Do you like learning English?
11 Have you got a dictionary?
12 Do you have any brothers and sisters?

Tapescript 6

J = John   M = Martin   P = Pam

J Let me ask you two a question. You know the wonders of the ancient world were all buildings. Well, what would *your* wonders of the *modern* world be? And don't ... don't necessarily think about buildings, think about things, you know, our way of life at the end of the twentieth century.
M Well, I think for me definitely, what's changed my life more than anything else is the washing machine, er ..., I think it's ... marvellous! It's the best invention ever! It has extended human freedom, really! I think that the free time it creates is incredible!
P Yes. It's very convenient, it's true ...
J No more taking your clothes to the river.
P ... but I think we wash our clothes more often than necessary because we have the machines to do it. So we fill that free time with more washing.
M Ah! That's interesting!
P I... I... take your point about the washing machine, but, well I was thinking along more, slightly sort of intellectual lines perhaps ...
M Yeah, go on!

P Um, well I was thinking that for me the ... well ... the most wonderful thing is the fax machine, because of the way it ... it simply enables you to communicate with people in a way that you just couldn't contemplate even five years ago!
J Are you saying it's good for work, or for pleasure ... for keeping in touch with people?
P I think it's just the wonder of the machine, not work or pleasure, er ... it's simply amazing.
J Yes, I know what you mean. You watch your piece of paper going into the fax, and at the same time, on the other side of the world it's coming out of somebody else's machine. It's incredible!
P That's it!
M But it never leaves you alone, though, that's the problem. It never stops.
P Oh, possibly, yeah.
M You're never alone ...
P ... never alone with your fax ...
M ... with your fax machine. Well, this may be very obvious, but talking about keeping in touch with people a long way away, I... I'm still very, very impressed by planes, actually. Especially jumbo jets. I think I'm slightly obsessed by them.
J Yes. I can never understand how something so very, very big can actually take off.
M Absolutely!
P Mmm. It is incredible to be able to get almost anywhere in the world in less than twenty-four hours.
J I think we have to agree, though, that one of the greatest wonders of the modern world has to be the microchip, or the computer, and all the technology that that's opening up. I mean, almost weekly there's some new amazing bit of technology that was inconceivable five or ten years ago.
P Yes. I think a lot of the things we're talking about are to do with communication, aren't they? The ways we can communicate with each other, how much and how quickly. We could include the phone. The phone's pretty amazing.
J To sort of ... to take a slightly different view of the question, wouldn't you say that one of the wonders of our age is free time, actually having free time? Well, that's what you were saying about washing machines.
M Yes. Mmm, I, er ... yes. I think that has been the great revolution. I just ... my fear is ... that all these machines are beginning to erm ... attack people's free time. I think we are losing our free time, because these machines that communicate with us never leave us alone!
P Mmm. Very philosophical. What you're saying is that, for every machine that comes

along to give us more free time, something else comes along, possibly even the same thing, to fill it.

M Exactly.

Tapescript 7

a	bread	head	read (past)	read (present)
b	work	fork	talk	walk
c	done	phone	son	won
d	paid	made	played	said
e	good	food	wood	stood
f	ache	break	take	weak
g	dear	hear	pear	near
h	cows	knows	owes	rose

Tapescript 8

a	castle	e	knock	i	psychology
b	bomb	f	foreign	j	grandma
c	sandwich	g	heart		
d	island	h	knowledge		

Tapescript 9a

a 'Sorry I'm late. I got held up in the traffic.'
'Never mind. You're here now. Come and sit down.'

b 'Bye, Mum! I'm off to school now.'
'Take care, my love. Have a nice day!'

c 'Have you heard that Jenny's going out with Pete Boyd?'
'Really? I don't know what she sees in him.'

d 'How long did it take you to do the homework?'
'Ages. What about you?'

e 'I don't know about you, but I'm fed up with this weather.'
'Me, too. I'm just longing for some sunshine.'

f 'Who was that I saw you with last night?'
'Mind your own business!'

g 'I'm tired. I'm having next week off.'
'That's a good idea. The break will do you good.'

h 'Right! Let's go for a ten-mile jog in the park!'
'You must be joking!'

i 'Let me buy you a drink.'
'No, no. It's my round. What would you like?'

j 'Shall we meet this afternoon at 3.00?'
'Sorry. I can't make it then. What about a bit later?'

k 'What a fantastic coat! Was it expensive?'
'It cost an absolute fortune!'

Tapescript 9b

1 I'm having Friday and Monday off work next week. We're going away.
2 I'll see you at about 7.00.
3 This weather's depressing, isn't it?
4 Hey! Nice jeans!
5 Sorry I'm late. I overslept.
6 Alan's going to invite Suzie to the party next week.
7 For your homework tonight I want you to learn one hundred new words.

UNIT 2

Tapescript 10   See page 16

Tapescript 11

a 'Where does he live?'
'In a detached house in the south of England.'

b 'What does he do?'
'He's an accountant.'

c 'How many children does he have?'
'Two.'

d 'How does he relax after work?'
'He watches television or a video.'

e 'How much does he spend per week?'
'£120 on average.'

f 'What does he do at the weekend?'
'He eats in restaurants, goes to see shows, or plays golf. Most weekends he potters in the garden.'

g 'How often does he go on holiday abroad?'
'More than once a year.'

Tapescript 12

Roger the gardener

D'you know the best thing that ever happened to me? D'you know what it was? It was when I lost my last job. Yes, really! I never liked it – hated it in fact – stuck in an office all day with computers and a telephone. *Now* my hobby is my full-time job! I start work very early, er … in summer I usually leave home about 5.30 in the morning, but in winter not until about 8.00. I have a small van, and I carry all my tools and equipment in that. It's autumn now so I'm tidying the gardens – I'm picking up leaves and pulling up old summer flowers. Oh, and I'm planting bulbs as well. I'm planting lots of daffodils and tulips. Every season is so different, and I love them all. I just love working outside in the open air after all those years in a stuffy office. I never noticed the seasons there!
After work I always go home and relax in a hot bath. I have a flat in London but most of my work is outside of London, in the suburbs. I'm not married but I live with my girlfriend, Fiona. I usually cook our evening meal because she gets home from work after me. She's a graphic designer and earns a lot of money, much more than me! She *earns* more but I think I enjoy my work more.
At weekends we often drive into the country and go to antique shops and antique sales. I collect old radios, you see. We don't have a television! Can you believe it? Everybody has one these days but we don't! Yes, er …, er … I collect old radios and Fiona collects old cookery books. We take our dog, we have a lovely dog, and we like taking her on long walks. I've just bought two 1930s radios and I'm cleaning them and mending them. All my radios work, you know! I never play *any* sports. Is this unusual?
I think there is only one problem with my job. It's seasonal, so I don't earn much in the autumn and winter, so er … I'm not earning much at the moment. I earn most money in spring and summer. But it's OK, I earn enough, not enough to eat out often in expensive restaurants or go to shows, but enough for my dog and my hobby. I'm a very happy man!

Tapescript 13   See page 18

Tapescript 14

I = Interviewer   SW = Sister Wendy

I When did you become a nun, Sister Wendy?

SW When I was sixteen. Goodness, that's nearly fifty years ago!

I And where do you live?

SW In Norfolk. In a Carmelite monastery. Well, not actually in the monastery but in the grounds. I have a caravan.

I Do you travel all round the world?

SW No, I don't. Just in Europe – that's far enough!

I Why do you think your art programmes are so popular?

SW I don't really know. I'm not sure why they're popular. I feel that I look so silly, but perhaps people find it funny to watch a silly old nun!

I Do you enjoy going on tour?

SW Yes, I do. Of course I do. The tours are really interesting and everybody enjoys a life of luxury now and then. I love good food and drink, but you know I'm happiest on my own in my caravan.

I Do you watch yourself on television?

SW No, I don't! I look ridiculous. I never watch if I can help it!

I What are you doing with all the money you're earning?

SW I'm using it to help the monastery. Some new shower rooms are being built. That's good, isn't it?

Tapescript 15

1 Suzanne

I love many sports, but best of all – skiing. I first skied when I was six years old, and lived in Canada, and then for many years, in fact decades, I wasn't able to ski again because I was living in hot places. But since I've been living in England, I've resumed skiing and it's even better than it was. For me now the place to ski is the Alps, and particularly France. I live in England and the winters are gloomy, and there's not much sun, so one of the wonderful things about skiing for me, is the light and the brilliant sunshine that you find high, high up in the mountains. A lot of other people like it, too, and it can be rather crowded, especially around the lifts because you now have mechanical lifts that take you zooming up, flying up the mountains like a god, whereas in Canada I had to walk up if I wanted to ski down.
The equipment you need … skis, and boots, and poles. Many people own their own equipment but I hire mine in the resort. I do have my own clothes though, and clothes are very important because skiing is quite a fashion-conscious sport. Also, it's necessary to have

clothes that will protect you because the weather can be very severe. You need a ski-suit, a hat, goggles to protect your eyes, socks, mittens, and a rucksack is useful to carry around your bits and pieces. Now at this point, I have to confess that I am not the world's greatest skier. I would say I am a respectable skier, I'm a safe skier, but that doesn't stop you having a wonderful time. Also, there is the social life that is such an important part of skiing. You can eat and drink as much as you want because you know you're burning it all off. And then at the end of the day there's the evening, food and wine with friends and everybody talking about their excitements during the day. I love it!

2 Dorothy

I'm an elderly lady of eighty-three and I've always been interested in keep-fit, yoga and anything to keep myself mobile, and er … two years ago, I joined a little club run by the Salvation Army, where about eighteen of us meet together and we go through all our movements with music – it's very enjoyable. Needless to say, I am the eldest one there, but I'm able to do most of the exercises, when I feel OK. When I've got a bad bout of sciatica, I've got to ease up a bit.

How often? I go once a week on a Thursday for …, oh we exercise for about three quarters of an hour, and then we end up with having a nice lunch, which is always very good, and that is at the Salvation Army Hall in Branksome. Who with? Lots of my friends; I have made friends since joining because I was a complete stranger when I went there but now there's a lot of people I can call my friends. And for this keep-fit we just wear a leotard with a nice bright yellow top and feel very smart. And across the top it says, 'Branksome is fighting fit'. And am I good at it? Well – *I* think I am … and the instructress tells me, or tells the others rather, that I am an example to the rest of them.

3 I = Interviewer M = Martin

I So Martin, what sports do you play?

M I play football, volleyball, tennis, and table tennis but volleyball is my favourite game as it's a team game and you can play it with your friends, and enjoy it as a team.

I Is it quite a fast game as well?

M Yeah. It is a fast game and that's another reason why I enjoy it.

I How exciting …

M Yes.

I Where do you play, then?

M I play at local sports centres more during the winter and sort of play in tournaments around England. I also, in the summer, play beach volleyball.

I Is beach volleyball different from the volleyball you play in the centres?

M Yes, it's a very different game. Instead of six players on a team, it's only two players.

I You mentioned you played in tournaments – now do you do quite well in the tournaments?

M Yes, I've played for South West England and we've got through to the semi-finals of different England tournaments, and for Wessex, my other volleyball team, we've actually won a few tournaments. So yes, I have done quite well.

I Oh well done! What sort of equipment do you need?

M Well, first of all you need the ball and the net, and obviously the court … but you may also need knee pads and your volleyball kit.

I OK … knee pads because you fall on your knees a lot?

M Yes … 'cos you … when diving and things like that …

I Diving?

M Diving … yeah.

I It sounds like swimming. That means jumping to catch the ball?

M Yeah, jumping to get a ball up in the air.

I Yes, all right. So how often do you play volleyball then Martin?

M Well during the season, which is about September to June, I play twice a week. One of those is training, and one of those is a match. And during the summer I play beach volleyball, but that's only once a week.

Tapescript 16a   See page 23

Tapescript 16b

1 A When do you go away on holiday?
   B On the fifteenth. We're flying. The flight takes nine and a half hours.
   A And when are you back?
   B On the twenty-fourth. I'll give you a ring when we're back.
   A OK.

2 And now the business news. This month inflation is up 1.5%. This produces an annual figure of 9%. Unemployment has also risen. An estimated two and three quarter million people are out of work.

3 A Hello. Odeon Cinema.
   B Hello. Can I book a seat for tonight's film?
   A Certainly. Do you want to pay now or later?
   B I can pay by credit card, can't I?
   A Yes, sir. The seats are six pounds each. There's no booking fee.
   B OK. It's a Visa card, number 4929 502 428 508.
   A Expiry date?
   B 04/99.
   A That's fine. Your tickets will be ready for you tonight. The programme starts at 7.45.
   B Thanks. Bye.

4 A Hey! I like those shoes. Where did you get them?
   B In Ravel's.
   A How much, if you don't mind my asking?
   B £39.99. They're having a sale at the moment. Everything's half price.
   A That's really good.

5 A Hello. 4887621.
   B Hello, Tony. It's Lionel.
   A Hello, Lionel. How are things?
   B OK, thanks. Listen, I'm phoning to ask you to a party.
   A Oh, that's nice. Is it your hundredth birthday already?
   B Ha, ha. No, it's our wedding anniversary, actually. Rosemary and I want to have a little party.
   A That sounds lovely. When is it?
   B The eighteenth, at about three o'clock. Can you make it?
   A Hold on. Let me have a look. Yes, that seems fine. I really look forward to it.
   B That's great. See you then.
   A Bye, Tony. Thanks.
   B Bye!

UNIT 3

Tapescript 17

The Bald Knight

Once upon a time, a long time ago, there was a knight who, as he *grew older, lost* all his hair. He *became* as bald as an egg. He didn't want anyone to see his bald head so he *bought* a beautiful, black, curly wig.

One day some lords and ladies from the castle invited him to go hunting with them, so of course he *put* on his beautiful wig. 'How handsome I look!' he *thought* to himself *as he was dressing in front of his mirror.* Then he *set* off happily for the forest.

However, a terrible thing happened. *He was riding along, singing merrily to himself, when he passed under an oak tree, and* his wig *caught* on a branch and fell off in full view of everyone. How they all laughed at him! At first the poor knight *felt* very foolish but then he *saw* the funny side of the situation, and he started laughing, too.

They were all still laughing when they arrived back at the castle. The knight never *wore* his wig again.

The moral of this story is: When people laugh at us, it is best to *laugh with them.*

Tapescript 18

1 arrived	5 started	9 laughed
2 cooked	6 lived	10 danced
3 wanted	7 travelled	11 listened
4 finished	8 visited	12 invited

Tapescript 19

A life story

They met and fell in love while they were working together in Malaysia.

They got married during the Second World War.

They had their first son while they were living in Hong Kong.

They lived in Hong Kong for five years.

They had five more sons when they returned to Britain.

They sent their sons to boarding school while they were working abroad.

They lived in six different countries during their marriage.

They were happily married for over forty-five years.
My grandfather died during the summer of 1991.

Tapescript 20

The Farmer and his Sons

There was once an old, dying farmer *who had worked hard in his vineyard all his life*. Before he died he wanted to teach his three sons how to be good farmers. So he called them to him and said, 'My boys, before I die I want you to know that there is a great treasure buried in the vineyard. Promise me that you will look for it when I am dead.'
The sons promised and *as soon as their father had died*, they began looking for the treasure. They worked very hard in the hot sun *and all the time as they were working they wondered what their father had left for them*. In their minds they pictured boxes of gold coins, diamond necklaces and other such things. *Soon they had dug up every inch of the vineyard*. But they found not a single penny. They were very upset. *They felt that all their hard work had been for nothing*. But then the grapes started to appear on the vines and their grapes were the biggest and best in the neighbourhood, and they sold them for a lot of money.
Now they understood *what their father had meant by the great treasure*, and they lived happily and wealthily ever after.
The moral of this story is: Hard work brings *its own reward*.

Tapescript 21

1 'I went to the airport but I couldn't catch the plane.'
   'Oh dear! Had you forgotten your passport?'
2 'I was homesick while I was living in New York.'
   'Poor you! Had you never lived abroad before?'
3 'I met my girlfriend's parents last Sunday.'
   'Oh! Hadn't you met them before?'
4 'My grandfather had two sons from his first marriage.'
   'Really? I didn't know he'd been married before.'
5 'I told everyone the good news.'
   'Hadn't they heard it already?'
6 'As soon as I saw him I knew something was wrong.'
   'Oh dear! What had happened?'

Tapescript 22

Music from *The Entertainer*

Tapescript 23

J = Jack   L = Liza   I = Interviewer

J And it was really frightening, wasn't it?
L Well, yes, it was like something out of a horror movie. This woman was so thin and bent, she had long, straggly grey hair, and dirty old torn clothes. The smell was …
J But …, but the worst thing were the bandages!
L Oh, yes! She had bandages on her wrists and round her legs …
J … yes both legs. And these bandages looked as if they had been on her for weeks. They were grey, and absolutely covered in blood.
L Goodness knows what she'd done to herself, but the wounds obviously hadn't healed.
J And under one arm she was carrying a cat, and in her other hand there was a large glass of whisky! She could hardly stand up straight!
L Yes, she was swaying from side to side, spilling her whisky, wasn't she? Anyway, she asked us in, so we tried to hide how terrified we were, and we followed her in. The house was so old and dark and dirty …
J … and it absolutely stank of cats. There were cats everywhere. Up the curtains, on the bookshelves, on the stairs … It was unbelievable. And when she was leading us upstairs, suddenly two huge dogs, really huge dogs, the size of horses, came charging out of a room and nearly knocked us over!
L So you can imagine how we were starting to feel. Like, do you really have to stay here? At New Year? And pay for it?
J *But* the worst was still to come. When we got to the rooms, we couldn't believe it. All the furniture was broken, there were no curtains …
L It was absolutely freezing. There was no heating apart from one little electric fire for the whole place. In fact, there was only one power point, so you had to make a choice. You could either have the television, or the lamp, or the fire, but you couldn't have more than one.
J We just looked at each other and knew that we couldn't stay.
I So what did you do?
J Well, we didn't even try to be polite.
L We just said that it really wasn't what we wanted and we couldn't possibly stay there, and left.
J The lady said we'd lose our deposit …
L A £10 deposit … which was cheap at the price, I'll tell you!
J And we just ran!

Tapescript 24

1 'Did you like the film?'
   'It was excellent. Have you seen it yet? It stars Anthony Hopkins and Emma Thompson.'
2 'What did you think of the play?'
   'It was so boring I fell asleep in the first act.'
3 'Did you enjoy your pizzas?'
   'They were delicious. John had tomato and mozzarella topping and I had ham and mozzarella.'
4 'Do you like Ben Brown's novels?'
   'I didn't like his last one, but I couldn't put his latest one down until the last chapter.'
5 'What do you think of their children?'
   'I think they spoil them. They always give them whatever they want.'
6 'What was your holiday like?'
   'It was a good break, but the weather wasn't very good.'
7 'What did you think of Hannah Smart?'
   'She's usually very good but I don't think she was right for this part.'
8 'What was the match like?'
   'It was really exciting, especially when Smith scored in the closing minutes.'

UNIT 4

Tapescript 25

I = Interviewer   M = Megan   L = Laura

I What are some of the good things about being a teenager, not an adult?
M Um … well, you *don't have to* go out to work, for a start.
L And you *don't have to* pay bills. You *can* go out with your friends, go shopping, go to the cinema.
M But I always *have to* tell my Mum and Dad where I'm going first.
L So do I. Another thing is we *don't have to* do the housework and the washing and cleaning, and all that stuff, which is really boring.
M One problem is that you never have enough money. We get *some* money from our parents, but it's never enough. You *aren't allowed to* buy what you want.
I What do think it's like being an adult?
L Well, adults *have to* worry about bills and looking after their family. They can't do what they want when they want.
I They have responsibilities, you mean?
L Yeah. I feel more sorry for my Mum. She's always rushing around and she has to go to work as well. She doesn't have to work on Thursdays and Fridays, but she has loads of different things to do in a day, like shopping, er … cooking, taking me to dancing and swimming.
I So do you think your Dad has the easier life?
L Well, I don't know. He has to work full-time, and he drives over a thousand miles a week, but he doesn't have to do anything in the house. When he gets in at 7.30, everything's been done!
I Um, tell me about school. What are some of the school rules?
M Huh! We *have to* wear a stupid school uniform, and we're not allowed to wear white socks, they have to be black. We *can't* wear make-up, and we *aren't allowed to* chew gum!
L And if you break one of the rules, you get a Friday afternoon detention!

Tapescript 26

Bert Atkins talks about his school days

I = Interviewer   B = Bert

I   When did you start school, Bert?

B   Well, … er, I was born in 1919 and I started school when I was five, so that was 1924. It was just a little village school, only 20 of us in all. I don't think it had a name, we just called it 'The Little School'. And we stayed there till we were ten, and then we moved to 'The Big Boys School' in the next village. I don't think that had a name either, it was always just 'The Big Boys School.'

I   And what can you remember about your first school?

B   Well, you know the first thing they taught us, all of us, *boys* and girls? The *very* first thing they taught us … was *knitting*. It seems strange, doesn't it? But we all *had* to learn to knit. We couldn't learn to read and write till we'd learnt to knit!

I   Why was that? Was there a reason?

B   Oh yes, there was a reason all right. You see, we all had to knit our own cloth to clean our slate. We weren't allowed to use paper and pencils, at least not until we were seven years old. They were too expensive, so we had to use chalk and a slate for the first two years. So you see it was a good idea, knitting a cloth. I think that's what I remember most about the Little School.

I   And when you were ten you moved to the Big Boys? Did you have to take any exams to go there?

B   Oh no, I don't remember any exams. When you were ten you just started walking to the next village to 'The Big Boys'. There was no transport, you see, you had to walk. It was about four miles. I didn't get a bike till I was fourteen, and of course I'd left school by then. You had to leave at fourteen in those days.

I   And what about 'The Big Boys'? Did you enjoy it?

B   Ooh, in the beginning I was terrified. There were so many really big boys, and the teachers were really strict. You had to behave in 'The Big Boys'!

I   What did you have to do?

B   Well, we had to stand behind our desks at the start of every lesson, we weren't allowed to talk at all in class, ever, well … er, only if the teacher asked a question. The headmaster, Tom Bevan he was called – we called him *Bossy* Bevan. He was really strict, we were terrified of him, terrified. Once he hit a boy so hard he broke his nose. But he never hit me, no. The worst punishment I got was writing lines after school, and that was for coming late. In the winter, it was, and in all the snow and I arrived ten minutes late. Huh …, I had to write one hundred times, 'I must leave home early. I must not arrive late.' *One* hundred times. But I was never hit, never.

I   And did you have to do much homework?

B   Homework? No – we never got homework. I don't remember any homework. We didn't have to do any. The teachers never thought about it. I think they'd had enough of us after each day. They didn't want more work!

I   So were your schooldays the happiest days of your life?

B   Ooh no! Never. I don't think I had an education really. The happiest time of my life was when I was in India during the war. It's the only time I've been abroad.

Tapescript 27a   See page 37

Tapescript 27b

M = Mum   J = Jim

M   You must look after your money.

J   Yes, Mum! I will.

M   You mustn't go out when it's dark.

J   No, Mum! I won't.

M   You must make sure you eat well.

J   Yes, Mum! I will.

M   You must phone us if you're in trouble.

J   Yes, Mum! I will.

M   You mustn't talk to strangers.

J   No, Mum! I won't.

M   You mustn't drink too much beer.

J   No, Mum! I won't.

M   You must have a bath regularly.

J   Yes, Mum! I will.

M   You mustn't go anywhere that's dangerous.

J   No, Mum! I won't.

Tapescript 28a

J = Jim   A = Anthony

J   I think we should take our travellers' cheques in American dollars.

A   I don't think we should go to Thailand in September because it's the rainy season.

Tapescript 28b

J   I think we should take plenty of suncream. It'll be really hot.

A   I think we should buy a book called *See the World on $25 a Day*. It'll have some good ideas about where to go and where to stay.

J   I don't think we should put too much in our backpacks. We won't be able to carry it all.

A   I don't think we should take anything valuable. We might lose it.

J   I think we should go to Australia first. I've got some friends there who'll put us up.

A   I think we should go to Indonesia by boat. It'll be cheaper than flying.

J   I don't think we should wait too long before we go. I want to get started.

Tapescript 29

1   Sumie

In my country, Japan, usually we invite guests home at the weekend, in the early evening, about seven o'clock. Before they come, we must tidy the front garden and clean the entrance hall. Then we must spray it all with water to show that we welcome guests with cleanliness. The guests usually bring presents and when they give you the present they say, 'I'm sorry this is such a small present', but in fact they have chosen the present very carefully. When the meal is ready the hostess says, 'We have nothing special for you today but you are welcome to come this way.' You can see that in Japan you should try to be modest and you should not show off too much. If you don't understand our culture you will think this is very strange.

When we have foreign guests we try to serve traditional Japanese meals like *sushi*, *tempura*, or *sukiyaki* but when we have Japanese guests, we serve all kinds of food such as spaghetti, Chinese food, or steaks. When guests leave, the host and hostess see them out of the house and wait until their car turns the corner of the street; they wait until they can't see them any more.

2   Rosa

I come from Spain. At home what we love most is going out to eat in bars and restaurants. There is a big choice and we can go from one bar to another trying different things and having a few drinks, usually wine or beer. But sometimes we also like to invite people to our home.

I usually invite my friends for an informal meal. I cook Spanish omelette, which is made with potatoes, onions and eggs, fried in olive oil. Then we have things like cheese, ham – Spanish ham is very different from English ham, and if you buy the best one, called *Jabugo*, is something delicious, worth trying. And then things like olives, anchovies, mussels. We drink wine or beer. Some people may bring a bottle of wine or something for pudding. We usually meet late in the evening, about eight thirty or nine. Of course we dress casually; we just want to be relaxed and comfortable, and talk and laugh together.

3   Leslie

I'm from the United States. Sometimes when our family gets together with other families, we have what's called a 'pot luck supper', which can take place in the evening or even at lunchtime. This is an informal occasion held perhaps in someone's garden, so people dress casually but nicely. Invitations can be written or made by phone, and each person is asked to bring a dish of food. They're given a choice of starter, main course, salad or vegetable, or dessert. The hostess knows how many of each kind of dish she needs but not exactly what the guests will bring. This is why it's called 'pot luck', as it's a lovely surprise, holding a dinner party and not knowing what you're going to feed your guests. As the guests arrive, they put their dish, or pot as it used to be called, on the table and the meal is served buffet-style, and drinks are provided, although some guests might bring a bottle of wine as a present.

I really enjoy this kind of entertaining; it's a fun, relaxed way of getting together with friends.

Tapescript 30

a 'Could you fill it up, please?'
'Sure. Shall I check the oil as well?'

b 'Could I have the bill, please?'
'Certainly, sir. I'll bring it straight away.'

c 'It's a present. Do you think you could gift-wrap it for me?'
'Yes, indeed. I'll just take the price off.'

d 'Two lagers, please.'
'Halves or pints?'

e 'Can you tell me the code for Paris?'
'One moment. I'll just look it up.'

f 'I'll give you a lift if you like.'
'That's great. Would you drop me at the station?'

g 'Would you mind opening the window?'
'Not at all. It's very stuffy in here.'

h 'Could I have extension 2387, please?'
'I'm afraid the line's engaged at the moment. Do you want to hold?'

Tapescript 31

1 A So anyway, I said to him that I really didn't think it was right to change the arrangements without letting everyone know …
B Sorry to interrupt, darling, but I think the baby's crying. Do you think you could just go and see if she's all right? And perhaps give her some milk? Ooh, and check her nappy?

2 A Yes, madam. Can I help you?
B Yes, I bought these here two days ago and the heel's broken. Can you change them?
A Oh, dear. I'm so sorry. I'll just see if we've got another pair for you.

3 A Turn that wretched music down, will you? Or better still, turn it off!
B Oh, all right.

4 A I think we need an advertising campaign on television and in the press. I really want to push this project, John. Would you mind looking after the newspapers, and I'll deal with the television? Is that all right?
B Mm, fine. Er … when shall we start?

5 A Anita, will you come here a minute? Could you get me the file on sales in France? I just need to check something. Oh, and Anita, I'd love a cup of coffee, if that's at all possible.
B Yes, Mr Parkinson.

6 A I'm awfully sorry to bother you. I'm sure people are always asking you this as you're always standing here selling your newspapers, but you wouldn't have change for a five-pound note, would you? It's for the phone box.
B Here you are.
A Oh, that's terribly kind.

UNIT 5

Tapescript 32   See page 45

Tapescript 33   See page 45

Tapescript 34

1 A Well, darling. It's our big day soon.
B I know. I can't wait. I hope the weather's good.
A Yes, it makes such a difference, doesn't it?
B The church is looking beautiful.
A And the hotel is getting ready for the reception.
B And then there's our honeymoon.
A In Bali.
B Ah!

2 A How many people are coming?
B About twenty or thirty.
A What have we got to eat and drink?
B Caviar and champagne. What else could anyone ask for?
A Let's move all the furniture out of this room.
B So people can dance, you mean?
A Yeah. Good idea?
B Fine.

3 A Have you packed the books and the pictures from the living room?
B Yes. And all the kitchen things are packed, too.
A That's it, then. What time are the removal men coming?
B Early, I hope. About 7.00 in the morning.
A Good! It's a long drive to our new house, *and* it's right in the middle of the countryside. Do you think the driver will find it OK?
B Don't worry. I've told him to follow our car. Oh, I can't wait to be there.
A And I can't wait to get the baby's room ready.
B Tom if it's a boy and Natalie if it's a girl. It's so exciting! A new home and a new baby in the same month!

Tapescript 35

S = Nina Kendle's secretary
A = Alan Middleton

S Hello. Nina Kendle's office.
A Hello. Could I speak to Nina Kendle, please? This is Alan Middleton.
S I'm afraid she's out at the moment. She's *visiting* a factory.
A I see. What time *will* she *be* back in the office?
S I'm not sure. I don't know how long she's going to stay there.
A All right. What about lunch-time? Is she free then?
S Just one moment. I'll check. No, she's *having* lunch with a designer.
A Till what time? Do you know?
S Erm … Well, she's *seeing* a customer here in her office at 2.00.
A Ah! So when's a good time to try again?
S Any time after 2.30.
A Are you sure?
S Definitely. She'll be in her office for the rest of the afternoon.
A OK. I'll phone back then. Thank you.
S That's all right. Goodbye.

Tapescript 36a

The Geography of the British Isles

The British Isles can be divided into two, not only because of its geography but also because of its climate and agriculture. If you draw a line from about the Bristol Channel to the Wash, then to the south of this line there are mainly low lands and hills, and to the north there are higher lands and mountains. This includes the Welsh Mountains, the Highlands of north-west Scotland, and the Pennines, which is a range of mountains that runs north to south, and is known as the backbone of England. It is wetter in the north because of the higher land, and drier and sunnier in the south. This has an effect on the agriculture, of course. To the north there are sheep and cows because the grass grows so well, and to the south there are arable farms growing crops and cereal.

Tapescript 36b

The South West of England is famous for its beautiful countryside and dramatic coastline. One particular area of natural beauty is Dartmoor, which is inhabited by wild ponies. The countryside in the South East is more gentle, and there is a lot of fruit-growing. It is also the most heavily populated part of Britain. East Anglia is very flat, and is famous for its vast fields of wheat and potatoes. The Midlands used to have a lot of heavy industry, but much of this has disappeared over recent years. Wales is characterized by its mountains in the north and its valleys in the south. In the North West of England there is the beautiful Lake District, and the cities of Liverpool and Manchester. The North East used to have a lot of mining and ship building, but not any more, unfortunately. Scotland is famous for its lakes, of course, known as *lochs*. The moors and mountains are beautiful and empty. Ireland is famed for its rains and its rich green grass, its romance and its mists.

Tapescript 37

The Weather Forecast

And now here's the weather forecast for the next twenty-four hours. I'll divide the country into four, starting with the North West and the North East of England. Well, there'll be some early morning mists, and after that it'll be mainly dry and sunny, but quite chilly, with temperatures around six or seven. It should stay dry all day, but there'll be quite a wind, so wrap up warm.

And now the South West and Wales. You can expect some rain in the morning and afternoon. There might be some storms, as well, with thunder and lightning. There'll be quite strong winds, and the temperature will be lower than yesterday, around three or four degrees. I don't think you'll see much of the sun. Cloudy all day, I'm afraid.

The South East, the Midlands, and East

Anglia will see the best of today's weather. It'll be warmer than yesterday, no winds, and sunshine nearly all day, with temperatures around ten or eleven, so quite warm for the time of year.

In Scotland and Northern Ireland, however, there'll be heavy rain and maybe some snow during the afternoon, and on the hills temperatures will drop to below freezing, minus four or five, and on the highest spots minus ten. Over much of Scotland it will be cloudy, and windy, too, as the cold front moves in over the Atlantic. Northern Ireland can expect the same, but the rain will end before dark. But again, very cold, with temperatures not going above freezing. And that's all from me.

Tapescript 38   See pages 51–53

Tapescript 39

I would like to reserve some rooms at your hotel. We are arriving in Alicante on 28 July. We hope to stay for ten nights leaving on 7 August. My husband and I would like a double room, preferably with a balcony. Our two teenage daughters require a twin room. We understand that all your bedrooms are en-suite. Could you confirm this? Is it possible to have rooms with a sea view? Please let me know if you have rooms available for these dates. I would also be grateful if you could tell me the price of each room. I look forward to hearing from you.

Tapescript 40

a   'No, no! He said turn left at the pub, not right!'
    'Look! *You* drive and *I'll* navigate from now on! Right?'
b   'Can you take us to Euston Station, please?'
    'Yes, of course. Hop in!'
c   'I'll get a couple of coffees from the buffet car.'
    'Would you mind getting me a sandwich as well?'
d   'Excuse me, I think you'll find those seats facing the front are ours.'
    'I'm terribly sorry. We didn't notice that they were reserved.'
e   'Excuse me, are we landing on time?'
    'Yes. We're beginning our descent soon.'
f   'Do you think it'll be a rough crossing?'
    'Well, the forecast is good, so it should be very smooth.'
g   'Two to the British Museum, please. And could you possibly tell us when it's our stop?'
    'One pound eighty, please. Just sit near me and I'll give you a shout.'
h   'Which line is it for Oxford Circus?'
    'The Jubilee Line to Green Park. Then change to the Victoria Line.'
i   'That's all right, you can keep the change.'
    'Thanks a lot. Do want a hand with those bags?'

UNIT 6

Tapescript 41

A = Anna   N = Nina

A   My French exchange visitor came yesterday.
N   What's her name?
A   Marie-Ange.
N   What a pretty name! *What's she like?*
A   She's really nice. I'm sure we'll get on really well. We seem to have a lot in common.
N   Why do you say that? *What does she like doing?*
A   Well, she likes dancing, and so do I. And we both like tennis and listening to music.
N   That sounds great. I saw you with someone this morning. Was it Marie-Ange? *What does she look like?*
A   She's quite tall, and she's got long, dark hair.
N   No, it wasn't her, then. Now, we're all going out tomorrow, aren't we? Shall we go for a pizza, or shall we go to the cinema? *What would she like to do?*
A   Um, I'll ask her tonight and tell you tomorrow. By the way, someone told me your Mum's not very well. What's the matter? *How is she?*
N   Oh, she's OK. She's had a bad sore throat, that's all, but it's getting better now.
A   Oh, it's not too bad, then.

Tapescript 42

1   He's very nice, actually. You'd really like him. He's the kind of person you can always go to with a problem.
2   She is not very well. Still got a temperature, and a cough that she can't get rid of.
3   She loves riding her horse, Blackey. She's mad about horses. They're her greatest passion. She lives for horses from morning till night.
4   It isn't very nice, actually. It's raining, it's cold, and it's pretty miserable. What about where you are?
5   Mmm … a bit like you, actually. She's got the same build, about the same height, but your hair is longer and straighter than hers. Other than that, you two are pretty similar.
6   He's fine. Very happy since he met a French girl called Valerie. Those two are inseparable.
7   She's quite good-looking. The kind of girl you go for. But she's a bit too serious for me. You know, politics, literature, human rights, things like that.
8   It was great. Really relaxing. Lots of sunshine, good food. We did nothing but sit next to the pool and read books for a whole two weeks.
9   I like all sorts, but I suppose I like biographies and detective stories best.

Tapescript 43

Dear Dennis
We just wanted *to say* thank you for putting us up before we caught the plane last week. It was a lovely evening, and we enjoyed *meeting* your friends, Pete and Sarah. We managed *to get* to the airport with plenty of time to spare. We even tried *to get* an earlier flight, but it wasn't possible.

We had a wonderful holiday in Spain. We just loved *driving* through the countryside, and we often stopped *to walk* round a mountain village. We met our friends, Bill and Sue, and they invited us *to have* a meal with them. They wanted *us to stay* with them, but we couldn't, as we had already booked a hotel.

The weather was fantastic. The sun didn't stop *shining* all the time we were there. Leaving Spain was very sad. It made me *want* to cry.

Anyway, we're looking forward to hearing from you, and hope *to see* you soon. Let us *know* if you're ever in the area. You must call in.
Best wishes, Sandra

Tapescript 44

1   The teacher told me to do my homework.
2   I promised to do it carefully.
3   I finished painting my kitchen yesterday.
4   The baby continued to cry until his mother picked him up.
5   I can't stand queuing. It drives me mad. It's such a waste of time.
6   Please don't forget to post my letter. It's terribly important.
7   I refuse to lend you another penny! You'll just spend it on the horses!
8   I usually choose to have my holidays in winter because we all like skiing.
9   Excuse me. I just need to go to the loo. I won't be a minute.
10 I hate shopping for clothes. They never have my size.
11 She agreed to lend us her flat while she was away.
12 She just asked us to look after the plants and water them every day.
13 How will you manage to pay all your bills if you have no money in your bank account?

Tapescript 45

a   'What is Anna's brother like?'
    'Well, he is certainly *tall*, dark and handsome, but I didn't enjoy meeting him at all. He is even *ruder* than she is!'
b   'What was your meal like?'
    'Ugh! It was awful. The pizza was *disgusting*. We were absolutely *starving*, but we still couldn't eat it!'
c   'Did you have a good time in Amsterdam?'
    'Excellent, thank you. There's so much to do. It's a really *exciting* city. And there are so many people from all over the world; it's even *more cosmopolitan* than London.'
d   'Mmm! These courgettes are *delicious*. Did you grow them yourselves?'
    'Yes, we did. All our vegetables are *home-grown*.'

Tapescript 46a

Sheila and Bob talking about New York

I = Interviewer   B = Bob   S = Sheila

I   How long did you live in the States?

B   We were there for two years, in New York.

I   And did you enjoy it?

S   Oh, tremendously. We had a wonderful time.

B   Yeah, what we liked best was that we could work and yet still lead a normal life. I mean, the shops are open till ten o'clock.

I   All shops?

S   Yes, everything. Food shops, chemists …

B   There's even a huge department store called Gimbles on 86th Street that was open till nine o'clock.

S   And some supermarkets are open twenty-four hours a day. Most shops don't open as early as in England, well, they don't open until about erm … 10 or 11 in the morning.

B   Yes, that's right.

S   Because they all work much later. And everything's open on Sundays.

B   And the holidays, the public holidays are much shorter than here, and in the States only the banks are shut. Everything else stays open, so it makes life much easier. You could do what you liked *when* you liked.

I   I see, erm … Do you think New York is as cosmopolitan as London?

S   Oh, yes, but it's not as mixed. Nationalities stay in their own areas; like there's the Russian section …

B   … the German section. We were in German Town, York Town, which is called German Town. And there was a row of German shops, all German-speaking.

S   I think the major difference was the height of the place. Everything was up. We lived on the twenty-ninth floor.

B   Yes, and I worked on the sixty-third floor.

S   Yes, but I like heights. And of course everything is faster. And the people are much ruder.

I   Oh! In what ways?

B   Well, pushing in the street, fights about getting on the bus. People don't queue like they do in England. And of course the taxi drivers! New York taxi drivers must be the rudest in the world! Americans themselves are really friendly but the taxi drivers never speak. *And* they don't seem to know where anything is. I asked one of them to take me to the Guggenheim Museum once and he was really angry with me because he'd never heard of it!

I   *He* angry with *you?* Are all American taxi drivers like that?

S   Oh, yes. Well, in New York, anyway. Not so much in other places. When we went to California it was very different.

B   Yes, I think we were aware that New York is quite a dangerous place. We never had any problems ourselves at all, but when there *was* a crime, it was horrendous.

S   Oh, yes. The subways are unusable. They're dirty, uncomfortable.

I   Did you make many friends?

S   Well, that's what's interesting, really. We made more friends in our two years there than we have after two years of living back here near London. I think Americans are more … open, they … you know, they speak their minds, so if they don't like something, well, they actually tell you directly. Not like the British, who might think one thing and say another. So maybe the British are ruder than the Americans!

Tapescript 46b

Terry talking about London

I = Interviewer   T = Terry

I   So, Terry. You've been in London quite a long time now.

T   Mmm.

I   What differences do you notice between the two countries?

T   Obviously the biggest difference is the people. The average Englishman is … mmm … cold and not very open.

I   Oh!

T   In the States it's very different. We start conversations with people in the street. We're a lot more enthusiastic and spontaneous than people here. You know, when I first came, I couldn't understand what was wrong, but now I see that I was trying to be too friendly too soon.

I   But um, tell me, do the English improve as you get to know them?

T   Oh yes!

I   Oh, good!

T   Once you've made a friend, it's a friend for life, but it takes a very long time. I'll tell you something that I think is very important. English people in America are respected. Everyone wants to talk to them. We're inquisitive, we love the accent. But Americans in England are thought to be a little inferior because they get excited by everything. They think everything is so 'cute'. One thing I've learned – it's funny now, but it wasn't at the time – I couldn't understand why, when I was talking to someone, they would move away, you know, move backwards. I thought, 'Do I smell? Am I boring?' The reason was, you see, Americans stand closer when they're talking.

I   Ah, that's interesting. What about your impressions of living here? How does that compare with the States?

T   Well, mmm … I think life's a lot easier in the States. It's easier to *make* money and it's easier to *spend* it. Shops are open all the time over there. When I first came to England you had to race to reach the supermarket before 5.30, but this has changed. Some shops are open later now, and on Sundays, but they are still harder to find than in the States.

I   Yeah. But it *is* a lot better than it was.

T   Sure. And another thing is Americans *work* a lot harder than you do here. To the English, their private lives are important, their holidays are important, their gardens are important, their dogs are important, but for Americans, *work* is the most important thing in our lives. You know, holidays seem to be longer here, and around Christmas and New Year the whole country closes down for two weeks!

I   Oh, come on!

T   It's true! We Americans are like the Japanese in this respect. We live to work.

I   So you don't like London very much!

T   Oh, you would think so from what I'm saying, wouldn't you? No, in fact I really love it here. I go home once a year and I really look forward to coming back here. This is my home now. I find life safer, more relaxed, and much more enjoyable. The Underground isn't very clean but at least you can use it and feel safe. And your taxi drivers are wonderful! They tell you their life stories and know every street in London. Maybe I've gotten into English habits! England doesn't have the dramatic beauty of the States, but oh, it … it's very pretty and charming in a way that I find comforting.

Tapescript 47   See page 63

UNIT 7

Tapescript 48

I = Interviewer   N = Nancy Mann

I   Who *do* you work for at the moment, Ms Mann?

N   Um, I work for the BBC World Service.

I   Ah, and how long *have* you worked for the BBC?

N   I've been with the BBC for five years. Yes, exactly five years.

I   And how long *have* you been their German correspondent?

N   For two years.

I   And what *did* you do before the BBC?

N   I worked as an interpreter for the EU.

I   As you know, this job is based in Geneva. *Have* you ever lived abroad before?

N   Oh yes, yes I *have*.

I   And when *did* you live abroad?

N   Well, in fact, I *was* born in Argentina and I lived there until I was eleven. Also, I lived and worked in Brussels for two years when I *was* working for the EU.

I   Mmm … That's interesting. *Have* you travelled much?

N   Oh yes, yes indeed. I've travelled all over western and eastern Europe, and I've also been to many parts of South America.

I   Mmm … And why *did* you go to these places?

N   Well, mostly for pleasure, but three years ago I went back to Argentina to cover various political stories in Buenos Aires for the BBC.

Tapescript 49

a She was born in Argentina in 1959.
b She went to boarding school in England from 1970 to 1977.
c She studied French and German when she was at Oxford University.
d She hasn't spoken Spanish since she was in Buenos Aires three years ago.
e She's worked in both eastern and western Europe at various times in her life.
f She worked in Brussels for two years, from 1989 to 1991.
g She's worked for the BBC for the last five years.
h She hasn't worked abroad since her son was born four years ago.
i She married for the first time when she was twenty-one.
j She's been married three times.
k She married for the third time last year.

Tapescript 50a

The news

a The murderer Bruce Braden *has escaped* from Parkhurst Prison on the Isle of Wight.
b After the heavy rain of the last few days, floods *have brought* chaos to drivers in the West Country.
c Amy Carter, the kidnapped baby from Leeds, *has been found* safe and well in a car park in Manchester.
d Two thousand car workers from a US car factory *have been made* redundant.

Tapescript 50b

a Last night, the murderer Bruce Braden *escaped* from Parkhurst Prison. Prison officers *found* his cell empty at six o'clock this morning.
b Early this morning, floods *brought* chaos to many roads in Devon. Drivers left their cars and *walked* to work through the flood water.
c Late last night, the kidnapped baby, Amy Carter, *was found* safe and well in a car park in the centre of Manchester. The car park attendant *heard* a noise coming from a rubbish bin and he *found* Amy wrapped in a warm blanket.
d Two thousand car workers from the General Motors factory in Detroit *were made* redundant yesterday. The management *gave* them no warning. The men were shocked and furious when they *heard* the news yesterday evening.

Tapescript 51

Thomas Wilson – a retired man

T = Thomas Wilson   P = Philippa

P How long have you been retired now, Grandpa?
T Let me see. Er … it's four years. Yes, I've been retired nearly four years now. I suppose I'm used to it after all this time. But you know, I worked for *Courtaulds* for over forty years. Can you believe that? Forty years.
P One job for forty years. Incredible! I remember when you retired and they gave you that gold watch. Do you like being retired? I'd get bored. I'm sure I would. Don't you get bored?
T Well, I'm lucky. I've got my health so I can do a lot, I can get out at lot. I've just taken up golf, you know. It's a wonderful sport for an old man like me 'cos it's not really a sport at all, at least not the way your Grandpa plays it. It's just a good excuse for a walk, and I need an excuse since Rover died. I … I miss good old Rover; he and I were great friends … but I don't think I want another dog at my age. I go to the golf club twice a week. I've made some good friends there, you know. Have you met Ted and Marjorie? They're my age. Er … They're a lovely couple.
P Er, no … I don't think I've met them, but didn't you go on holiday with them?
T Yes, that's right. We went to Wales together last Easter. Oh … and we had a lovely time, a lovely time. I do appreciate company since your Grandma died … you know, I really miss your Grandma. Thirty-five years we were married, thirty-five years and still as much in love as the day we met. She was a wonderful lady, your Grandma.
P Oh I know that, Grandpa. We all miss her so much. We all loved her so much.
T So I like to keep busy. I've been on all sorts of special holidays, you know. Package holidays for senior citizens, and I …
P Well, I know you went to visit Uncle Keith in Australia. *And* you've just come back from a cruise round the Caribbean. You're so brown.
T I know. My word, that was an experience. I loved every minute of it! When you're older, I'll tell you about the American widow I met! … Miriam, she was called. Oh, just a baby of fifty-five, but she seemed to like me.
P Grandpa!
T And yes, of course, Keith. I saw him two years ago. You've not met your Australian cousins yet, have you? Oh, you'd love the baby, Kylie, she's beautiful. Looks just like your Grandma. But you know, I've also been to Spain and Morocco, *and* Turkey. These package holidays are so good for people like me.
P Grandpa, next time, please think of me. Don't you want a companion? Can I come with you? I'd love a suntan like yours! We never go anywhere interesting.
T Oh, Philippa, you know your mum and dad wouldn't let me. Not until you've finished your exams. Helen says I am a bad influence on you.
P Well, I think *you* have more fun than *I* do! All I have to look forward to is exams and more exams and then years and years of work!
T Oh Philippa. Don't wish your life away. Just enjoy it all. You only get one go at it!

Tapescript 52

On the telephone

a Hello, this is Chesswood 285120. I'm afraid I'm not at home at the moment, but please leave your name and number after the tone and I'll get back to you as soon as I can. 'Hi, Annie. This is er … Pete here. Pete Nealy. Er … I need to speak to you about next weekend. Can you give me a ring? Erm … I'm at home, by the way. It's ten o'clock now and I'll be here all morning, er … at least until two o'clock. Yeah, thanks. Bye.'
b 'I'm afraid Mr Barrett's in a meeting. Can I take a message?'
'Yes, please. This is Pam Haddon. He rang me earlier and left a message on my answer phone and I'm returning his call. Can you tell him I'm back in my office now?'
c 'Shall I ask Miss Jackson to give you a call when she gets back?'
'Yes, please. I'm sure she's got my number but I'll give it to you again, just in case. It's 01924 561718.'
d 'Good morning. Payne and Stracey Advertising.'
'Good morning. Can I have extension 321, please?'
e 'Hello, Mrs Barrett … I'm afraid Mr Barrett's on another line at the moment. Do you want to hold or …? Oh, he's free now. I'm putting you through.'
'Thank you very much.'
'Hello …'
'Hello, Frank? It's me, Diana …'
f 'Hello. Is that Sandra?'
'No, I'm sorry, it isn't. She's just gone out. Can I take a message? She'll be back in a minute.'

UNIT 8

Tapescript 53a

M = Mum   J = Jim

M Oh, dear! I hope everything will be all right. You've never been abroad before.
J Don't worry, Mum. I*'ll be* OK. I can look after myself. Anyway, I*'ll be* with Anthony. We *won't do* anything stupid.
M But what *will you do* if you run out of money?
J We*'ll get* a job of course!
M Oh. What about if you get lost?
J Mum! If we *get* lost, we*'ll ask* someone the way, but we *won't get* lost because we know where we're going!
M Oh. All right. But what if you can't read the directions?

Tapescript 53b

M But how will I know that you're all right?
J When we *get* to a big city, I*'ll send* you a postcard.
M Oh. But Jim, it's such a long flight to Istanbul!

J Mum! As soon as we *arrive* in Turkey, I'*ll give* you a ring!
M I'*ll be* so worried until I *hear* from you.
J It'll be OK, Mum. Honest!

Tapescript 54

J = Joe   S = Sue

J Goodbye, darling! Good luck with the interview!
S Thanks. I'll need it. I hope the trains are running on time. *If* the trains *are* delayed, I'*ll get* a taxi. *If* I'*m* late for the interview, I'*ll be* furious with myself!
J Just keep calm! Phone me when you can.
S I will. *As soon as* I *come* out of the interview, I'*ll* give you a ring.
J When *will* you *know if* you've got the job?
S They'*ll send* me a letter in the next few days. *If* they *offer* me the job, I'*ll accept* it, and *if* I accept it, we'*ll have to* move house. You know that, don't you?
J Sure. But we'll worry about that later.
S OK. What are you doing today?
J I can't remember. *When* I *get* to the office, I'*ll look* in my diary. I don't think I'm doing much today.
S Don't forget to pick up the children *as soon as* you get back from work.
J I won't. You'd better go now. *If you don't hurry*, you'*ll miss* the train.
S OK. I'*ll see* you this evening. Bye!
J Bye, my love. Take care, and good luck!

Tapescript 55

1 A I'd go on a boat trip around the world.
  B Oh, I *wouldn't*. I'd get so bored. I'd *rather* fly. It'*d be* so much quicker.
  A No, I'd like to relax on the boat, sunbathe all day long, and have a waiter bring me a cold drink just when I want one. Ah, Heaven!
2 I *wouldn't mind* taking things easy for a bit, but then I'*d like* to just get on with my life, 'cos I'm very happy, really, with what I've got.
3 I'd buy all the toys in the world.
4 I would buy a field with the most beautiful view I could find, not very far away from where we live, if possible, and move my own house that I live in stone by stone and build it in that field.
5 I would first of all resign from my job as a teacher, and I would take the kids to Disneyland, and make sure they had the time of their life, and then I'd probably buy a property in Europe somewhere, just so we had the chance to go away for different holidays.
6 I would buy a football team.
7 Well, I wouldn't give up my job, because I've heard too many stories about people who go completely mad when they do that. I think I'd try to spend it all in a week or a month, and then I could forget all about it.
8 Erm … I would go ice-skating, go to the moon, on a rocket of course, and … go to the circus.

Tapescript 56a

a If Tony rings, tell him I'm at Andy's. He can get hold of me there.
b If you've finished your work, you can have a break. But you must be back here in fifteen minutes.
c If I'm not back by eight o'clock, don't wait for me. Go without me. I'll join you at the party.
d If you've got the 'flu, you should go to bed. Keep warm and have plenty of fluids.
e If you're ever in London, you must give me a ring. We could go out somewhere.
f If you go to Australia, you have to have a visa. You can get one from the Embassy.
g I'd buy a word processor if I could afford it. It would be really useful for work.
h If I had more time, I might do an evening class. I'd love to be really good at photography.

Tapescript 56b

1 What do you do if you can't get to sleep at night?
2 What will you do if the teacher gives us a lot of homework tonight?
3 What would you do if you saw someone stealing in a shop?
4 What will you do if the weather's good this weekend?
5 What would you do if you were in a place where smoking was forbidden, and someone started to light a cigarette?
6 What do you do if you're reading something in English and you come across a new word?
7 What would you do if you found a wallet with a lot of money and an address in it?
8 What do you do if you get a headache?
9 What would you do if you needed £1,000 very quickly?

Tapescript 57

Who wants to be a millionaire?

Who wants to be a millionaire?
I don't.
Have flashy flunkies everywhere.
I don't.
Who wants the bother of a country estate?
A country estate is something I'd hate.

Who wants to wallow in champagne?
I don't.
Who wants a supersonic plane?
I don't.
Who wants a private landing field, too?
I don't.
And I don't 'cos all I want is you.

Who wants to be a millionaire?
I don't.
Who wants uranium to spare?
I don't.
Who wants to journey on a gigantic yacht?
Do I want a yacht? Oh, how I do not!

Who wants a fancy foreign car?
I don't.
Who wants to tire of caviar?
I don't.
Who wants a marble swimming pool, too?
I don't.
And I don't 'cos all I want is you.

Tapescript 58

1 'I went to Alice's flat last night.'
  'Oh, really! What was it like?'
  'Well, it was absolutely wonderful.'
2 'When I got home, I told my parents that I'd failed the exams.'
  'Oh, dear. What did they say?'
  'Well, my mother was OK, but my father, he went mad!'
3 'We went out for a meal last night.'
  'Where did you go?'
  'That new restaurant near the station.'
  'What was the food like?'
4 'We had a great time skiing in Switzerland.'
  'Where did you go?'
  'Zermatt.'
  'Was the weather good?'
  '…'
5 'It took hours to get here.'
  'Why?'
  'The traffic! It was incredible!'

Tapescript 59

1   Amnesty International

Amnesty International is a world-wide organization, independent of any government or political party. It is our aim to release prisoners of conscience. These are men and women who are in prison not because they have broken the law, but because of their beliefs, colour, language, or religion. We try to get fair and early trials by publicizing their cases and by putting pressure on their governments to practise basic human rights.

Amnesty International has been in operation for over twenty years, and in that time we have helped prisoners in over sixty countries. We have won several peace prizes, including the Nobel Peace Prize in 1978.

Each year we handle, on average, nearly 5,000 individual cases. Please help us. We need your donations to make us unnecessary in this world.

2   The RSPCA

Founded in 1824, the RSPCA is the world's oldest animal welfare organization. We work to promote kindness and to prevent cruelty to animals within all lawful means throughout England and Wales. Every year we find new homes for about 80,000 animals, we treat over 200,000 sick animals ranging from hedgehogs to horses, and we investigate over 100,000 complaints of cruelty.

We also work for the welfare of animals in the wild, such as whales and badgers. We are the world experts at cleaning and rehabilitating birds that have been damaged in oil spills. Every year nearly 3 million animals are used in research laboratories, and we oppose all experiments that cause pain and suffering.

We work with both governments and the farming industry to promote humane methods in the rearing of farm animals. Intensive farming methods can cause many animal welfare problems.

The society is a charity, and receives no aid from the government. Our running costs amount to £38 million a year. Please give generously.

3 Drought and Famine in Africa

Drought and famine have come to Africa again this year, just as they have every year for the past fifteen years. In some parts of Africa it hasn't rained for three years. There have been no crops, and the animals on which many people depend died long ago. Refugees are pouring from the countryside into the towns in their desperate search for food, and it has been estimated that over a thousand people are dying every day.

We are supplying towns and camps with food and medical supplies, but our efforts are drops in the ocean. We need a hundred times more food and medical supplies, as well as doctors, nurses, blankets, tents, and clothes. Your help is needed now before it is too late. Please give all you can. No pound or penny will ever be better spent or more appreciated.

Tapescript 60

M = Maggie   A = Anna

M I'm bored!
A Well, it's a lovely day. Why don't we take the dog for a walk?
M No, I don't feel like going for a walk. I'm too tired.
A You need to get out! Let's go shopping!
M Oh, no! I couldn't bear it! I'd rather do anything but that!
A OK, then. Shall we watch the telly?
M That's a good idea!
A Do you want the news on ITV?
M Mmm, I'd rather watch *Neighbours* on BBC1. It's just started.

P = Paul   B = Billy

P I'm broke, and I don't get paid for two weeks! What am I going to do?
B If I were you, I'd get a job that paid more money.
P Oh, why didn't I think of that? Thanks, Billy. It doesn't help me now, does it?
B Well, then, you'd better get a loan from the bank.
P No, I couldn't do that. I owe them too much already.
B Why don't you ask your parents? They'd help you.
P No, I'd rather not. I'd rather sort out my problems on my own.
B Then you ought to ask your boss for a pay rise.
P Good idea, but I've already tried that and it didn't work.
B Oh. Well, I suppose I could lend you some.
P Really? That would be great! Thanks Billy. You're a real mate. I'll pay it back, honest!

UNIT 9

Tapescript 61

a 'Mr and Mrs Brown never go on holiday.'
   'They can't have much money.'
b 'The phone's ringing!'
   'It might be Jane.'
c 'Paul's taking his umbrella.'
   'It must be raining.'
d 'There are three fire engines!'
   'There must be a fire somewhere!'
e 'I don't know where Hannah is.'
   'She could be in her bedroom.'
f 'My aunt isn't in the kitchen.'
   'She can't be cooking dinner.'
g 'Whose coat is this?'
   'It might be John's.'
h 'We've won the lottery!'
   'You must be joking!'

Tapescript 62

a A A half of lager and a fizzy mineral water, please.
   B Ice and lemon with the water?
   A Yes, please. And do you do bar meals?
   B Yes, we do.
b I don't work regular hours and I like that. I'd hate one of those nine to five office jobs. Also, I meet a lot of really interesting people. Of course, every now and then there's a difficult customer, but most times people are really nice. I took that really famous film star to the airport last week, now what was her name? Er … you know, she's in that film – er, what's it called? Anyway she was really nice. Gave me a big tip!
c A So how did you get on?
   B Oh it was good. They're very nice actually.
   A Were you nervous?
   B Yeah, a bit. Michael really wanted them to like me. I think they did. They were very kind anyway.
   A And did you tell them that you and Michael are going to get married?
   B No, next time. I just wanted to get to know them first.
d A We've never had one before.
   B Really? We've always had them in our family. We're all mad about them.
   A Well, we are now. The kids love her. And she is so good with them, ever so good-natured. But it wasn't fair to have one when we lived in town.
   B It's OK if they're small and you live near a park, but I know what you mean. What's she called?
   A Trudy.
e A Pull! Pull! Not too quickly!
   B I can't. It's really strong.
   A Come on. In then out. You're doing fine. Careful!
   A Yaow!
   A The one that got away!

Tapescript 63a   **See page 88**

Tapescript 63b

A = Andy   C = Carl

A Hi! Carl? It's Andy.
C Andy!
A Yeah. How are you? Feeling better?
C No! Not a lot. I have to sit down most of the time. It's too tiring – walking with a crutch.
A Really? Still using a crutch, eh? So you're not back at work yet?
C No. And I'm bored to death. I don't go back to the hospital for two more weeks.
A Two more weeks! That's when the plaster comes off, is it?
C I hope so. I can't wait to have two legs again! Anyway. How are you? Still missing all that snow and sun?
A No, I'm fine. The suntan's fading though. Josie's is too. She sends love, by the way.
C Love to her, too. I miss you all. By the way, have you got any holiday photos back yet?
A Yes, yes, I have. I got them back today. They're good. I didn't realize we'd taken so many.
C What about that one you took of that amazing sunset behind the hotel?
A Yes, the sunset. It's a good one. All of us together on Bob and Marcia's balcony, with the mountains and the snow in the background. It's beautiful. Brings back memories, doesn't it?
C Yeah. The memory of me skiing into a tree!
A Yes, I know. I'm sorry. At least it was towards the end; it could have been the first day. You only came home two days early.
C OK, OK. Oh, Andy, have you written to the tour operator yet to complain about that car we hired? They did promise us a bigger one.
A Yes, we have. Yesterday, in fact. Bob wrote it and we all signed it. I don't know if it'll do any good, but it's worth a try.
C And Marcia's suitcase, did that turn up?
A Yeah. They found it. It arrived on the next flight. Marcia was delighted.
C I'll bet she was! I suppose it was a good two weeks really, wasn't it?
A Sure. Some ups and downs, but generally I think we all got on well and had a great time. Shall we go again next year?
C I'd like to. All six of us again. Julie wants to, too. She fell in love with Switzerland, but she says she'll only come if I don't break a leg!
A Good! Great! It's a date. Next time, look out for the trees! I'll ring again soon, Carl. Take care!

Tapescript 64

a 'John didn't come to school yesterday.'
   'He must have been ill.'
b 'Look at my new gold watch!'
   'Wow! You can't have bought it yourself.'
c 'Why is Isabel late for class?'
   'Um … She might have overslept.'
d 'I can't find my homework.'
   'You must have forgotten it.'
e 'The teacher's checking Maria's work.'
   'She can't have finished already!'

f 'Did you know that Charles got top marks in the exam?'
   'He must have cheated!'
g 'Where's my umbrella?'
   'Oh! You could have left it on the train.'

Tapescript 65
Brothers and sisters

1 A large family

J = Jillie I = Interviewer

J I'm the youngest of nine children. My eldest sister is still alive, age ninety-three and there are sixteen years between us. We were four girls, four boys, and then me.

I And how well did you all get on together when you were children?

J Really, amazingly well. Being the youngest, I and my two young brothers rather looked on the rest of the family as 'the others', 'cos by that time they were either away at school or working. But we were always fond of one another and now of course, the roles have rather reversed because they were inclined to keep an eye on us and now — we younger ones, the two youngest, are very busy looking after the remainder, 'the ancient ones'.

I Tell me how your relationship with your sister, Joy, has changed over the years.

J Joy was the sister who used to ... in her holidays ... used to take me off er ... for lovely walks and teach me a great deal about the countryside. And she eventually became a nun and disappeared to Australia for twenty-three years. And we wrote to one another and I was still her little sister. When she came back, shortly after my husband died and the whole relationship changed enormously, and we became tremendous friends, we've never looked back.

I What do you see as the main advantage and disadvantage of coming from such a large family?

J I think the main advantage was this marvellous example of our parents, of how to enjoy life on a shoestring, because we were very much the poor relations, and it always amused us that our wealthy young cousins envied us so much. We had the old bikes and all the freedom in the world, and they were stuffed into Eton suits and expected to behave themselves.

I Disadvantages?

J I think it was very tough at a certain stage to have hand-me-down clothes, especially for a vain little girl, and not to have much in the way of parties and perhaps not to be able to go abroad, as other children did. But the advantages outweighed the disadvantages enormously, there's no doubt about that.

I Six out of the nine of you are still alive. How closely have you kept in touch over the years?

J Very closely. For many years now we've had an annual family party of three generations. And the touching thing is that the two younger generations just love to come, and there are anything up to sort of thirty-five of us meet up, once a year, in one or other of the houses, and have this marvellous lunch and tea-party, and lots of photographs are taken. And we've now got baby twins that were handed round this time. D'you know, and all this sort of thing ... marvellous!

2 An only child

P = Philippa I = Interviewer

P I'm an only child and basically I think the disadvantages far outweigh the advantages of being an only child. I was erm ... relatively happy as a young child but as you get older, I think being an only child gets more difficult to deal with.

I When you were little it wasn't too bad being an only child?

P No, but I was very lucky; I had lots of cousins. I had fourteen first cousins and most of them lived in the same town that I grew up in until I was ten, so we all played together and what have you. And I had a friend who lived next door to me, who was my best friend, who was the same age as me and so she was a bit like a sister then I suppose, and it wasn't until we moved away from there that I think it became more difficult being an only child.

I You said to me once that it was when you were a teenager that it was particularly hard. Why was that?

P Yes. I think ... I think when you're a teenager, you're quite unsure of how to deal with things, especially your parents anyway, and when you're on your own, you have nobody to compare notes with or to sort of say, are my parents being unreasonable or not, you just have to work it out for yourself, and that I think is quite hard really.

I Some people who come from large families might envy you because you had all of your parents' attention.

P Yes. That of course has its negatives as well as its positives, doesn't it? I think. You have all of their attention but you don't always want it, especially as a teenager. I think at that point in your late teens, you want to move away from your family a little bit, and ... and sort of explore other relationships, and if you have all of your parents' attention, you can't necessarily do that very well.

I What about now that you're an adult? Does the fact of being an only child have any impact on your life at all?

P Er ... yes. I think it's probably again quite difficult really. Erm ... my father died about ten years ago, so of course I'm the one who's left totally responsible for my mother. I'm the one that has to look after her if she has a problem, and help her if she needs help in any way. There's nobody else to help at all. So yes, I think it does have problems then, too.

I You have two children of your own. Was that a conscious decision because you decided that you didn't want one of your children to be an only child?

P Yes, very definitely. Yes, yes, I didn't want that to happen and I feel sorry for other children who are only children. I must say, I think that's ... at this age at the age of my children, it's probably fine but as they get older, I think it gets more difficult.

I So all in all, being an only child is not something you'd recommend.

P No, certainly not, no, no.

Tapescript 66a–d See pages 92–93

Tapescript 67
Polly and her friends

P = Polly A–J = Polly's friends

A I want to travel the world.
P So do I.
B I don't want to have lots of children.
P Neither do I.
C I can speak four languages.
P I can't.
D I can't drive.
P Neither can I.
E I'm not going to marry until I'm 35.
P Neither am I.
F I went to America last year.
P So did I.
G I have never been to Australia.
P I have.
H I don't like politicians.
P Neither do I.
I I am bored with the British Royal family.
P So am I.
J I love going to parties.
P I don't.

UNIT 10

Tapescript 68 See pages 96–97

Tapescript 69

a How long has he been learning to drive?
b How many lessons has he had?
c How much has he spent on tuition?
d How many instructors has he had?
e How many times has he crashed?
f How long has he been praying for a driving-licence?
g What have his instructors been telling him?
h How many times has he taken his test?
i How has he been celebrating?

Tapescript 70

A *Can you* drive?
B Oh, yes.
A How long *have you been driving?*
B Since I was seventeen. About ten years.
A *Have you got* a car?
B Yes, I have. It's a Renault.
A How long *have you had it?*

B About a year.
A How much *did you* pay *for it?*
B Well, I got it second-hand, and I think I paid about six thousand pounds.
A How many kilometres *has it done?*
B Ooph! I'm not sure.
A About how many?
B About forty thousand kilometres, I'd say.
A *Have you* ever *had an accident?*
B Not in this car, no, but I had one in the car I had before.
A What happened?
B Well, the roads were wet because it had been raining, and I skidded into another car.
A Whose fault *was it?*
B Oh, it was my fault. I was going too fast.

Tapescript 71

A You look tired! What have you been doing?
B I've been getting ready to go on holiday.
A Have you done everything?
B Well, I've packed the cases and I've been to the bank, but I haven't booked the taxi yet.

Tapescript 72

a A When was she born?
  B In 1950.
b A When was her collection of poems published?
  B In April 1958, when she was just eight years old.
c A When did her mother die?
  B On 16 September 1961.
d A When did she get married for the first time?
  B While she was still at university – in spring 1970.
e A When did she graduate?
  B On 20 June 1971.
f A When was her daughter born?
  B On 14 June 1972.
g A When did she go to India and the Far East?
  B After her divorce. She was twenty-nine at the time.
h A When did she get married for the second time?
  B At 10.30 on 3 August 1988.
i A How long did her first marriage last?
  B Nine years.
j A How long has she been living in Paris?
  B Since 1988.

Tapescript 73

I = Interviewer   J = Joanna

1 I How long are you in the States for?
  J Two weeks.
2 I How long have you been in the States?
  J Eight days.
3 I When do you go back to England?
  J At the end of the week, in five days' time.
4 I Where were you the day before yesterday?
  J I was in Chicago.
5 I Where were you this time last week?
  J Er, I was in New York.
6 I Where will you be the day after tomorrow?
  J I'll be in Denver.

Tapescript 74

driving-licence   chain smoker   postbox
driving test   business partner postman
wallpaper   ashtray   postcode
press conference   postcard   post office

Tapescript 75a

I = Interviewer   M = Margaret Tyler

I Margaret, may I ask you what you do for a living?
M Well, I work for a children's charity. That's a full-time job, but I also have guests coming to stay with me at weekends.
I You mean ... paying guests?
M Yes. This house, which is called Heritage House, is a bed-and-breakfast place, too.
I What I can see around me, Margaret, is amazing! How long have you been collecting all this royal memorabilia?
M Well, I first got interested in the Royal family when I saw the wedding of Princess Margaret on TV in 1960. Um, my father wouldn't let us have a television in the house because he said it would stop me doing my homework, so on the day of the wedding, I went round to a friend's house, and I just sat in front of the screen, mesmerized. But it wasn't until later that I started collecting. I've been collecting for eighteen years. The first things I bought were a dish with the Queen's head in the centre, and a few Coronation mugs to go with it.
I What sort of things have you got?
M Oh, everything! Oh, pictures, paintings, ashtrays, hundreds of mugs, um ..., er ... tea-pots, tea-cloths, biscuit tins, posters, books, flags, toast racks, egg cups, candle sticks, the lot! I've got over four thousand Royal souvenirs.
I All in this house?
M All in this house, yes. The house has been extended three times to fit it all in. They're in all the rooms downstairs, and in the four bedrooms upstairs, and in the attic, too.
I Incredible!
M It takes all my spare time to keep everything clean and dusted. I'm always playing around, making a special area for one of the Royals or another. Er ... It keeps me amused for hours, and the visitors who come, mainly foreign visitors, never get tired of talking about our Royal family.
I Is there one piece that's your favourite?
M Yes. I was desperately upset when Princess Diana and Prince Charles split up, and I wrote to Princess Diana, saying I hoped they might get together again. I got a lovely letter back from her Lady-in-Waiting, Sarah Campden, and that's the most important part of my whole collection.
I Have you had to spend a lot of money on your collection?
M Oh, I don't know. I've never thought about it. No, I don't think so. Once, when Prince Andrew married Fergie, a shop filled its windows with nothing else but mementoes of them, and I walked in and bought the lot.

But I ... I can't remember how much it was.
I And where do you get it all from?
M All over the place. There are lots of people who collect this stuff. I go up and down the country. We have conventions where we swap things. And there are specialist magazines and shops, and ... and jumble sales.
I Have you ever had to fight to get something you really wanted?
M Well, once I was in a shop and the shop keeper was drinking his tea from a lovely Coronation mug. I offered to buy it from him but he wasn't interested. So off I went to a shop nearby and bought a plain mug and presented it to him. 'Now will you do a swap?' I said to him. And he did. Oh, it was driving me mad, the thought of him using this mug every day! I wanted to give it a proper home!
I Is there anything you haven't got that you'd really like to have?
M Not a thing, but a person. Princess Diana is my favourite Royal. She's warm, wonderful, giggly, real. I'd love to meet her.
I Well, I hope your dream comes true! If she ever came to your house, she'd feel very at home!

Tapescript 75b

I = Interviewer   T = Ted Hewitt

I Ted, we're sitting in your dining-room, surrounded by a wonderful collection of miniature coaches. When did you start collecting them?
T Well, some of them date back to when I was a child, and they were given to me as toys, so ... at the age of five or six. But the bulk of them I've added er ... in the last ten, fifteen years.
I Now, I can understand a child enjoying playing with them, but why did you carry on, and actually make this collection?
T Well, it's because of my family background, erm ... I'm the third generation in a family coach business, so I've been ... lived with and been brought up with coaches all my life.
I Mmm. So you've got the real thing, and ... and the miniatures as well?
T That's right, yes.
I How many miniatures do you think you've got?
T I haven't counted them for a long time, but there must be at least five hundred, I should think.
I Which is your favourite?
T Well, my favourite is probably what is also the oldest, and that's a er ... little tin-plate double-decker bus, loosely based on a London Transport double-decker of the period.
I And how old is that?
T Er ... that would have been manufactured in the ... in the late thirties, early forties ...
I And ...
T ... I think.
I And we've got it here. It's lovely. And it ... and it ... it winds up. Will you ... will you ...?

T Yes. It's ...
I ... do it for us?
T It's a clockwork. So, er ... winds up like that.
I Oh, it's marvellous. How long have you had that? Did you have it as a child?
T Er ... no, no. That one doesn't date from that period. Erm ... probably about ten years I've had that one.
I Hmm. Do you keep your collection all in here? Is this the complete collection?
T The bulk of it is here, but er ... I have others in other rooms of the house, and some stored up in the attic, as well.
I Do many people collect miniature coaches? Where ... where do you get your coaches from? Where do you find them?
T Yes, there are a surprisingly huge number of people collect buses and coaches, and erm ... there are specialist shops that sell them. And then there's also a ... a network of what are called swapmeets, where people go and trade in either current models or old models. So there's no difficulty in finding ... models at all.
I Are they expensive? If I decided that I wanted to collect ...?
T No, not necessarily. You can ... you can buy contemporary models ... anything from about two ninety-nine upwards. And the sky's the limit.
I Give me a figure.
T Oh, some people pay thousands and thousands for a specific model.
I Which do you think was your most expensive?
T I don't really know. Erm ... I've never paid more than ... probably about fifty, sixty pounds. I think, yes.
I Have you got any very rare ones that people would fight for?
T I've got some that have ... have become rare. Weren't particularly rare when ... when I bought it. It's ... there's no rhyme or reason, but there ... there is one that I bought probably for seven or eight pounds which is now worth about a hundred and eighty. And that's quite good in ... sort of seven or eight years. That's not bad.
I Would you ever ... would you ever sell it?
T No, I don't think so. Unless I had to. No.
I No.
T No. I'm too attached to them to sell them. It's like the real ones.
I Are there any that you would really like to have that you haven't got, that you ... you look for when you go to these swapmeets?
T There's a lot that I'm tempted by, but er ... no, no one specific model erm ... financial constraint is the ... is the problem, I'm afraid. However, if a model appears of an actual vehicle that I ... that I own, then financial constraint or not ... no, I would have to have it, I think.
I Well, I think they're all lovely. Thank you very much, Ted.
T Thank you.

UNIT 11

Tapescript 76   See page 107

Tapescript 77

A = Clerk in the tourist office R = Rosie

A Good afternoon.
R Hello. I wonder if you could help me. I've just arrived here, and I'm looking for somewhere to stay.
A Uh huh.
R Can you tell me where I can find a cheap hotel?
A Certainly. There are a few around here, but the nearest and one of the nicest is just around the corner. It's called the Euro Hotel. Would you like me to phone to see if they have a room?
R No, that's OK. I'll just wander round there myself. Ah! Another thing. I need to change some travellers' cheques, but I don't know what time the banks close.
A They close at 7 o'clock in the evening.
R Right, thanks. This is a very pretty town, isn't it? It looks terribly old. Have you any idea how old this town is?
A Yes, it was founded in the thirteenth century.
R Really? As old as that? Wow! Well, I'd better get going. Oh, I'm not sure if we're near the centre of town, because I've only just arrived.
A Yes, this square out here is just about the centre.
R Thanks very much. Thanks for your help. I'll go to ... oh, sorry, I can't remember which hotel you suggested.
A The Euro Hotel.
R The Euro. Thanks a lot. Bye.

Tapescript 78

The news

There's been a train crash in the north of the country, and there are fears that up to five people have been killed. It happened at XXXX o'clock this morning. The train was going from London to XXXX.

Lucie Courtney, the six-year-old girl from XXXX who went missing from her home last Thursday, has been found safe and well. She was found by XXXX. She'd gone to stay with her grandparents.

There's been a robbery at a bank in Manchester. About XXXX men dressed as policemen went into the bank and stole XXXX pounds. They escaped in a XXXX.

And finally sport. Liverpool played Real Madrid in the European Cup last night. It was a closely fought match, and the final score was XXXX.

And in boxing, Louis Henderson is the new heavyweight champion. He beat XXXX in Las Vegas last night. He said after the fight XXXX. And that's the end of the news.

Tapescript 79   See page 109

Tapescript 80

C = Caroline Bailey   N = Norma, her secretary

C Now, what's happening today? I've got a meeting this afternoon, *haven't I*?
N Yes, that's right. With Henry and Ted.
C And the meeting's here, *isn't it*?
N No, it isn't. It's in Ted's office, at 3.00.
C Oh! I'm not having lunch with anyone, *am I*?
N No, you're free all morning.
C Phew! I'll start on that report, then. Er ... I signed all my letters, *didn't I*?
N No, you didn't, actually. They're on your desk, waiting for you.
C Ah, right! And er ... tomorrow I'm going to Scotland, *aren't I*?
N Yes. You're booked on the early morning shuttle.
C OK. It doesn't leave until 8.00, *does it*?
N 8.15, to be precise.
C Gosh, Norma! Where would I be without you?

Tapescript 81a

R = question tag rises; F = question tag falls

a It isn't very warm today, *is it*? (F)
b The weather forecast was wrong again, *wasn't it*? (F)
c You can cook, *can't you*? (R)
d You don't eat snails, *do you*? (R)
e You've got a CD, *haven't you*? (R)
f Sally's very clever, *isn't she*? (F)
g There are a lot of people here, *aren't there*? (F)
h The film wasn't very good, *was it*? (F)
i I am a silly person, *aren't I*? (F)
j You aren't going out dressed like that, *are you*? (R)

Tapescript 81b

a 'It isn't very warm today, is it?' (F)
  'No, it's freezing.'
b 'The weather forecast was wrong again, wasn't it?' (F)
  'Yes! It always is, though, isn't it?'
c 'You can cook, can't you?' (R)
  'Me? No! I can't even boil an egg.'
d 'You don't eat snails, do you?' (R)
  'Yuk! No, I don't! They're disgusting!'
e 'You've got a CD, haven't you?' (R)
  'Believe it or not, I haven't. I've got a tape recorder, though.'
f 'Sally's very clever, isn't she?' (F)
  'Yes. She's as bright as a button.'
g 'There are a lot of people here, aren't there?' (F)
  'I know! It's absolutely packed! I can't move!'
h 'The film wasn't very good, was it?' (F)
  'Terrible! The worst I've seen for ages.'
i 'I am a silly person, aren't I?' (F)
  'No, you're not. Just because you made one mistake doesn't mean you're silly.'
j 'You aren't going out dressed like that, are you?' (R)
  'Why? What's wrong with it? I thought I looked really smart.'

Tapescript 82

1 A You broke that vase, didn't you?
   B Yes, I did. I dropped it. I'm sorry.
   A You'll buy another one, won't you?
   B Yes, of course. How much was it?
   A £200.
   B It *wasn't* £200, was it?!
   A Yes, it *was*.

2 A It's so romantic, isn't it?
   B What is?
   A Well, they're really in love, aren't they?
   B Who are?
   A Paul and Mary.
   B Paul and Mary *aren't* in love, are they?!
   A Oh, yes, they are. They're mad about each other.

3 A Have you paid the electricity bill?
   B No, *You've* paid it, haven't you?
   A No, I haven't!
   B But you *always* pay it, don't you?
   A No, I don't. *I* always pay the telephone bill.
   B Oh, yes. Sorry.

4 A We love each other, don't we?
   B Er … I think so.
   A We don't ever want to part, do we?
   B Well …
   A We'll get married and have six children, won't we?
   B What!? You haven't bought me a ring, have you?
   A Yes, I have. Diamonds are forever.
   B Oh, dear!

5 A Helen didn't win the lottery, did she!?
   B Oh, yes, she did. She won £2,000,000!
   A She isn't going to give it all away, is she?
   B Oh, yes, she is.
   A She's very kind. Not many people would do that, would they?
   B Well, *you* certainly wouldn't, would you?

6 A That *isn't* a letter from Bertie, is it?
   B Yes, it is. He hasn't written for six months, has he?
   A What does he want?
   B He wants to borrow some money, doesn't he?
   A I'm not lending him another penny!
   B You've already lent him £2,000, haven't you?
   A I certainly have.

7 A You *haven't* forgotten the map, have you?
   B Oh, dear. Yes, I have.
   A But I put it next to your rucksack.
   B I didn't see it, did I?
   A So, how can we find the village?
   B We could ask a policeman, couldn't we?
   A There *aren't* many policemen on this mountain!

8 A We can't afford that new car, can we?
   B Are you sure? Haven't we saved a lot of money?
   A Yes, but, we need that money, don't we?
   B What for?
   A Our old age.
   B You're joking, aren't you?
   A Yes, I am. I've just bought it for you!
   B Wow!

Tapescript 83a

The Forgetful Generation

Presenter
Hello and welcome to Worldly Wise. How's your day been so far? Have you done all the things you planned? Kept all your appointments? Collected that parcel from the Post Office? Oh – and have you remembered to send your mother a birthday card? If so, well done! If not – you're not alone. Many of us are finding it more and more difficult to remember everything. Once upon a time we all just blamed getting older for our absent-mindedness, but now experts are blaming our modern lifestyle. They say that we've become 'the forgetful generation' and that day after day we try to do too much!

Tapescript 83b

Ellen
Last year I finished university and I got a job in the same town, Canterbury, where I was at university. And one day, for some reason, rather than go to work for nine o'clock, I got the bus and went to the university for an eleven o'clock lecture. I was sitting there, in the lecture room, and I thought to myself, 'Why don't I know anybody?' Then suddenly I remembered that I'd finished university and that I was two hours late for work!

Josh
I'm studying law in London now, and um, at the end of last term I packed my suitcase as usual, and went to King's Cross Station to catch the train home. I was sitting reading on the train, revising for my exams, and the inspector came to check my ticket. He looked as it and said, 'Thank you, sir. We'll be in Newcastle in about an hour.' And suddenly I thought, 'Newcastle!?! But I don't want to go to Newcastle. My parents live in Plymouth!' You see, when I was a child I lived with my parents in Newcastle, but we moved to Plymouth when I was ten. I couldn't believe it. How could I be so stupid?

Fiona
Some time ago I got dressed, ready to go to work. I put on my smart black suit. I'd been working at home the night before – preparing for a very important meeting the next day, and I remembered to put all the right papers into my briefcase. I left home and walked down to the bus stop. Just before I got on the bus, I looked down, and I was still wearing my fluffy, pink bedroom slippers!

Tapescript 83c

P = Presenter   A = Alan Buchan

P Stories of forgetfulness like these are familiar to many of us and experts say that such cases as Ellen's, Josh's and Fiona's show that loss of memory is not just related to age, but can be caused by our way of life. Professor Alan Buchan, a neuro-psychologist, explains why.

A One of the problems, these days, is that many companies have far fewer employees and this means that one person often does several jobs. Jobs that before were done by many people are done by a few and they haven't been trained to do this. If you have five things to do at once, you become stressed and forgetful. I think many people in work situations, at a meeting or something, have the experience where they start a sentence and half-way through it, they can't remember what they're talking about, and they can't finish the sentence. It's a terrible feeling – you think you're going mad. I remember one lady who came to me so distressed because at three important meetings in one week, she found herself saying, mid-sentence, 'I'm sorry, I can't remember what I'm talking about.' And, this was a lady in a new job, which involved a lot of travelling. She also had a home and family to look after, *and* she'd recently moved house. She had so *many* things to think about that her brain couldn't cope. It shut down.

P I can see the problem but what's the solution? How did you help that lady?

A Well, part of the solution is recognizing the problem. Once we'd talked to this lady about her stressful lifestyle, she realized that she wasn't going crazy, and she felt more relaxed and was able to help herself. But do you know one of the best ways to remember things, even in these days of personal computers and filofaxes?

P What's that?

A Well, in fact, it's a notebook – and a pencil of course! At the beginning of every day, write yourself a list of things you have to do, and it gives you a really good feeling when you cross things off the list as you do them! Psychologically, it's *very* satisfying to complete things.

P Well, there you have it! I hope I can remember how not to forget! Thank you very much indeed Professor … er … er … Oh! Professor Alan Buchan!

Tapescript 84

a A Oh, let's have a break, shall we?
   B All right. I'm dying for a cuppa.

b A My old man isn't at work today.
   B Why? What's up with him?
   A He was walking to work yesterday when this guy in a car knocked him over.
   B Really! Is he OK?
   A Well, he was very lucky. He just got a few cuts and grazes.

c A Can I have one of your fags?
   B Sure. Help yourself. I've got loads.
   A Ta! Do *you* want one?
   B No. I've just put one out.

d A Gimme your homework so I can copy it.
   B No way! You can do it yourself!

e A Did you manage to fix the telly?
   B Kind of. The picture's OK, but the sound isn't quite right.
   A What's on tonight?
   B Dunno. Look in the paper.

f A What's that stuff called that you use to clean between your teeth?
    B What do you mean?
    A Oh, you know! It's like string. White.
    B Oh! You mean dental floss.
    A That's it!

UNIT 12

Tapescript 85

The Marriage Proposal

J = John   M = Moira

J Hello, Moira. How are you?
M I'm fine. How are you?
J I feel wonderful because we're together again. It's been a long time since our holiday in Paris.
M Oh, I loved every minute of it. I'll never forget it. Can we go back there next spring?
J I love you, Moira. Will you marry me and come to Paris with me for our honeymoon?
M Oh, yes, yes, I will. I love you, too.

Tapescript 86a

The Wedding Reception

A = Adam   B = Beatrice

A Are you on your own?
B No, I'm not. I'm with my husband.
A How do you know John and Moira, then?
B I was at university with Moira.
A Do you like big weddings?
B I prefer smaller ones.
A Where did you meet your husband, then?
B Actually, I met him at a wedding.
A Why aren't you drinking?
B Because I'm driving.
A Er … Have you travelled far to get here?
B Yes, we have. We flew in from New York yesterday.
A Hey, why aren't you wearing a hat?
B I never wear hats.
A Where are you staying tonight?
B We're at the *Red Lion*.
A Oh! Can you give me a lift there?
B Yes, we can. Are you staying at the *Red Lion*, too?
A Yes, I am. Will there be enough room in your car?
B Oh, yes, lots. There won't be a problem.

Tapescript 86b

Beatrice talking to her husband

I've just met this really friendly young man. Do you know what he said to me? First he asked me if I was on my own and of course I said that I wasn't, I was with you. Then he asked me how I knew John and Moira and I told him I had been at university with Moira. He asked me if I liked big weddings, and I said no, I preferred smaller ones. Then he asked me where I'd met you, which was a bit of a funny question, so I told him that we'd met at a wedding. He asked me why I wasn't drinking, and I said that it was because I was driving. He asked me if we'd travelled far to get here, so I explained that we'd flown in from New York yesterday.

Then he asked something strange. He asked me why I wasn't wearing a hat, so I said I never wore hats. He then went on to ask me where we were staying tonight, and I told him we were at the *Red Lion*. He asked me if we could give him a lift there, and I said yes. I asked him if he was staying at the *Red Lion*, too, and he said he was. He asked if there would be enough room in our car, and I told him that there wouldn't be a problem.

Tapescript 87

a A He loves living in London.
    B But he told me he *hated* it!
b A He's moving to Canada.
    B But he told me that he was moving to *Australia*!
c A His girlfriend has left him.
    B But he told me that he'd left *her*!
d A He'll be thirty next week.
    B But he told me he'd be *twenty-one*!
e A He went to Amsterdam for his last holiday.
    B But he told me he'd gone to *Barbados*!
f A He can't give up smoking.
    B But he told me that he'd given up *three years ago*!
g A He was given the sack last week.
    B But he told me he'd been given *promotion*!
h A He's fallen in love with a French girl.
    B Oh! But he told me that he'd fallen in love with *me*!

Tapescript 88a

Pauline Peters

OK. We argue sometimes but not often. Usually we just sit quietly and watch television in the evenings. But sometimes … sometimes we argue about money. We don't have very much because neither of us has a job at the moment, and I get very upset when Patrick spends the little we have at the pub or on the horses. He promised to stop drinking but he hasn't stopped. It's worse since he lost his job. OK. We were shouting but we didn't throw a chair at Mr Fish. It … er … it just fell out of the window. And I'm really sorry that we woke the baby. We won't do it again. We love children. We'll babysit for Mr and Mrs Fish anytime if they want to go out.

Tapescript 88b

Iris Fish

Every night it's the same. They argue every night. And we can hear every word they say. During the day it's not so bad because they're both out at work. But in the evenings it's terrible. Usually, they start arguing about which television programme to watch. Then he bangs the door and marches down the road to the pub. Last night he came back really drunk. He was shouting outside his front door. 'Open the door you … er … so and so.' I won't tell you the language he used! But she wouldn't open it, she opened a window instead and threw a plant at him. Tonight she threw a chair at my poor husband. They're so selfish. They don't even care about the baby.

Tapescript 89a,b   See pages 121–122

Tapescript 90   See page 123

Tapescript 91a

a 'Excuse me, can you tell me where the post office is?'
    'Sorry, I'm a stranger here myself.'
b 'Ouch! That's my foot!'
    'Oh, I'm sorry. I wasn't looking where I was going.'
c 'Er … Excuse me, what's that creature called?'
    'It's a Diplodocus.'
    'Pardon?'
    'A Diplodocus. D-I-P-L-O-D-O-C-U-S.'
    'Er … Thank you very much.'
d 'I failed my driving test for the sixth time!'
    'I am sorry.'
e 'Excuse me! We need to get past. My little boy isn't feeling well.'
f 'Do you want your hearing aid, Grandma?'
    'Pardon?'
    'I said: *Do you want your hearing aid?*'
    'What?'
    'DO YOU WANT YOUR HEARING AID?'
    'I'm sorry, I can't hear you. I need my hearing aid.'
    'Oooh!'

Tapescript 91b

a Hello, Elana? Hello, again! I don't know what happened. I think we must have been cut off. I'm sorry about that. Never mind. Now, where were we?
b Excuse me! Hello! Excuse me! Excuse me, please! Hi! Yes, please! Can we have another large bottle of fizzy mineral water, please? Thanks.
c Oh, I *am* sorry to hear about that. Of course I understand. We'll go out another time.
d What! You want to go where? And with a bottle of whisky? How old do you think you are? Huh! You can think again!
e Excuse me! I wonder if you could help me. I bought this jumper, and I thought it was medium, but when I got home I saw it was the wrong size. Can I change it?
f Pardon? Could you say that again, please. I didn't understand.
g Excuse me, please! Thank you. Oh! Excuse me. I'm getting off at the next stop. Sorry. I've got a big suitcase.
h Oh, no! Of course, you're vegetarian! I *am* sorry! How awful of me. Don't worry, there are lots of other things for you to eat.

Grammar Reference

UNIT 1

Auxiliary verbs

Introduction

There are three classes of verbs in English.

1 The auxiliary verbs *do*, *be* and *have*
These are used to form tenses, and to show forms such as questions and negative. They are dealt with in this unit.

2 Modal auxiliary verbs
These are verbs such as *must, can, should, might, will,* and *would*. They are auxiliary verbs because they 'help' other verbs, but unlike *do, be* and *have*, they have their own meanings. For example, *can* expresses ability, and *must* expresses obligation. (See Units 4, 8, and 9)

3 Full verbs
These are all the other verbs in the language, for example, *play, run, help, think, want, go,* etc.
Remember that the verbs *do, be* and *have* can also be used as full verbs with their own meanings.
*I **do** my washing on Saturdays.*
*She **does** a lot of business in the Far East.*
*I want **to be** a teacher.*
*We **are** in class at the moment.*
*They **were** at home yesterday.*
*He **has** a lot of problems.*
*They **have** three children.*
*What do you **do**?* = What's your job? (The first *do* is an auxiliary; the second is a full verb.)

Auxiliary verbs and tenses

When *be* and *have* are used as auxiliary verbs, they make different verb forms.

be

1 *Be* with verb + *-ing* is used to make *continuous* verb forms.
*He's **washing** his hair.* (Present Continuous)
*They **were going** to work.* (Past Continuous)
*I've **been learning** English for two years.* (Present Perfect Continuous)
*I'd like **to be lying** on the beach right now.* (Continuous infinitive)

Continuous verb forms describe activities in progress and temporary activities.

2 *Be* with the past participle (*-ed* etc.) is used to form the *passive*.
*Paper **is made** from wood.* (Present Simple Passive)
*My car **was stolen** yesterday.* (Past Simple Passive)
*The house **has been redecorated**.* (Present Perfect Passive)
*This homework needs **to be done** tonight.* (Passive infinitive)

There is an introduction to the passive on page 144.

have

Have with the past participle is used to make *perfect* verb forms.
*He **has worked** in seven different countries.* (Present Perfect)
*She was crying because she **had had** some bad news.* (Past Perfect)
*I'd like **to have met** Napoleon.* (Perfect infinitive)

Perfect means 'before', so Present Perfect means 'before now'. (See Units 7 and 10). Past Perfect means 'before a time in the past'. (See Unit 3)

Auxiliary verbs and negatives

To make a negative, add *-n't* to the auxiliary verb. If there is no auxiliary verb, use *don't/doesn't/didn't*.

	Negative
He's working.	*He **isn't** working.*
I was thinking.	*I **wasn't** thinking.*
We've seen the play.	*We **haven't** seen the play.*
She works in a bank.	*She **doesn't** work in a bank.*
They like skiing.	*They **don't** like skiing.*
He went on holiday.	*He **didn't** go on holiday.*

Note the following points.
– We can't say *~~I amn't working~~*. We have to say *I'm not working*.
– It is possible to contract the auxiliaries *be* and *have* and use the uncontracted *not*.
*He's **not** playing today.* (= He *isn't* playing today.)
*We're **not** going to Italy after all.* (= We *aren't* going to Italy…)
*I've **not** read the book yet.* (= I *haven't* read the book yet.)

Auxiliary verbs and questions

1 To make a question, invert the subject and the auxiliary verb. If there is no auxiliary verb, use *do/does/did*.

	Question
She's wearing jeans.	*What **is she** wearing?*
You aren't working.	*Why **aren't you** working?*
Peter's been to China.	***Has Peter** been to China?*
You were born in Paris.	*Where **were you** born?*
I know you.	***Do I** know you?*
He wants an ice-cream.	*What **does he** want?*
They didn't go out.	*Why **didn't they** go out?*

2 Question tags are very common in spoken English. (See Unit 11)
*It's a lovely day, **isn't it**?*
*You've never tried curry, **have you**?*
*You love learning English, **don't you**?*

3 There is usually no *do/does/did* in subject questions.
Who wants an ice-cream?
What happened to your eye?
Who broke the window?

Compare the questions above to the following:
*What flavour ice-cream **do** you want?*
*What **did** you do to your eye?*
*How **did** you break the window?*

Auxiliary verbs and short answers

1 Short answers are very common in spoken English. If you just say *Yes* or *No*, it can sound rude.
We use short answers after 'yes/no' questions, and also in reply to statements.
To make a short answer, repeat the auxiliary verb. If there is no auxiliary verb, use *do/does/did*.

	Short answer
Are you coming with us?	*Yes, **I am**.*
Have you had breakfast?	*No, **I haven't**.*
It's a lovely day!	*Yes, **it is**, isn't it?*
Kate likes walking.	*No, **she doesn't**. She hates it.*
Did you go out last night?	*Yes, **we did**.*
Mary didn't phone.	*Yes, **she did**. You were out.*
Don't forget to write.	*No, **I won't**.*
Can you cook?	*Yes, **I can**.*

2 We often use a short question to reply to something someone has said. In this way, we use the short question to express our interest, concern, surprise, or whatever emotion we feel. We are not asking a question.

	Reply question
I went shopping today.	***Did you**, dear?*
I've bought you a present.	***Have you?** Thank you.*
David's going to Berlin.	***Is he?** How interesting!*
I love classical music.	***Do you?** I can't stand it.*

Auxiliary verbs and emphasis

Special emphasis can be put on an auxiliary verb when we speak. This can give more emotional force to the whole sentence, or it can express a contrast, for example, between true or false. If there is no auxiliary, use *do/does/did*.

*The house is so tidy! You **have** been working hard.*
*Mmm! That was delicious. I **do** like your cooking!*
*'It's time you cleaned your room.'   'I **have** cleaned my room.'*
*'Why didn't you ring me last night?'   'I **did** ring, but you were out.'*

have/have got

There are two forms of the verb *have*: *have* as a full verb with *do/does/did* for questions, negatives and short answers, and *have got* where *have* is an auxiliary.

*I **have** three sisters.*	*I've **got** three sisters.*
***Does** she **have** any children?*	***Has** she **got** any children?*
*I **don't have** any meetings today.*	*I **haven't got** any meetings today.*
*'**Do** fish **have** lungs?'*	*'**Have** fish **got** lungs?'*
*'Yes, they **do**.'*	*'Yes, they **have**.'*

Have and *have got* can mean the same. Note the following points:

– *Have got* is more informal, and spoken. When we write, we normally use *have*.

– We cannot use *have got* to talk about a habit.
   *I've **got** a meeting this afternoon.*
   *I always **have** a meeting on Monday afternoon.* (habit)

– For the past, we use forms of *have* only with *did/didn't*, NOT *~~had got~~*.
   *I **had** a headache yesterday.*
   ***Did** you **have** any pets as a child?*
   *I **didn't have** any money when I was a student.*

UNIT 2

Present states and actions

Present Simple

The Present Simple is one of the most common tenses in English. It can refer to the present (now), but it can also refer to *all time* and *regular time* (permanent situations and habits).

*I **want** a cup of tea.* = now
*The sun **rises** in the east.* = all time
*I **play** tennis on Sunday mornings.* = regular time

• Form

Positive and negative

I We You They	work don't work	hard.
He She It	works doesn't work	

Question

Where	do	I we you they	live?
	does	she he it	

• Use

The Present Simple is used:

1 to express an action that happens again and again, that is, a habit.
   *I **go** to work by car.*
   *She **smokes** ten cigarettes a day.*
   *I **wash** my hair twice a week.*

2 to express a fact which is always true.
   *Rolf **comes** from Germany.*
   *Some birds **fly** south in winter.*
   *My daughter **has** brown eyes.*

3 to express a fact which stays the same for a long time (a state).
   *He **works** in a bank.*
   *I **live** in a flat near the centre of town.*
   *I **prefer** coffee to tea.*

Adverbs of frequency

1 We often use adverbs of frequency with the Present Simple.

0%			50%			100%
never	rarely	not often	sometimes	often	usually	always

2 They go before the main verb, but after the verb *to be*.
   *I **usually** go to bed at 11.00.*
   *I don't **often** go swimming.*
   *She **never** eats meat.*
   *I **rarely** see Peter these days.*
   *He is **never** late for school.*
   *I am **usually** in a hurry in the morning.*

3 *Sometimes* and *usually* can also come at the beginning or the end.
   ***Sometimes** we play cards.*   *We play cards **sometimes**.*
   ***Usually** I go shopping with friends.*   *I go shopping with friends **usually**.*

4 *Never, always, rarely*, and *seldom* cannot move in this way.
   NOT *~~Never I go to the cinema.~~*
       ~~Always I have tea in the morning.~~

5 *Everyday*, etc. goes at the end.
   *He phones me **every night**.*

Spelling of verb + -s

1 The normal rule is to add *-s* to the base form of the verb.
   wants   eats   helps   drives

2 Add *-es* to verbs that end in *-ss, -sh, -ch, -x*, and *-o*.
   kisses   washes   watches   fixes   goes

3 Verbs that end in a consonant + *y* change to *-ies*.
   carries   flies   worries   tries
   But verbs which end in a vowel + *y* only add *-s*.
   buys   says   plays   enjoys

Present Continuous

• Form

Positive and negative

I	'm 'm not	
He She It	's isn't	eating.
We You They	're aren't	

Question

What	am	I	doing?
	is	she he it	
	are	we you they	

• Use

The Present Continuous is used:

1 to express an activity that is happening now.
Don't turn the TV off. I'm watching it.
You can't speak to Jane. She's having a bath.

2 to express an activity or situation that is true now, but is not necessarily happening at the moment of speaking.
Don't take that book. Jane's reading it.
I'm doing a French evening course this year.

3 to express a temporary activity.
Peter is a student, but he's working as a barman during the holidays.
I'm living with friends until I find a place of my own.

4 to express a planned future arrangement.
I'm having lunch with Glenna tomorrow.
We're meeting at 1.00 outside the restaurant.

Spelling of verb + *-ing*

1 The normal rule is to add *-ing* to the base form of the verb.
going   wearing   visiting   eating

2 Verbs that end in one *-e* lose the *-e*.
smoking   coming   hoping   writing

But verbs that end in *-ee* don't lose an *-e*.
agreeing   seeing

3 In verbs of one syllable, with one vowel and one consonant, the consonant is doubled.
stopping   getting   running   planning   jogging

But if the final consonant is *-y* or *-w*, it is not doubled.
playing   showing

Note *lie   lying*

State verbs

1 There are certain groups of verbs that are usually only used in the Present Simple. This is because their meanings are related to states or conditions which are facts and *not* activities. This is a feature of the use of the Present Simple. The groups of verbs are:

Verbs of thinking and opinions

believe	think	understand	suppose	expect
agree	doubt	know	remember	forget
mean	imagine	realize	deserve	prefer

I believe you.
Do you understand?
I know his face, but I forget his name.

Verbs of emotions and feeling

| like | love | hate | care | hope | wish | want | admit |

I like black coffee.
Do you want to go out?
I don't care.

Verbs of having and being

| belong | own | have | possess | contain | cost | seem | appear |
| need | depend on | weigh | come from | resemble |

This book belongs to Jane Leadbetter.
How much does it cost?
He has a lot of money.

Verbs of the senses

| look | hear | taste | smell | feel |

The food smells good.

When the subject is a person, we often use *can*.
Can you see that bird?
Can you smell something burning?
I can hear someone crying.

2 Some of these verbs can be used in the Present Continuous, but with a change of meaning. In the Continuous, the verb expresses an activity, not a state.
I think you're right. (= opinion)
We're thinking of going to the cinema. (= mental activity)
He has a lot of money. = (possession)
She's having a bath. = (activity)
I see what you mean. (= understand)
Are you seeing Nigel tomorrow? (= activity)
The soup tastes awful. (= state)
I'm tasting the soup to see if it needs salt. (= activity)

The passive

Introduction to the passive

The passive is dealt with in Units 1, 2, 3, and 7 of *New Headway Intermediate*.

• Form

The tense of the verb *to be* changes to give different tenses in the passive. This is followed by the past participle.

It	is was has been	
They	are were have been	mended.

Notice the passive infinitive.
I'd love to be invited to their party.
This homework must be done by tomorrow.

• Use

1 Passive sentences move the focus from the subject to the object of active sentences.
Shakespeare wrote Hamlet in 1599.
Hamlet, one of the great dramatic tragedies, was written by Shakespeare.

The passive is not another way of expressing the same sentence in the active. We choose the active or the passive depending on what we are more interested in. In the first sentence, we are more interested in Shakespeare; in the second sentence, *Hamlet* has moved to the beginning of the sentence because we are more interested in the play.

2 Very often *by* and the agent are omitted in passive sentences. This might be because:

– the agent is not known.
My flat was burgled last night.

– the agent is not important.
This bridge was built in 1886.

– we understand who the agent is.
I was fined £100 for speeding.

3 The passive is associated with an impersonal, formal style. It is often used in notices and announcements.
Customers are requested to refrain from smoking.
It has been noticed that reference books have been removed from the library.

4 In informal language, we often use *you*, *we*, and *they* to refer to people in general or to no person in particular. In this way we can avoid using the passive.

They're building a new department store in the city centre.
You can buy stamps in lots of shops, not just post offices.
We speak English in this shop.

The same meaning is expressed in formal language using *one*.
One should dress to suit the occasion.

5 Be careful! Many past participles are used more like adjectives.

I'm very interested in modern art.
I was surprised by her behaviour.
We were very worried about you.
Aren't you bored by the news?
I'm exhausted! I've been working all day.

Present Simple and Continuous passive

The uses are the same in the passive as in the active.

My car is serviced regularly. (= habit)
Computers are used in all areas of life and work. (= fact which is always true)
Sorry about the mess. The house is being redecorated at the moment. (= activity happening now)

UNIT 3

Past tenses

Look at the diagram.
When Sylvia arrived home at 8.00 last night …

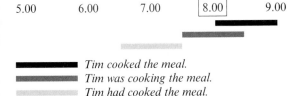

| 5.00 | 6.00 | 7.00 | 8.00 | 9.00 |

━━━━ *Tim cooked the meal.*
━━━━ *Tim was cooking the meal.*
━━━━ *Tim had cooked the meal.*

Past Simple

• Form

The form of the Past Simple is the same for all persons.

Positive

| I You He/She/It We They | finished arrived left | yesterday. three weeks ago. |

Negative

| I She You (etc.) | didn't | finish. arrive yesterday. leave. |

Question

| Did | you he they (etc.) | finish? enjoy the meal? |

• Use

The Past Simple is used:

1 to express a finished action in the past.
We met in 1987.
I went to Manchester last week.
John left two minutes ago.

2 to express actions which follow each other in a story.
Mary walked into the room and stopped. She listened carefully. She heard a noise coming from behind the curtain. She threw the curtain open, and then she saw …

3 to express a past situation or habit.
When I was a child, we lived in a small house by the sea. Every day I walked for miles on the beach with my dog.

This use is often expressed with *used to*.
We used to live in a small house … I used to walk miles …

Past Simple and time expressions

Look at the time expressions that are common with the Past Simple.

| I did it | last night. two days ago. yesterday morning. in 1990. in summer. when I was young. |

Spelling of verb + -ed

1 The normal rule is to add *-ed* to the base form of the verb.
worked   wanted   helped   washed

2 When the verb ends in *-e*, just add *-d*.
liked   used   hated   cared

3 If the verb has only one syllable, with one written vowel + one written consonant, the consonant is doubled.
stopped   planned   robbed   tinned

But we write *cooked*, *seated* and *moaned* because there are two vowels.

4 The consonant is not doubled if it is *y* or *w*.
played   showed

5 In most two-syllable verbs, the end consonant is doubled if the stress is on the second syllable.
pre'ferred   ad'mitted

But we write *'entered* and *'visited* because the stress is on the first syllable. The exception is the final consonant *-l*, as in *travelled* in British English. (In American English the spelling is *traveled*.)

6 Verbs that end in a consonant *+y* change to *-ied*.
carried   hurried   buried

But we write *enjoyed*, because it ends in a vowel + *y*.

Past Continuous

• Form

Positive and negative

| I He She It | was wasn't | working. |
| We You They | were weren't | |

Question

| What | was | I she he it | doing? |
| | were | we you they | |

• Use

We often use the Past Continuous in sentences together with the Past Simple. When this happens, the Past Continuous refers to longer, 'background' activities, whilst the Past Simple refers to shorter actions that happened in the middle of the longer ones.

*When I **woke** up this morning ...*

*... the birds **were singing** and the sun **was shining**.*

The Past Continuous is used:

1 to express an activity in progress before, and probably after, a particular time in the past.
   *I walked past your house last night. There was an awful lot of noise. What **were** you **doing**?*
   *At 7.00 this morning, I **was having** breakfast.*

2 to describe a situation or activity during a period in the past.
   *Jan looked lovely. She **was wearing** a green cotton dress. Her eyes **were shining** in the light of the candles that **were burning** nearby.*

3 to express an interrupted past activity.
   *When the phone rang, I **was having** a bath.*
   *We **were playing** tennis when it started to rain.*

4 to express an incomplete activity in the past in order to contrast with the Past Simple which expresses a completed activity.
   *I **was reading** a book during the flight. (I didn't finish it.)*
   *I **watched** a film during the flight. (the whole film)*

5 The Past Simple is usually used to express a repeated past habit or situation.
   *I **went out** with Jack for years.*

   But the Past Continuous can be used if the repeated habit becomes a longer 'setting' for something.
   *I **was going out** with Jack when I first met Harry.*

Past Simple versus Past Continuous

1 The Past Simple expresses past actions as simple facts. The Past Continuous gives past activities time and duration.

   Compare the following pairs of sentences:

   A *I didn't see you in the pub last night.*
   B *No. I **stayed** at home and **watched** the football.*

   A *I rang you last night, but there was no reply.*
   B *Sorry. I **was watching** the football. I didn't hear the phone.*

2 The questions refer to different time periods: the Past Continuous asks about activities before; the Past Simple asks about what happened after.
   When the war broke out, Peter was studying medicine at university. He decided that it was safer to go home to his parents and postpone his studies.

   What was Peter **doing** when the war broke out?   *He was studying.*
   What did Peter **do** when the war broke out?   *He went home to his parents.*

Past Perfect

Perfect means 'completed before', so Past Perfect refers to an action in the past which was completed before another action in the past.

• Form

The form of the Past Perfect is the same for all persons.

Positive and negative

I		
You	had	seen him before.
We	hadn't	finished work at 6.00.
(etc.)		

Question

	you	
Where had	she	been before?
	they	
	(etc.)	

• Use

1 The Past Perfect is used to look back to a time in the past and refer to an action that happened *before* then.

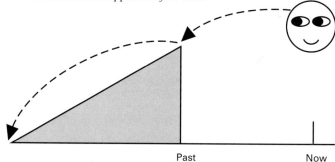

Past	Now

*When I got home, I found that someone **had broken** into my flat and **had stolen** my stereo.*

*I didn't want to go to the cinema with the others because **I'd seen** the film before.*

2 Notice the difference between the following sentences:
   *When I got to the party, Peter **went** home.*
   (= After I arrived, Peter left.)
   *When I got to the party, Peter **had gone** home.*
   (= Before I arrived, Peter left.)

Past tenses in the passive

The uses are the same in the passive as in the active.
*The bridge **was built** in 1876.* (Past Simple – finished action in the past)
*The bomb **was being defused** when it exploded.* (Past Continuous – interrupted past activity)
*The letter I was waiting for didn't arrive because it **had been sent** to my old address.* (Past Perfect – one action before another action in the past)

UNIT 4

Modal verbs (1)

Introduction to modal verbs

The modal verbs are *can, could, may, might, must, will, would, shall, should, ought*. They are known as modal auxiliary verbs because they 'help' another verb. (See also Units 1,5,8,9)
*I **can** swim.*
*Do you think I **should** go?*

- **Form**

1 There is no *-s* in the third person singular.
   She **can** *ski.*   *He* **must** *be tired.*   *It* **might** *rain.*

2 There is no *do/does* in the question.
   Shall *we go for a walk?*   **Can** *I help you?*   *What* **should** *I do?*

3 There is no *don't/doesn't* in the negative.
   He **can't** *dance*   *I* **won't** *be a minute*   *You* **mustn't** *steal!*

4 Modal auxiliary verbs don't usually have past forms. Other expressions are used instead.
   I **had to** *work hard at school.*

   Could is used with a past meaning in some cases. Compare the following sentences:
   I **could** *swim when I was six.* (= general ability)
   The prisoner **was able to/managed to** *escape by climbing onto the roof of the prison.* (NOT *could escape*) (= ability/performance on one occasion)

5 They have no infinitives and no *-ing* forms. Other expressions are used instead.
   I'd love **to be able to** *ski.*
   I hate **having to** *get up on cold, winter mornings.*

6 They are followed by an infinitive without *to*. The exception is *ought to*.
   You **must** *go.*   *I'll* **help** *you.*   *You* **ought to see** *a doctor.*

7 They can be used with perfect infinitives to talk about the past.
   You **should have told** *me that you can't swim. You* **might have drowned***!*

- **Use**

1 Each modal verb has at least two meanings. One use of all of them is to express possibility or probability.
   I **must** *post this letter!* (= obligation)
   You **must** *be tired!* (= deduction, probability)
   Could *you help me?* (= request)
   We **could** *go to Spain for our holidays.* (= possibility)
   May *I go home now?* (= permission)
   'Where's Anna?'   *'I'm not sure. She* **may** *be at work.'* (= possibility)

2 Modal verbs express our attitudes, opinions and judgements of events. Compare the dialogues.
   'Who's that knocking on the door?'
   'It's John.' (This is a fact.)
   'Who's that knocking on the door?'
   'It **could/may/might/must/should/can't/'ll** *be John.'*
   (These all express our attitude or opinion.)

Expressing obligation

Have to, *must*, and *should* are used to express obligation.

- **Form**

Positive and negative

I / You / We / They	have to / don't have to	work hard.
He / She	has to / doesn't have to	

Question

Do	you (etc.)	have to work hard?

Must and *should* are modal verbs. See the Introduction to modal verbs.

Positive and negative

I / You / They (etc.)	must / mustn't / should / shouldn't	do that!

Note the following points:

1 *Must I ...?* is possible, but question forms with *have to* are more common.
   Do *I* **have to** *do what you say, or can I do what I want?*

2 *Should I /she/we ...?* is possible. We often use *Do you think ...?*
   Should *I try to eat less?*
   Do you think *I* **should** *see a doctor?*

3 *Have to* has all the forms that *must* doesn't have.
   I **had to** *work until midnight last night.* (Past)
   You'll **have to** *study hard when you go to university.* (Future)
   She's a millionaire. She's never **had to** *do any work.* (Present Perfect)
   I hate **having to** *get up on cold, winter mornings.* (*-ing* form)
   If you were a policeman, you would **have to** *wear a uniform.* (Infinitive)

- **Use**

1 *Must* and *have to* both express strong obligation.
   Must is used to express an obligation that involves the speaker's opinion. It is personal.
   I **must** *get my hair cut.* (This is me talking to me.)
   You **must** *do this homework carefully.* (A teacher talking to students.)
   Must is also associated with a formal, written style.
   Candidates **must** *write in ink and answer four questions.* (Instructions on an exam paper.)
   Books **must** *be returned on or before the due date.* (Instructions in a library.)

2 *Have to* expresses a general obligation based on a law or rule, or based on the authority of another person. It is more objective.
   I can't play tennis tomorrow. I **have to** *go to the dentist.* (I have an appointment.)
   Children **have to** *go to school until they are sixteen.* (A law)
   Mum says you **have to** *tidy your room before you go out.* (Mother's order!)
   Must and *have to* are sometimes interchangeable.
   I **must** *be home by midnight.*   *I* **have to** *be home by midnight.*

   But, *have to* is used more often than *must*. If you are unsure which to use, it is probably safer to use *have to*.

3 Be careful! The negatives *mustn't* and *don't have to* are completely different.
   Mustn't expresses negative obligation – it is very important **not** to do something.
   Don't have to expresses the absence of obligation – you can if you want to but it isn't necessary.
   You **mustn't** *steal other people's things. It's wrong.*
   You **mustn't** *drive if you've been drinking. You could kill someone!*
   Some people iron their socks, but you **don't have to***. I think it's a waste of time.*
   When you go into a shop, you **don't have to** *buy something. You can just look.*

4 *Have got to* is also common in British English but it is more informal than *have to*.
   I've **got to** *go now. See you!*
   Don't go to bed late. We've **got to** *get up early tomorrow.*
   'Go and tidy your room.'   *'***Have** *I* **got to***?'*   *'Yes, you have!'*

5 *Should* and *ought to* express mild obligation, or advice. They both express what, in the speaker's opinion, is the right or best thing to do.

*You're always asking me for money. I think you **should** spend less.*
*You **ought to** be more careful with your money.*
*I know I **shouldn't** keep buying you presents, but I just love you!*
*You **shouldn't** sit so close to the television! It's bad for your eyes.*

Expressing permission

Can, *may*, and *be allowed to* are used to express permission. *Can* is more informal and usually spoken.

*You **can** borrow my bike, but you **can't** have the car. I need it.*
***May** we smoke in here?*
*You **can't** come in here with those muddy shoes!*
*You're **allowed to** get married when you're sixteen.*
*Are we **allowed to** use a dictionary for this test?*

Making requests

1 There are many ways of making requests in English.

Can Could Will Would	you	help me, please? pass the salt, please?

Would you mind helping me, please?

Can Could	I	speak to you, please? ask you a question?

Do you mind if I open the window?
Would you mind if I opened the window?

Can, *could*, *will*, and *would* are all modal verbs. For an introduction to modal verbs, see page 146.

2 *Could* is (a little) more formal; *can* is (a little) more familiar.
Could I ...? and *Could you ...?* are very useful because they can be used in many different situations.

3 Here are some ways of responding to requests:
A *Excuse me! Could you help me?*
B *Sure.*
   Of course.
   Well, I'm afraid I'm a bit busy at the moment.
A *Would you mind if I opened the window?*
B *No, not at all.*
   No, that's fine.
   Well, I'm rather/a little chilly, actually.

Making offers

1 *Will* and *shall* are used to express offers. They are both modal verbs. For an introduction to modal verbs, see page 146.

2 The contracted form of *will* is used to express an intention, decision or offer made at the moment of speaking.
Come over after work. I'll make a meal for you.
'It's Jane's birthday today.'   'Is it? I'll buy her some flowers.'
Give him your suitcase. He'll carry it for you.
Don't worry about the bus. Dave'll give you a lift.
Give it back or we'll call the Police!

In many languages, this idea is often expressed by a present tense, but in English this is wrong.

NOT *~~I give you my number~~*

NOT *~~I carry your suitcase~~*

Other uses of *will* are dealt with in Unit 5.

3 *Shall ...?* is used in questions with the first person, *I* and *we*. It expresses an offer, a suggestion, or a request for advice.
*'**Shall** I carry your bag for you?'   'That's very kind. Thank you.'*
*'**Shall** we go out for a meal tonight?'   'Mmm. I'd love to.'*
*'What **shall** we do? We haven't got any money.'   'We could ask Dad.'*

We use *should* to make an informal suggestion.
*What **should** we have for dinner?*
*What **should** we do tonight?*

UNIT 5

Future forms

There is no future tense in English as there is in many European languages. However, English has several forms that can refer to the future. Three of these are *will*, *going to*, and the Present Continuous.
I'll see you later.
We're going to see a film tonight. Do you want to come?
I'm seeing the doctor tomorrow evening.

The difference between them is *not* about near or distant future, or about certainty. The speaker chooses a future form depending on when the decision was taken, and how the speaker sees the future event. There is more about this in **Use** below.

• Form
Positive and negative

I He They	'll won't	help you.
I'm/I'm not She's/She isn't We're/We aren't	going to	watch the football tonight.
I'm/I'm not He's/He isn't You're/You aren't	catching the 10.00 train.	

Question

What time	will you are you going to	arrive?
	are you meeting the manager?	

Note that we avoid saying *going to come* or *going to go*.
We're coming tomorrow.
When are you going home?

• Use
1 **Prediction** (*will* and *going to*)

will

The most common use of *will* is as an auxiliary verb to show future time. It expresses a future fact or prediction. It is called the pure future, or the Future Simple.
We'll be away for two weeks.
*Those flowers **won't grow** under the tree. It's too dark.*
*Our love **will last** forever.*
You'll be sick if you eat all those sweets!

Will for a prediction can be based more on an opinion than a fact.
*I think Laura **will do** very well in her exams. She works hard.*
*I am convinced that inflation **will fall** to 3 per cent next year.*

going to

Going to can also express a prediction, especially when it is based on a present fact. There is evidence now that something is certain to happen.

She's going to have a baby. (We can see she's pregnant.)
Liverpool are going to win the match. (It's four nil, and there's only five minutes left.)
It isn't going to rain today. (Look at that lovely blue sky.)

Sometimes there is no difference between *will* and *going to*.

This government	will ruin	the country with its stupid
	is going to ruin	economic policies.

2   **Decisions and intentions (*will* and *going to*)**

Will is also used as a modal auxiliary verb to express a decision, intention or offer made at the moment of speaking. We saw this use in Unit 4. (See page 148)

I'll have the steak, please.
I'll see you tomorrow. Bye!
Give me a ring some time. We'll go out for a drink.
'Jeff, there's someone at the door!'   'OK, I'll get it.'

Remember that you can't use the present tense for this use.

NOT *~~I have the steak.~~*   *~~I see you tomorrow.~~*

Going to is used to express a future plan, decision or intention, made *before* the moment of speaking.

When I grow up, I'm going to be a doctor.
Jane and Peter are going to get married after they've graduated.
We're going to paint this room blue.

3   **Arrangements (Present Continuous)**

The Present Continuous can be used to express a future arrangement between people. It usually refers to the near future.

We're going out with Jeremy tonight.
I'm having my hair cut tomorrow.
What are we having for lunch?

Think of the things you might put in your diary to remind you of what you are doing over the next few days and weeks. These are the kinds of events that are often expressed by the Present Continuous for the future. The verbs express some kind of activity or movement.

I'm meeting Peter tonight.
The Taylors are coming for dinner.
I'm seeing the doctor in the morning.
We're going to a party on Saturday night.
We're catching the 10.00 train.

Remember, that you can't use the present tense for this use.

NOT *~~I meet Peter tonight.~~*
        ~~I see the doctor in the morning.~~
        ~~What do you do this evening?~~

Sometimes there is no difference between an agreed arrangement (Present Continuous) and an intention (*going to*).

We're going to get	married in the spring.
We're getting	

UNIT 6

like

1   Be careful not to confuse *like* as a verb and *like* as a preposition.
Like as a verb has a person as subject:

I like modern art.
I don't like the way he looks at me.
Do you like fish?
Would you like a drink?

Like as a preposition has an object after it:
She's wearing a hat like mine.
He's nothing like his father.
That sounds like the postman.
You're behaving like children.
This new girlfriend of his – what's she like?

2   *What's London like?* is a very general question. It means 'Describe London to me because I don't know anything about it', or 'What are your impressions of London compared to other cities?'. The answer can be a description or a comparison.

It's quite big, and it's very interesting. (= description)
It's like New York, but without the tall buildings. (= comparison)

Be careful not to confuse a description and a comparison.
What's Peter like? (asks for a description)
He's tall and good-looking.   NOT *~~He's like tall....~~*

3   *What ... like?* asks about the permanent nature of people and things.
What's your mother like?
What's the health system like in your country?

4   *How ...?* is used to ask about the present condition of something that can change.
How's work these days?
How was your journey?
How was the traffic this morning?

To ask about the weather, we can use both questions.

What's the weather like	
How's the weather	where you are?

5   *How ...?* is also used to ask about people's health and happiness. Compare the following.
How's Peter?
He's fine.

What's Peter like?
He's a nice guy. Quiet but funny. He's quite tall, has dark hair ...

6   *How ...?* is also used to ask about people's reactions and feelings.
How was the party?
How's your meal?
How's your new job?

Sometimes we can use *What ... like?* or *How ...?*, but they aren't the same. *What ... like?* asks for an objective description. *How ...?* asks for personal feelings.
How's the party?
It's great!

What's the party like?
It's very noisy, but there's lots to eat and drink.

Verb + *-ing* or infinitive?

See Appendix 2 on page 158 for a list of verb patterns.

Relative clauses

1   Relative clauses are used to tell us which person or thing we are talking about. It makes it possible to give more information about the person or thing being spoken about.

'The boy has gone into hospital.'
(Which boy?)
'The boy **who lives next door** has gone into hospital.'

'The book is very good.'
(Which book?)
'The book **that I bought yesterday** is very good.'

'This is a photo of the hotel.'
(Which hotel?)
'This is a photo of the hotel **where we stayed**.'

2 We use *who* to refer to people (and we can also use *that*). We use *that* to refer to things (and we can also use *which*).
*The book is about a girl **who/that** marries a millionaire.*
*What was the name of the horse **that/which** won the race?*

3 When *who* or *that* is the object of a relative clause, it can be left out.
*The person **you need to talk to** is on holiday.*
*This is the best wine **I've ever tasted**.*
*The book **I bought yesterday** is very good.*
*Have you found the keys **you lost**?*

But when *who* or *that* is the subject of a relative clause, it **must** be used.
*I like people **who are kind and considerate**.*
*I want a car **that is cheap to run**.*

4 *Which* can be used to refer to the whole previous sentence or idea.
*I passed my driving test first time, **which surprised everyone**.*
*Jane can't come to the party, **which is a shame**.*

5 We use *whose* to refer to someone's possessions.
*That's the woman **whose son won the lottery**.*

6 We can use *where* to refer to places.
*The hotel **where we stayed** was right on the beach.*
*We went back to the place **where we first met**.*

UNIT 7

Present Perfect

The same form (*have* + past participle) exists in many European languages, but the uses in English are different. In English the Present Perfect is essentially a *present* tense but it also expresses the effect of past actions and activities on the present.

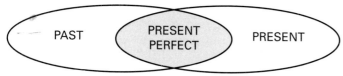

Present Perfect means 'before now'. The Present Perfect does not express *when* an action happened. If we say the exact time, we have to use the Past Simple.
*In my life I **have travelled** to all five continents.*
*I **travelled** round Africa **in 1988**.*

• Form

Positive and negative

I We You They	've haven't	
		lived in Rome.
He She	's hasn't	

Question

How long have	I we you	
		known Peter?
How long has	she he	

• Use

The Present Perfect has three main uses.

1 It expresses an action which began in the past and still continues.
*We've **lived** in the same house for twenty-five years.*
*Peter's **worked** as a teacher since 1991.*
*How long **have** you **known** each other?*
*They've **been** married for twenty years.*

Many languages express this idea with a present tense: 'Peter is a teacher; Peter is a teacher for ten years', but in English the second sentence is wrong.
~~Peter is a teacher for ten years.~~ ✗
Peter has been a teacher for ten years. ✔

Note the time expressions that are common with this use. We use *for* with a period of time, and *since* with a point in time.

for	two years a month a few minutes half an hour ages	since	1970 the end of the lesson August 8.00 Christmas

2 It expresses an experience that happened at some time in one's life. The action is in the past and finished, but the effects of the action are still felt. *When* the action happened is not important.
*I've **been** to the States.* (I still remember.)
*She's **written** poetry, children's stories, and biographies.* (In her writing career)
*Have you ever **had** an operation?* (At any time in your life up to now)
*How many times **has** he **been** married?* (In his life)

Note the adverbs that are common with this use.
*Have you **ever** been to Australia? I've **never** tried bunjee jumping.*
*I haven't tried sake **before**. It's very nice.*

Note that questions and answers about definite times are expressed in the Past Simple.
*When **did** you **go** to the States?*
*Was her poetry **published** while she was alive?*
*I **broke** my leg once, but I **didn't** have to stay in hospital.*
*He **met** his second wife in the dry cleaner's.*

3 It expresses a past action that has a present result. The action is usually in the recent past.
*I've **lost** my wallet.* (I haven't got it now.)
*The taxi **hasn't arrived**.* (We're still waiting for it.)
*What **have** you **done** to your lip?* (It's bleeding.)
*Peter **has shaved** his beard off.* (He looks different.)

We often announce news in the Present Perfect, because the speaker is emphasizing the event as a present fact.
*Have you **heard**? The Prime Minister **has resigned**.*
*Susan's **had** her baby!*
*I've **ruined** the meal. It's burnt.*

Note the adverbs that are common with this use.
*I haven't done my homework **yet**.* (Negative)
*Has the postman been **yet**?* (Question)
*I've **already** done my homework.*
*I've **just** seen some scissors. Now where did I put them?*

Again, details about definite time will be in the Past Simple.
*She **resigned** because she lost a vote of no confidence.*
*She **had** a baby boy this morning. It **was** a difficult birth.*
*I **didn't watch** it carefully enough.*

Final notes

1 Be careful with *been* and *gone*.
*He's **been** to America.* (= experience – he isn't there now.)
*She's **gone** to America.* (= present result – she's there now.)

2 Compare the following sentences.
   a   *I've lived in Paris for six years.* (I still live there.)
       I lived in Paris for six years. (Now I live somewhere else.)
   b   *Shakespeare wrote thirty plays.* (He can't write any more.)
       I've written several books. (I can still write some more.)
   c   *Have you seen Billy this morning?* (It's still morning.)
       Did you see Billy this morning? (It's the afternoon or evening.)

3 Compare the following right and wrong sentences.

RIGHT	WRONG
a When did you go to Greece?	* When have you been to Greece?
b I saw him yesterday.	* I have seen him yesterday.
c I've studied English for three years.	* I study English for three years.
d Where did you buy your jumper?	* Where have you bought your jumper?
e I haven't brought my dictionary to class.	* I didn't bring my dictionary to class.

4 We can see how the Present Perfect refers to indefinite time and the Past Simple refers to definite time by looking at the time expressions used with the different tenses.

Present Perfect – indefinite		**Past Simple – definite**	
I've done it	for a long time. since July. before. recently.	I did it	yesterday. last week. two days ago. at eight o'clock. in 1987. when I was young. for a long time.
I've already done it. I haven't done it yet.			

5 American English is different from British English. In American English, the following sentences are correct.
   Did you hear the news? The President resigned!
   Did you do your homework yet?
   Your father just called you.
   I already had breakfast.

Multi-word verbs

There are four types of multi-word verbs.

Type 1

Verb + particle (no object)

   a   *He put on his coat and went out.*
   b   *I didn't put enough wood on the fire and it went out.*

In a, the verb and particle are used literally. In b, they are used idiomatically. *To go out* means to stop burning.

Examples with literal meaning:
Sit down.
She stood up and walked out.
Please go away.
She walked right past the shop without noticing it.

Examples with idiomatic meaning:
The meat has gone off. (= go bad)
The marriage didn't work out. (= succeed)
Our plans fell through. (= fail)

Type 2

Verb + particle + object (separable)

   a   *I put up the picture.*
   b   *I put up my sister for the night.*

In a, the verb and particle are used literally. In b, they are used idiomatically. *To put up* means to give someone food and a place to sleep usually for the night or a few days.

Type 2 multi-word verbs are separable. The object (noun or pronoun) *can* come between the verb and the particle.

I put up the picture.	*I put up my sister.*
I put the picture up.	*I put my sister up.*

But if the object is a pronoun, it *always* comes between the verb and the particle.

I put it up.	NOT * I put up it.
I put her up.	NOT * I put up her.

Examples with a literal meaning:
The waiter took away the plates.
Don't throw it away.
They're pulling that old building down.

Examples with an idiomatic meaning:
I put off the meeting. (= postpone)
She told her boyfriend off for being late. (= be angry with)
Don't let me down. (= disappoint)

Type 3

Verb + particle + object (inseparable)

   a   *She came across the room.*
   b   *She came across an old friend while she was out shopping.*

In a, the verb and particle are used literally. In b, they are used idiomatically. *To come across* means to find by accident.

Type 3 multi-word verbs are inseparable. The object (noun or pronoun) *always* comes after the particle.
NOT *She came an old friend across. or *She came her across.

Examples with a literal meaning:
I'm looking for Jane.
They ran across the park
We drove past them.

Examples with an idiomatic meaning:
I'll look after it for you. (= care for)
She takes after her father. (= resemble)
He never got over the death of his wife. (= recover from)

Type 4

Verb + particle + particle

I get on very well with my boss.
I'm looking forward to it.
How can you put up with that noise?

Type 4 multi-word verbs are nearly always idiomatic. The object cannot change position. It cannot come before the particles, or between the particles.

NOT *I'm looking forward it to.

UNIT 8

Conditionals

There are many different ways of making sentences with *if*. It is important to understand the difference between sentences that express *real* possibilities, and those that express *unreal* situations.

Real possibilities

*If it **rains**, we'll stay at home.* (*if* + Present Simple + *will*)
*If you've **finished** your work, you **can** go home.* (*if* + Present Perfect + modal auxiliary verb)
*If you're **feeling** ill, go home and **get** into bed.* (*if* + Present Continuous + imperative)

Unreal situations

*You **would understand** me better if you **came** from my country.* (*would* + *if* + Past Simple)
*If I **were** rich, I **wouldn't have** any problems.* (*if* + *were* + *would*)
*If I **stopped** smoking, I **could run** faster.* (*if* + Past Simple + modal auxiliary verb)

There are several patterns which you need to know to understand the variations. Note that a comma is usual when the *if* clause comes first.

First Conditional

- **Form**

If + Present Simple + *will*

Positive

*If I **find** your wallet, I'll let you know.*
We'll come and see you on Sunday if the weather's good.

Negative

*You **won't** pass the exams if you **don't revise**.*
*If you **lose** your ticket, you **won't be** able to go.*

Question

*What **will** you do if you **don't find** a job?*
*If there **isn't** a hotel, where **will** you stay?*

Note that we do not usually use *will* in the *if* clause.

NOT *If you will leave now, you'll catch the train.
     *If I'll go out tonight, I'll give you a ring.

If can be replaced by *unless* (= if … not) or *in case* (= because of the possibility …).
***Unless** I hear from you, I'll arrive at 8 o'clock.*
*I'll take my umbrella **in case** it rains.*

- **Use**

1 First Conditional sentences express a possible condition and its probable result in the future.

Condition (*if* clause)	Result (Result clause)
If I find a jumper that suits you,	*I'll buy it for you.*
If you can do the homework,	*give me a ring.*
If you can find my purse,	*I might buy you an ice-cream.*
If you've never been to Wales,	*you should try to get there one day.*

2 We can use the First Conditional to express different functions (all of which express a possible condition and a probable result.)
If you do that again, I'll kill you! (= a threat)
Careful! If you touch that, you'll burn yourself! (= a warning)
I'll post the letter if you like. (= an offer)
If you lend me £100, I'll love you forever. (= a promise)

Second conditional

- **Form**

If + Past Simple + *would*

Positive

*If I **won** some money, **I'd** go round the world.*
*My father **would** kill me if he **could** see me now.*

Negative

*I'd give up my job if I **didn't like** it.*
*If I **saw** a ghost, I **wouldn't** talk to it.*

Question

*What **would** you do if you **saw** someone shoplifting?*
*If you **needed** help, who **would** you ask?*

Note that *was* can change to *were* in the condition clause.

| If I / If he | were rich, | I / he | wouldn't have to work. |

- **Use**

1 We use the Second Conditional to express an unreal situation and its probable result. The situation or condition is improbable, impossible, imaginary, or contrary to known facts.
If I were the president of my country, I'd increase taxation. (But it's not very likely that I will ever be the president.)
If my mother was still alive, she'd be very proud. (But she's dead.)
If Ted needed any money, I'd lend it to him. (But he doesn't need it.)

2 Other modal verbs are possible in the result clause.
*I **could** buy some new clothes if I had some money.*
*If I saved a little every week, I **might** be able to save up for a car.*
*If you wanted that job, you'**d have** to apply very soon.*

3 *If I were you, I'd* … is used to give advice.
***If I were you, I'd** apologize to her.*
*I'd take it easy for a while **if I were you.***

First or Second Conditional?

Both conditionals refer to the present and future. The difference is about probability, not time. It is usually clear which conditional to use. First Conditional sentences are real and possible; Second Conditional sentences express situations that will probably never happen.
If I lose my job, I'll … (My company is doing badly. There is a strong possibility of being made redundant.)
If I lost my job, I'd … (Redundancy probably won't happen. I'm just speculating.)
If there is a nuclear war, we'll all … (Said by a pessimist.)
If there was a nuclear war, … (But I don't think it will happen.)

Zero Conditional

Zero Conditional sentences refer to 'all time', not just the present or future. They express a situation that is always true. *If* means *when* or *whenever*.
If you spend over £20 at that supermarket, you get a 5% discount.

Time clauses

Conjunctions of time (*when, as soon as, before, until, after*) are not usually followed by will. We use a present tense even though the time reference is future.
*I'll phone you **when I get** home.*
***As soon as** dinner **is** ready, I'll give you a call.*
*Can I have a word with you **before I go**?*
*Wait **until I come** back.*

We can use the Present Perfect if it is important to show that the action in the time clause is finished.
*When **I've read** the book, I'll lend it to you.*
*I'll go home after **I've done** the shopping.*

would

Notice the use of *would* in the following sentences:
She'd look better with shorter hair. (= If she cut her hair, she'd look better.)

would to express preference
I'd love a cup of coffee.
*Where **would** you like to sit?*
I'd rather have coffee, please.
I'd rather not tell you, if that's all right.
*What **would** you rather do, stay in or go out?*

would to express a request
***Would** you open the door for me?*
***Would** you mind lending me a hand?*

UNIT 9

Modal verbs (2) *must, could, might, can't*

There is an introduction to modal auxiliary verbs on page 146. Modal verbs can express ability, obligation, permission, and request. They can also express the idea of probability, or how certain a situation is.

Expressing possibility/probability

1 We use ***must*** and ***can't*** to express the logical conclusion of a situation: *must* = logically probable; *can't* = logically improbable. We don't have all the facts, so we are not absolutely sure, but we are pretty certain.
*He's very fit, though he **must be** at least sixty!*
*Suzie **can't have** a ten-year-old daughter! She's only twenty-five herself!*
*Is there no reply? They **must be** in bed. They **can't be** out at this time of night.*
*A walk in this weather! You **must be joking**!*

2 We use ***may/might*** and ***could*** to express possibility in the present or future. *May/Might + not* is the negative. *Couldn't* is rare in this use.
*Take your umbrella. It **might rain** later*
*Dave and Beth aren't at home. They **could be** in the pub, I suppose.*
*We **may go** to Greece for our holidays. We haven't decided yet.*
*You know we're going out tonight? Well, I **might not be able** to make it. I **might have to work** late.*

3 We use ***will*** to express what we believe to be true about the present. We are guessing based on what we know about people and things, their routines, character, and qualities.
*'There's a knock on the door.' 'That**'ll be** the postman. He always calls at this time.'*

Infinitives

Notice the different infinitives.

Continuous infinitive
*You must **be joking**!*
*Peter must **be working** late.*
*She could **have been lying** to you.*

Perfect infinitive to express degrees of probability in the past
*He **must have been** drunk.*
*She **can't have got** home yet.*
*He **might have got** lost.*
*They **could have moved** house.*

Asking about possibilities

Question forms with the above modal verbs are unusual. We usually use *Do you think …?*
*'**Do you think** she's married?'   'She can't be.'*
*'Where **do you think** he's from?'   'He might be French. He's very handsome.'*
*'**Do you think** they've arrived yet?'   'They may have. Or they might have got stuck in the traffic.'*

So do I! Neither do I!

Notice how we repeat the auxiliary verbs when we agree or disagree by using *So . . ./Neither . . . I*. If there is no auxiliary, use *do/does/did*. Be careful with sentence stress.

AGREEING		DISAGREEING	
I like ice-cream.	So do I.	I don't like Mary.	I do.
I don't like working.	Neither do I.	I like blue cheese.	I don't.
I can swim.	So can I.	I can speak Polish.	I can't
I can't drive.	Neither can I.	I saw Pat yesterday.	I didn't.
I'm wearing jeans.	So am I.	We're going now.	We aren't.
I went out.	So did I.	I haven't been skiing.	I have.
I haven't been to Paris.	Neither have I.	I'm going to have a coffee.	I'm not.

There are several ways of expressing the same ideas.
*'I like ice-cream.'   '**I do, too.**' / '**Me too.**'*
*'I don't like working.'   '**I don't, either.**' / '**Me neither.**'*

UNIT 10

Present Perfect Continuous

Remember the ideas expressed by all continuous forms.

1 **Activity in progress**
*Be quiet! **I'm thinking**.*
*I **was having** a bath when the phone rang.*
*I**'ve been working** since nine o'clock this morning.*

2 **Temporary activity**
*We**'re staying** with friends until we find our own place to live.*
*We**'ve been living** with them for six weeks.*

3 **Possibly incomplete activity**
*I**'m writing** a report. I have to finish it by tomorrow.*
*Who**'s been eating** my sandwich?*

● Form
Positive and negative

I We You They	've haven't	been working.
He She It	's hasn't	

Question

How long	have	I you we	been working?
	has	she it	

- ## Use

1 The Present Perfect Continuous expresses an activity which began in the past and is still continuing now.

   *I've **been learning** English for three years.*
   *How long **have** you **been working** here?*

   There is sometimes no difference between the Simple and the Continuous.

   I've played
   I've been playing the piano since I was a boy.

   If the Continuous is possible, English has a preference for using it.

   The Continuous can sometimes express a temporary activity, and the Simple a permanent state.

   *I've **been living** in this flat for the past few months.* (= temporary)
   *I've **lived** here all my life.* (= permanent)

   Remember that state verbs rarely take the Continuous (See page 144).

   *I've **had** this book for ages.*
   *I've always **loved** sunny days.*

2 The Present Perfect Continuous expresses a past activity which has caused a present result.

   *I've **been working** all day.* (I'm tired now.)
   ***Have** you **been crying**?* (Your eyes are red.)
   *Roger's **been cutting** the grass.* (I can smell it.)

   The past activity might be finished or it might not. The context usually makes this clear.

   *Look outside the window! It's **been snowing**!* (It has stopped snowing now.)
   *I've **been writing** this book for two years.* (It still isn't finished.)
   *I'm covered in paint because I've **been decorating** the bathroom.* (It might be finished or it might not. We don't know.)

Present Perfect Simple or Continuous?

1 The Simple expresses a completed action.

   *I've **painted** the kitchen, and now I'm doing the bathroom.*

   The Continuous expresses an activity over a period, and things that happened during the activity.

   *I've got paint in my hair because I've **been decorating**.*

2 Think of the verbs that have the idea of a long time, for example, *wait*, *work*, *play*, *try*, *learn*, *rain*. These verbs are often found in the Continuous.
   Think of the verbs that *don't* have the idea of a long time, for example *find*, *start*, *buy*, *die*, *lose*, *break*, *stop*. These verbs are more usually found in the Simple.

   *I've **been cutting** firewood.* (Perhaps over several hours.)
   *I've **cut** my finger.* (One short action.)

3 The Simple expresses a completed action. This is why we use the Simple if the sentence gives a number or quantity, and the Continuous isn't possible.

   *I've **been reading** all day. I've **read** ten chapters.*
   *She's **been smoking** ever since she arrived. She's **had** ten already.*

Time expressions

Here are some time expressions often found with certain tenses.

Past Simple

*I lived in Rome **for six years**.*
*I saw Jack **two days ago**.*
*They met **during the war**.*
*She got married **while she was at university**.*

Present Perfect

*We've been married **for ten years**.*
*They've been living here **since June**.*
*She hasn't been working **since their baby was born**.*

Future

*We're going on holiday **for a few days**.*
*The lesson ends **in twenty minutes' time**.*
*I'll be home **in half an hour**.*

Prepositions with dates, months, years, etc.

in	September 1965 summer the 1920s the twentieth century the holidays the interval	on	Monday Monday morning 8 August Christmas Day holiday	at	seven o'clock Christmas the end of May the age of ten tea time

UNIT 11

Questions

Look at the following question words. Notice that *What*, *Which* and *Whose* can combine with a noun, and *How* can combine with an adjective or an adverb.

***What sort** of music do you like?*
***What kind** of cigarettes do you smoke?*
***What size** shoes do you take?*
***What colour** are your eyes?*
***Which pen** do you want?*
***Which way** is it to the station?*
***Whose book** is this?*
***How much** do you weigh?*
***How many** brothers and sisters have you got?*
***How many times** have you been on a plane?*
***How much** homework do you get every night?*
***How tall** are you?*
***How often** do you go to the cinema?*
***How long** does it take you to get to school?*

Indirect questions

1 Indirect questions have the same word order as the positive and there is no *do/does/did*.

Tom lives in Wimbledon.

I don't know where Tom lives.

NOT *I don't know ~~where does Tom live~~.

Here are some more expressions that introduce indirect questions.

I wonder	
I can't remember	
I've no idea	how long the journey takes.
I'd like to know	
I'm not sure	

If there is no question word, use *if* or *whether*.

*I don't know **if** I'm coming or not.*
*I wonder **whether** it's going to rain.*

2 We often make direct questions into indirect questions to make them sound 'softer' or more polite.

Could you tell me	
Do you know	
Do you happen to know	what time the banks close?
Have you any idea	
Do you remember	

Question tags

1 Question tags are very common in spoken English. We use them to keep conversation going by involving listeners and inviting them to participate. The most common patterns are: positive sentence – negative tag, or negative sentence – positive tag.

*You're Jenny, **aren't** you?*
*It **isn't** a very nice day, **is** it?*

2 We repeat the auxiliary verb in the tag. If there is no auxiliary, use *do/does/did*.

*You **haven't** been here before, **have** you?*
*You **can** speak French, **can't** you?*
*We **must** take the dog out, **mustn't** we?*
*She eats meat, **doesn't** she?*
*Banks close at four, **don't** they?*
*You went to bed late, **didn't** you?*

Careful with question tags with *I'm …*

*I'm late, **aren't** I? (NOT ~~*am't I~~)*

3 Notice the meaning of *yes* and *no* in answer to question tags.

'You're coming, aren't you?'   *'Yes.'* (= I **am** coming.)
                                  'No.' (= I**'m not** coming.)

4 The meaning of a question tag depends on how you say it. If the tag falls, the speaker expects people to agree with him/her.

Beautiful day, isn't it?

It's just the sort of weather for swimming, isn't it?

I'm a silly person, aren't I?

You don't like my mother, do you?

If the tag rises, the speaker is asking for confirmation. The speaker thinks he/she knows the answer, but isn't absolutely sure.

Your name's Abigail, isn't it?

You're in advertising, aren't you?

You work in the city, don't you?

5 We can also use question tags with negative sentences to make a polite request for information or help.

You couldn't lend me your car this evening, could you?

UNIT 12

Reported speech

Reported statements

1 If the reporting verb is in the past tense (e.g. *said*, *told*), it is usual for the verb in the reported clause to move 'one tense back'.

present ————▶ past
present perfect ————▶ past perfect
past ————▶ past perfect

*'**I'm going**.'*   *He said he **was going**.*
*'She**'s passed** her exams.'*   *He told me she **had passed** her exams.*
*'My father **died** when I was six.'*   *She said her father **had died** when she was six.*

2 If the reporting verb is in the present tense (e.g. *says*, *asks*), there is no tense change.

*'The train **will be** late.'*   *He says the train **will be** late.*
*'I **come** from Spain.'*   *She says she **comes** from Spain.*

3 The 'one tense back' rule does have exceptions. If the reported speech is about something that is still true, the tense remains the same.

*Rainforests **are being destroyed**.*   *She told him that rainforests **are being destroyed**.*
*'I **hate** football.'*   *I told him I **hate** football.*

4 The 'one tense back' rule also applies to reported thoughts and feelings.

*I thought she **was** married, but she isn't.*
*I didn't know he **was** a teacher. I thought he **worked** in a bank.*
*I forgot you **were coming**. Never mind. Come in.*
*I hoped you **would** ring.*

5 Some modal verbs change.

can ————▶ could
will ————▶ would
may ————▶ might

*'She **can** type well.'*   *He told me she **could/can** type well.*
*'**I'll** help you.'*   *She said she**'d** help me.*
*'I **may** come.'*   *She said she **might** come.*

Other modal verbs don't change.

*'You **should** go to bed.'*   *He told me I **should** go to bed.*
*'It **might** rain.'*   *She said she thought it **might** rain.*
Must can stay as must, or it can change to had to.

*'I **must** go!'*   *He said he **must/had to** go.*

6 In more formal situations, we can use *that* after the reporting verb.

He told her (that) he would be home late.
She said (that) sales were down on last year.

7 There are many reporting verbs.

We rarely use *say* with an indirect object (i.e. the person spoken to).

She said she was going.
NOT *~~She said to me she was going~~.*

Tell is always used with an indirect object in reported speech.

She told	**me**	
	the doctor	the news.
	us	
	her husband	

Many verbs are more descriptive than *say* and *tell*, for example, *explain, interrupt, demand, insist, admit, complain, warn.*

Sometimes we report the idea, rather than the actual words.

'I'll lend you some money.'   *He offered to lend me some money.*
'I won't help you.'   *She refused to help me.*

Reported questions

1   The word order in reported questions is different in reported speech. There is no inversion of subject and auxiliary verb, and there is no *do/does/did*. This is similar to indirect questions (page 155).

'Why have you come here?'   *I asked her why she had come here.*
'What time is it?'   *He wants to know what time it is.*
'Where do you live?'   *She asked me where I lived.*

Note
We do not use a question mark in a reported question.
We do not use *say* in reported questions.

He said, ' How old are you?'   *He asked me how old I am.*

2   If there is no question word, use *if* or *whether*.

She wants to know | whether / if | she should wear a dress.

Reported commands, requests, etc.

1   Reported commands, requests, offers and advice are formed with a verb + person + *to* + infinitive.

*They **told us to** go away.*
*We **offered to take them** to the airport.*
*He **urged the miners to** go back to work.*
*She **persuaded me to** have my hair cut.*
*I **advised the Prime Minister to** leave immediately.*

Note
say is not possible. Use *ask ... to* or *told ... to*, etc.

2   Notice the negative command. Use *not* before *to*.
*He told me **not to tell** anyone.*
*The police warned people **not to go** out.*

3   Notice we use *tell* for both reported statements and reported commands, but the form is different.

Reported statements
He told me that he was going.
They told us that they were going abroad.
She told them what had been happening.

Reported commands
He told me to keep still.
The police told people to move on.
My parents told me to tidy my room.

4   We use *ask* for both reported commands and reported questions, but the form is different.

Reported commands
I was asked to attend the interview.
He asked me to open my suitcase.
She asked me not to smoke.

Reported questions
He asked me what I did for a living.
I asked her how much the rent was.
She asked me why I had come.

Appendix 1

Irregular verbs

passive

Base form	Past Simple	Past Participle
be	was/were	been
beat	beat	beaten
become	became	become
begin	began	begun
bend	bent	bent
bite	bit	bitten
blow	blew	blown
break	broke	broken
bring	brought	brought
build	built	built
burn	burned/burnt	burned/burnt
burst	burst	burst
buy	bought	bought
can	could	been able
catch	caught	caught
choose	chose	chosen
come	came	come
cost	cost	cost
cut	cut	cut
dig	dug	dug
do	did	done
draw	drew	drawn
dream	dreamed/dreamt	dreamed/dreamt
drink	drank	drunk
drive	drove	driven
eat	ate	eaten
fall	fell	fallen
feed	fed	fed
feel	felt	felt
fight	fought	fought
find	found	found
fly	flew	flown
forget	forgot	forgotten
forgive	forgave	forgiven
freeze	froze	frozen
get	got	got
give	gave	given
go	went	gone/been
grow	grew	grown
hang	hanged/hung	hanged/hung
have	had	had
hear	heard	heard
hide	hid	hidden
hit	hit	hit
hold	held	held
hurt	hurt	hurt
keep	kept	kept
kneel	knelt	knelt
know	knew	known
lay	laid	laid
lead	led	led
learn	learned/learnt	learned/learnt
leave	left	left
lend	lent	lent

Base form	Past Simple	Past Participle
let	let	let
lie	lay	lain
light	lit	lit
lose	lost	lost
make	made	made
mean	meant	meant
meet	met	met
must	had to	had to
pay	paid	paid
put	put	put
read /ri:d/	read /red/	read /red/
ride	rode	ridden
ring	rang	rung
rise	rose	risen
run	ran	run
say	said	said
see	saw	seen
sell	sold	sold
send	sent	sent
set	set	set
shake	shook	shaken
shine	shone	shone
shoot	shot	shot
show	showed	shown
shut	shut	shut
sing	sang	sung
sink	sank	sunk
sit	sat	sat
sleep	slept	slept
slide	slid	slid
smell	smelled/smelt	smelled/smelt
speak	spoke	spoken
spend	spent	spent
spill	spilled/spilt	spilled/spilt
spoil	spoiled/spoilt	spoiled/spoilt
stand	stood	stood
steal	stole	stolen
stick	stuck	stuck
swim	swam	swum
take	took	taken
teach	taught	taught
tear	tore	torn
tell	told	told
think	thought	thought
throw	threw	thrown
understand	understood	understood
wake	woke	woken
wear	wore	worn
win	won	won
write	wrote	written

Appendix 2

Verb patterns

Verbs + -ing

like love adore enjoy prefer hate can't stand don't mind finish look forward to	doing cooking sightseeing

Note

Like, love, adore, prefer, hate are sometimes used with *to* but *-ing* is more usual and more general in meaning.
*I like **cooking**.*
*I like **to cook** beef on Sundays.*

Verbs + to + infinitive

agree choose dare decide expect forget help hope learn manage need offer promise refuse seem want would like would love would prefer would hate	to do to come to cook

Notes

1 **Help** and **dare** can be used without *to*.
   *We **helped tidy** the kitchen.*
   *They didn't **dare disagree** with him.*

2 **Have to** for obligation
   *I **have to wear** a uniform.*

3 **Used to** for past habits.
   *I **used to smoke** but I gave up last year.*

Verbs + somebody + to + infinitive

advise allow ask beg encourage expect help need invite order remind tell want warn (+ not) would like would love would prefer would hate	me him them someone	to do to go to come

Verbs + somebody + infinitive (no *to*)

let make help	her us	do

Notes

1 *To* is used with **make** in the passive.
   *We were **made to work** hard.*

2 **Let** cannot be used in the passive.
   Allowed to is used instead.
   *She **was allowed** to leave.*

Verbs + -ing or to + infinitive (with no change in meaning)

begin start continue	raining to rain

Verbs + -ing or to + infinitive (with a change in meaning)

remember stop try	doing to do

Notes

1 *I remember **posting** the letter.*
   = I have a memory now of a past action: *posting the letter.*

   *I remembered **to post** the letter.*
   = I reminded myself to post the letter.

2 *I stopped **smoking**.*
   = I gave up the habit.

   *I stopped **to smoke**.*
   = I stopped doing something else in order to have a cigarette.

3 *I tried **to sleep**.*
   = I wanted to sleep but it was difficult.

   *I tried **counting** sheep and **taking** sleeping pills.*
   = these were possible ways of getting to sleep.

Index

An index of grammatical items and functional areas

(SB 1 = Student's Book Unit 1; WB 3 = Workbook Unit 3; p 2 = page 2)

Acknowledgements

The authors would like to thank all the staff at Oxford University Press, especially the editor of this book, Elana Katz, for their help, encouragement and dedication throughout the writing of the series. We are deeply indebted to them.

The publishers and authors are very grateful to the following teachers and institutions for reading and/or piloting the manuscript, and for providing invaluable comment and feedback on the course:

Alex Boulton
Henny Burke
Antonio Marcelino Campo
Anna Gawrys-Stosio
John Golding
Bernie Hayden
Felicity Henderson
Amanda Jeffries
Heather Jones
Paula Jullian
David Massey
Paul Packer
Jeremy Page
Stephanie Richards
Nina Rosa da Silva
Ricardo Sili da Silva
Russell Stannard
Sylvia Wheeldon

Akcent Language School, Prague; Aximedia Idiomas, Madrid; The Bell School, Prague; British School of Verona; CLM Bell, Riva del Garda TN; CLM Bell, Trento; EFIP Groupement des Chambres de Commerce et d'Industrie de Castres et de Mazamet; English Language Centre, Ferrara; The 'English Plus' Director and teaching staff at the Colchester English Study Centre; Escola d'Idiomes Moderns, Universitat de Barcelona; The Institute of English, University of Bari; Instituto de Idiomas, Universidad de Navarra, Pamplona; International House, Budapest; International House, Livorno; International House, London; The Oxford Academy; Richard Language College, Bournemouth; Southbourne School of English, Bournemouth; Universidad de los Andes, Santiago.

The authors and publisher are grateful to those who have given permission to reproduce the following extracts and adaptations of copyright material:

p 15   Adapted from 'The happiest person in Britain', The Daily Mail, © The Daily Mail/Solo Syndication, by permission.

p 42   Extract from 'Oxford Wordpower Dictionary', © Oxford University Press.

p 60   Adapted from 'English food: bad taste?', © Focus.

p 70   Taken from ' The modern servant', The Daily Mail, © The Daily Mail/Solo Syndication, by permission.

p 80   Adapted from 'Who wants to be a millionaire?' by Martin Plimmer, SHE Magazine, © National Magazine Company.

p 92   Adapted from 'The Man Who Planted Trees', by Jean Giono, with kind permission of Peter Owen Publishers, London.

p 96   From 'Here Endeth the Lessons', © The Sun.

p 100 Extract from 'Here Have One of Mine', © The Telegraph plc, London, 1994.

p 123 From 'Funeral Blues', Collected Poems by WH Auden edited by Edward Mendelson, with kind permission of Publishers Faber and Faber Ltd.

p 135   T.57 'Who wants to be a millionaire?', (Cole Porter) © 1956 Buxton Hill Music Corp, USA and Warner Chappell Music Ltd, London W1Y 3FA, reproduced by kind permission of International Music Publications.

Every endeavour has been made to identify the sources of all material used. The publisher apologizes for any omissions.

Illustrations by:

Richard Allen pp 92, 93
Stephan Chabluk pp 64, 67, 74
Nicky Cooney pp 10, 29, 42, 103, 116, 120
Paul Dickinson pp 32, 33
Sue Faulks/Eikon Ltd pp 17, 18, 46
Rosamund Fowler pp 12, 28, 44, 63, 111
Gay Galsworthy p 37
Clive Goodyer pp 22, 80, 91
Hardlines pp 22, 36, 50, 83
Gordon Hendry p 146
Peter Hudspith pp 39, 72, 75, 106
Conny Jude p 14
Ian Kellas pp 6, 15, 38, 45, 55, 65, 77, 107, 125
Frances Lloyd pp 8, 48, 88, 89
Andrew Morris pp 40, 41, 85, 95, 113
Tracy Rich pp 24, 26, 123
Sue Sheilds pp 121, 122
Margaret Wellbank pp 24, 26, 56, 76, 96, 116, 117

Handwriting by: Kathy Baxendale

Studio photography by: Mark Mason pp 8, 13, 29, 43, 101, 102

Location Photography by:

Emily Anderson pp 23, 37, 47, 52, 53, 57, 65, 73, 76, 77, 96, 107, 118, 119
Christine Kelly p 78
Norman McBeath pp 17, 35, 104
John Walmsley pp 16, 124

The publishers would like to thank the following for their permission to reproduce photographs and other copyright material:

Ace Photo Library p 9 (A Mauritius)
All Action Pictures p 81 (pools win)
The Ancient Art and Architecture Collection p 7 (statue)
BBC Photo Library pp 20 (caravan), 21 (portrait)
Madeleine Black p 66
The Anthony Blake Photo Library pp 7 (sushi), 60 (meat pie, Rosenfeld – rosemary), 61 (Tim Imrie)
The Bridgeman Art Library p 29 Guernica 1937 by Pablo Picasso © Succession Picasso/DACS 1996
Derek Cattani p 104 (royalist)
Verity Cooke and family p 88
The Mary Evans Picture Library pp 6 (printing), 7 (Lincoln)
Hulton Deutsch p 31 (Picasso and Joplin)
The Image Bank pp 49 (Bokelberg – flowers), 95 (J Alvarez – man)
Impact Photos pp 15 (C Cormack – old man), 34 (E Houssein – outdoor café, P Cavendish – indoor café, S Fear – old men), 54 (G Sweeney)
Life File pp 51 (E Lee – cuckoo clock), 114 (K Curtis – 'Ellen')
Little Boats Model Agency p 56
Billie Love Historical Collection p 37 (schoolroom)
Magnum Photo Library p 83 (C Steele–Perkins – meals on wheels)
Mousetrap Productions p 30 (St Martin's and cast)
Network Photo Library pp 19 (B Lewis – whisky and sorting post), 51 (W Buss – Madrid), 62 (G Sioen/Rapho – NY Manhattan), 68 (M Goldwater), 83 (G Mendel – homeless person), 115 (H Salvadori – commuters)
Oxford Photo Library p 95 (C Andrews – skyline)
Popperfoto p 108 (Madame Tussaud)
Rex Features pp 20 (portrait), 81 (A Books – lottery win)

Liz and John Soars p 26
Solo Syndication/Mail Newspapers pp 70, 71
Frank Spooner pp 100 (Gamma), 108 (A Berg – Bill Clinton, Gamma – The Beatles), 112 (old man)
Tony Stone Images pp 6 (Olympics), 10 (F Ivaldi), 11 (T Beddow – sunbathers, M Kezar – harvesters), 15 (P Tweedie – teenager, D Stewart – man with glasses, V Oliver – old lady, K Fisher – young woman and man with moustache), 34 (B Ayres – businesswoman), 49 (H Grey – men embracing), 51 (R Grosskopf – Venice, AB Wadham – David, A Smith – Big Ben, T Craddock – Belgian lace), 57 (P Webster – Indian food), 62 (D Hughes – London view, A Sotirou – NY café), 98 (Dale Durfee), 115 (J Garrett – opera house)
Topham Picture Source pp 30 (portrait), 69, 108 (Queen Victoria)
The Times p 9 (Masthead)
John Walmsley Photo Library pp 34 (neighbours), 49 (arranging to meet), 74, 114 ('Josh' and 'Fiona')
Zefa Photo Library pp 19 (long hair), 49 (Mugshots – men shaking hands), 51 (Munich, Eiffel Tower, and Pisa), 62 (Oxford St), 83 (classroom), 86, 109, 111, 112 (Earth), 113 (Dolphin)

We would also like to thank the following for their help:
Eurostar, Waterloo; Joel and Son Fabrics; Little Boats Model Agency; Oxford Tourist Information office; The Times for the use of their Letter's page masthead on page 9. (The Editor referred to in the article is fictional.)

Oxford University Press
Great Clarendon Street, Oxford OX2 6DP

Oxford   New York
Athens Auckland Bangkok Bogotá Buenos Aires
Calcutta Cape Town Chennai Dar es Salaam
Delhi Florence Hong Kong Istanbul Karachi
Kuala Lumpur Madrid Melbourne Mexico City
Mumbai Nairobi Paris São Paulo Shanghai
Singapore Taipei Tokyo Toronto Warsaw

and associated companies in
Berlin Ibadan

OXFORD and OXFORD ENGLISH are trade marks of Oxford University Press

ISBN 0 19 470223 5   International Edition
ISBN 0 19 435727 9   German Edition

© Oxford University Press 1996

First published 1996
2000 impression
Printing ref. (last digit): 6 5 4
German Edition first published 1996
Sixth impression 2000